Preparing Students for Life and Work

Preparing Students for Life and Work

Policies and Reforms Affecting Higher Education's Principal Mission

Edited by

Walter Archer and Hans G. Schuetze

BRILL SENSE

LEIDEN | BOSTON

All chapters in this book have undergone peer review.

Library of Congress Cataloging-in-Publication Data

Names: Archer, Walter, editor. | Schütze, Hans Georg, editor.
Title: Preparing students for life and work : policies and reforms affecting
  higher education's principal mission / edited by Walter Archer and Hans G.
  Schuetze.
Description: Leiden ; Boston : Brill Sense, [2019] | Includes bibliographical
  references. |
Identifiers: LCCN 2019000995 (print) | LCCN 2019002720 (ebook) | ISBN
  9789004393073 (ebook) | ISBN 9789004393066 (hbk. : alk. paper) | ISBN
  9789004393059 (pbk. : alk. paper)
Subjects: LCSH: Education, Higher--Aims and objectives. | Education,
  Higher--Cross-cultural studies | College students--Political activty. |
  Student participation in administration. | Comparative education.
Classification: LCC LB2322.2 (ebook) | LCC LB2322.2 .P74 2019 (print) | DDC
  378/.01--dc23
LC record available at https://lccn.loc.gov/2019000995

Typeface for the Latin, Greek, and Cyrillic scripts: "Brill". See and download: brill.com/brill-typeface.

ISBN 978-90-04-39305-9 (paperback)
ISBN 978-90-04-39306-6 (hardback)
ISBN 978-90-04-39307-3 (e-book)

Copyright 2019 by Koninklijke Brill NV, Leiden, The Netherlands.
Koninklijke Brill NV incorporates the imprints Brill, Brill Hes & De Graaf, Brill Nijhoff, Brill Rodopi,
Brill Sense, Hotei Publishing, mentis Verlag, Verlag Ferdinand Schöningh and Wilhelm Fink Verlag.
All rights reserved. No part of this publication may be reproduced, translated, stored in a retrieval system,
or transmitted in any form or by any means, electronic, mechanical, photocopying, recording or otherwise,
without prior written permission from the publisher.
Authorization to photocopy items for internal or personal use is granted by Koninklijke Brill NV provided
that the appropriate fees are paid directly to The Copyright Clearance Center, 222 Rosewood Drive, Suite
910, Danvers, MA 01923, USA. Fees are subject to change.

This book is printed on acid-free paper and produced in a sustainable manner.

Contents

List of Figures and Tables VII
Notes on Contributors IX
Introduction XIV
    Walter Archer and Hans G. Schuetze

1 How Central Is the "Principal Mission" of the University Today? 1
    Chris Duke

PART 1
Canada

2 Access to and Participation in Higher Education in Canada 19
    Hans G. Schuetze and Walter Archer

3 Aboriginal Higher Education and Indigenous Students 42
    Michelle Pidgeon

4 Minding the Gap: Perspectives on Graduate Education for Students with
Disabilities 64
    Mahadeo A. Sukhai

5 Student Affairs and Services in Canadian Higher Education 78
    Kyle D. Massey

PART 2
The World

6 Reforms and Myths: University Graduates and the Labor Market in
Mexico 101
    Wietse de Vries

7 Policies for Adult Students in Mexican Higher Education and Motives for
Returning to Study 122
    Germán Álvarez Mendiola and Brenda Yokebed Pérez Colunga

8 The Value of Degrees and Diplomas in Japan   141
   Shinichi Yamamoto

9 MOOCs, Students, Higher Education and Their Paradoxes   157
   Maureen W. McClure

10 The Expansion of Higher Education and First Generation Students in
    Germany: Increasing Participation or Continuing Exclusion?   179
    Andrä Wolter

11 The Abolition of Tuition Fees in Germany: Student Protests and Their
    Impact   204
    Dieter Timmermann

12 Conditions of Learning at High-Ranked Universities in Four Countries: An
    International Student's Perspective   220
    Jade Zhao

PART 3
Students and Their Influence on Higher Education Policies

13 Student Policies and Protests: The Student Movements of the 1960s and the
    2012 Canadian "Maple Spring"   239
    Hans G. Schuetze

14 Collective Student Action and Student Associations in Quebec   255
    Alexandre Beaupré-Lavallée and Olivier Bégin-Caouette

15 European Higher Education Reforms and the Role of Students   272
    Pavel Zgaga

Figures and Tables

Figures

8.1 Higher education – generic skills versus special skills.   153
9.1 Google searches for "Massive open online course" or "MOOC" 2012–2016   161
10.1 Level of education of students' parents in European countries, 2014. (The country abbreviations are listed before the references.)   184
10.2 Representation of students from families with high, medium or low educational background in European countries, 2014.   186
10.3 Percentage of new entrants in higher education related to the age cohort, 1950–2017, Germany.   188
10.4 Study probability of school leavers with a study entitlement in Germany, differentiated according to the highest qualification of their parents, 1996–2015.   191
10.5 Social composition of students in Germany according to the highest qualification of parents, 1991–2016.   192
10.6 Probability of studying in correlation with the highest educational background of students' parents in Germany, 2016.   194

Tables

2.1 Area, population (2016), university and college enrolment (2015) by province and territory.   21
2.2 The changing undergraduate student profile.   24
2.3 Highest post-secondary credential earned by NHS 2011 respondents.   26
2.4 Weighted average undergraduate tuition fees for Canadian full-time students, by province, 2016/2017.   30
2.5 Weighted average undergraduate tuition fees for Canadian full-time students, by field of study, 2016/2017.   31
2.6 Sources of post-secondary student financial assistance (2011).   33
2.7 Median cumulative (1991–2010) earnings by sex, level of education, and field of study.   34
3.1 Highest post-secondary credential earned by NHS 2011 respondents.   45
6.1 Do you currently hold a paid job (Percentage)?   107
6.2 Employment and unemployment (Percentage).   108
6.3 Conditions of employment by educational level, 4th trimester of 2013 (Percentage).   108
6.4 Do you currently hold a paid job (Percentage)?   110

6.5	What is your average monthly income (USD, 2008) (Percentage)?	110
6.6	Please indicate the level of your competencies (Percentage).	111
6.7	To what degree does your current job match your studies (Percentage)?	112
6.8	What level of studies is required for your current job (Percentage)?	113
6.9	How satisfied are you with your current job (Mean) (Percentage)?	113
6.10	Job satisfaction by areas of knowledge and gender (Mexico).	114
7.1	Mexico: Adult population by age group, 2015–2050 (total numbers and percentage).	126
7.2	Mexico: Distribution of student population in higher education by area of knowledge and age (Percentages).	127
7.3	Mexico: Total enrollment of adult students by age, 2000–2015. On-site and open and distance modalities combined, cumulative growth.	131
7.4	Mexico: Total enrollment of adult students by age, 2000–2015. On-site and open and distance modalities combined (Percentages).	132
8.1	Number of entrants by age and program levels (2015).	142
8.2	Distribution of enrolment per 1,000 students in 2010.	143
8.3	Top 50 universities which sent many graduates to 400 leading companies in 2015.	147
8.4	Economic benefit of higher education.	152
9.1	Basic MOOC trends.	158
11.1	Dates of introduction/abolition of student fees, by state	212

Notes on Contributors

Walter Archer
is Professor Emeritus in the Faculty of Extension at the University of Alberta. He was previously the Dean of Extension at the University of Saskatchewan. He has served as President of the Canadian Society for the Study of Higher Education, and as Editor of the *Canadian Journal of University Continuing Education*. His recent research interests include the effects of English Medium Instruction (EMI) in international higher education, and the education of older adults.

Germán Álvarez Mendiola
is Professor and Head of the Department of Educational Research at the Centre for Advanced Research and Studies in Mexico City. His research interests are public policies and organizational change in higher education; private higher education; lifelong learning policies and institutions; and adult learners in higher education. He coordinates the book series *Higher Education Library* of the Mexican National Association of Universities and Higher Education Institutions.

Alexandre Beaupré-Lavallée
is Professor of Higher Education Administration at Université de Montréal's Department of Educational Administration and Studies. He pursues two main research and teaching subjects: management processes and practices in higher education institutions, and stakeholders' participation in said institutions.

Olivier Bégin-Caouette
is Assistant Professor of Comparative Higher Education at the Université de Montréal. His research focuses on higher education systems, academic research production and the internationalization of higher education institutions. He co-authored with Glen A. Jones (2014) the article "Student organizations in Canada and Quebec's Maple Spring," published in *Studies in Higher Education*. More information can be found at http://olivierbegincaouette.yolasite.com

Wietse de Vries
is Professor at the Institute for Government Sciences and Strategic Development at the Benemérita Universidad Autónoma de Puebla (BUAP) in Mexico. His research interests concern higher education policies and reform, and the effects of these reforms for students, alumni and academics. Among his recent publications: De Vries, W., & Álvarez, G. (2019). Can reform policies

be reformed? An analysis of the evaluation of academics in Mexico. In P. Zgaga, U. Teichler, H. G. Schuetze, & A. Wolter (Eds.), *Higher education reform: Looking back – looking forward* (2nd ed., pp. 277–292). Frankfurt: Peter Lang.

Chris Duke

is Cambridge and London UK educated. He is a visiting emeritus professor at several universities following retirement. He created and led adult/continuing education and lifelong learning departments in universities in Australia, New Zealand and the UK, and held senior and top university management positions in these countries. He has held leadership positions in international and country adult education organizations, including ICAE and ASPBAE, and is currently Secretary-General of the international civil society NGO body PIMA. He has published widely as a historian, sociologist and policy analyst on adult and higher education, university engagement, community and regional development.

Kyle D. Massey

is a higher education administrator, researcher, and educator. He has worked in various administrative and teaching roles at several colleges and universities in Canada and the United States, including roles within student affairs and curricular management of academic programs. He now works at Memorial University of Newfoundland where he has been a professor in the Faculty of Education, and is currently the Curriculum and Accreditation Advisor in the Faculty of Medicine. Kyle's research interests are focused on student affairs in the Canadian context, teaching and learning in higher education, and faculty development.

Maureen W. McClure

is Director of the Institute for International Studies in Education (IISE) in the School of Education, University of Pittsburgh, Associate Professor and former Chair of the Department of Administrative and Policy Studies. Her research centers on the wicked problems of education in the generational interest. It ranges from shifting tax capacities in the US, to education in nations with disasters, to extending the reach of Massive Open Online Courses (MOOCS) and their derivatives, by acting locally and sharing globally. She teaches courses in fiscal and strategic management, and comparative, international and global education.

Brenda Yokebed Pérez Colunga

earned her undergraduate diploma in Psychology at Metropolitan Autonomous University (UAM) and a master's degree in Educational Research at the Center for Advanced Research and Studies (CINVESTAV) in Mexico. Currently, she is a

NOTES ON CONTRIBUTORS

doctoral student whose research interests are young people and adult students in higher education institutions.

Michelle Pidgeon

of Mi'kmaq ancestry from Newfoundland and Labrador, is Associate Professor in the Faculty of Education at Simon Fraser University, British Columbia. Her research is focused on higher education, student services, and Indigenity. Theoretically and methodologically, her work is guided by an Indigenous wholistic framework with the intentional goals of: (1) transforming the educational system for Aboriginal peoples and (2) empowering the cultural integrity of all students. She is also the Director of the Centre for Educational Leadership and Policy Studies at SFU and the Editor of the *Canadian Journal of Higher Education*.

Hans G. Schuetze

is Professor Emeritus of the Department of Educational Studies at the University of British Columbia. He has a PhD in international and comparative public law from the University of Göttingen, Germany, and a LL.M. from the University of California at Berkeley. After work as a lawyer for the city of Hannover, Germany, he was a policy analyst at the Centre for Educational Research and Innovation (CERI), Organization for Economic Cooperation and Development (OECD) in Paris, France (1977 to 1985). From 1991 he was Professor of Higher Education Research and Policy, and Research Associate, Centre for Policy Studies in Higher Education and Training, University of British Columbia. As an emeritus, he worked as a lawyer in private practice and a part-time lecturer at the University of Oldenburg. He is presently a Visiting Professor at the Renmin University of China in Beijing, China.

Mahadeo Sukhai

is the world's first congenitally blind biomedical research scientist. He is the Head of Research and Chief Accessibility Officer for the CNIB (Canadian National Institute for the Blind), having previously served as a research scientist at the University Health Network in Toronto. Dr. Sukhai is the Principal Investigator for and lead author of *Creating a Culture of Accessibility in the Sciences*, a book based on his groundbreaking work on access to science within higher education, and serves as the principal investigator for national projects to examine accessibility and inclusion within science education and healthcare.

Dieter Timmermann

an economist of education, studied in the 1960s at Bonn University, received his PhD at Technical University Berlin, wrote his habilitation thesis at Stanford

University, and taught a course at UBC in Vancouver as a visiting professor. He is Professor Emeritus at Bielefeld University, Faculty of Education. He was Vice-Rector of Student Affairs at Bielefeld University from 1996 to 2001, and from 2001 until 2009 he served as the Rector of that institution. From 2012 to 2018 he was the President of the German Student Services. From 2001 to 2004 he was the Chair of the National Expert Commission on "Financing Lifelong Learning." He is author of numerous publications. He was editor of the journal *Beiträge zur Bildungsplanung und Bildungsökonomie* [Contributions to Educational Planning and the Economics of Education], and co-editor of the series *Wissenschaft – Praxis – Dialog: Berufliche Bildung* [Science – Practice – Dialogue: Vocational Education]. His scientific work was and still is focused on the economics of education.

Andrä Wolter

was Professor for Research on Higher Education at the Humboldt-Universität Berlin, Germany (2010–2017). He previously worked at the universities of Oldenburg and Hanover (1976–1993). From 1993 until 2010 he was professor for policy studies in education, Dresden University of Technology, and head of the higher education research department at HIS Hochschul-Informations-System, Hanover (2004–2006). He is co-author of the national educational report in Germany. His main research fields are higher education policy, participation in higher education, graduate studies, lifelong learning and educational monitoring.

Shinichi Yamamoto

is Professor of Higher Education Systems at J. F. Oberlin University in Tokyo, Japan. After graduation from the University of Tokyo, he worked for the Ministry of Education for 20 years before joining academia. He served Hiroshima University as its Director of Research Institute for Higher Education 2007–2012. His books and papers on higher education include "Doctoral Education in Japan" in S. Powell & H. Green (Eds.), *The doctorate worldwide* (pp. 181–193) (2007).

Pavel Zgaga

is Professor of Philosophy of Education at the University of Ljubljana, Slovenia. He has held several research grants and directed or contributed to a number of national and international research projects mainly focused on contemporary higher education issues, education policy and reforms in the contemporary European context and to teacher education as a specific field within higher education. In his field of expertise, he has also been co-operating with international organisations, e.g. the Council of Europe, the European

Commission, UNESCO, and the OECD and has been a consultant and invited speaker to a number of countries.

Jade Zhao
studied at the University of British Columbia in Vancouver, and at the Institut d'études politiques ('Science Po') in Paris for her undergraduate studies in International Relations. She did her graduate studies in International Studies and History at Peking University and the London School of Economics (LSE). Presently she is the Program Coordinator for the Global Malaria Access Program at the Clinton Health Access Initiative (CHAI). Prior to assuming this role, she served as Project Coordinator for the International Growth Centre at the LSE.

Introduction

Walter Archer and Hans G. Schuetze

Background

This volume consists partly of papers that were originally presented at an international workshop on Higher Education (HE) reforms that took place in August, 2014 at Memorial University of Newfoundland and Labrador, located in the city of St. John's, Canada. Those papers were later amended and expanded in the light of the discussions at that workshop. Some more papers were contributed by authors who had an interest in student issues and policies but had been unable to attend the workshop. We, as participants in the workshop and editors of this volume, would like to express our appreciation to Rob Shea and Angie Clarke of Memorial University, who organized and hosted the workshop and began the process of soliciting contributions to this book.

The St. John's workshop was the eleventh in a series of International Workshops on Higher Education Reform (HER). The first was organized at the University of British Columbia (UBC) in Vancouver, on the Pacific coast of Canada, in 2003. The St. John's workshop took place 11 years later at the most easterly point in Canada, on the Atlantic coast.

Other HER workshops have taken place in Dublin, Vienna, Berlin, Ljubljana, Pittsburgh, Tokyo, Shanghai, Tianjin and Hiroshima. The hallmark of the HER workshops is their small size, which is deliberate to allow for in-depth discussions. With normally not more than half of the participants from the hosting country and the other half from other countries, the discussions are naturally comparative, even if presentations or panels occasionally focus on just one country. There are, of course, large learned societies which are also providing international and comparative perspectives, for example the Comparative & International Education Society (CIES) and the International Consortium of Higher Education Researchers (INCHER), but their annual conferences normally involve hundreds if not thousands of participants, which makes in-depth and continuous discussions difficult.

Higher Education Reform

Originally, the definition of "Higher Education Reform" was rather narrow: "Reforms are intended, purposeful changes to public policies that are directed towards HE, or have a major impact on HE." This was meant to exclude discussions on developments and changes that were not part of the public policy agenda, or the consequence of public policy – e.g., demographic changes, new technologies and social media, or the globalization of markets.

It soon became clear that such a limitation of focus was difficult, since most of the public policies were, in fact, effects of changes in the environment of Higher Education. And as we know from organizational theory as well as practice, universities and other HE Institutions (HEIs) must, if they are to survive and thrive, both adapt to their changing environments and, at the same time, try to influence them.

Thus, any discussion of "reform in higher education" must include an understanding of their larger environments and the particular context (national, political, social, economic) in which HEIs exist. It is for this reason that each of the HER workshops has tended to focus on the particular context of the host country, although in the wider perspective of international trends.

The Theme of the St. John's Workshop

The overall theme of the St. John's workshop was "Higher education and its principal mission: Preparing students for life, work, and civic engagement." Contributions were invited on issues related to reforms and changes regarding accessibility and affordability of post-secondary studies, conditions and modes of learning, the transition from study to work, and, for adult students, the integration of higher education with other aspects of their professional, personal and civic life. As the relationship between HE and labor markets and employment systems is changing and the borders of HE expanding, there are many new institutional innovations, programs, forms of learning, and transition mechanisms and routes both into HE, from HE to the world of work, and, for continuing lifelong learners, from employment and domestic and civic duties back into HE.

The following section consists of very brief summaries of the chapters, including some comments on how the themes of each chapter relate to each other and the overall theme of this book.

The first chapter, by Chris Duke, quite appropriately questions and challenges the central assertion of the conference theme, namely that "preparing students for life and work" is, in fact, still the principal mission of the university today. He looks at this question horizontally, considering similarities and differences in the HE situations in different countries, and historically, considering how the roles of universities and the balance among them have shifted over recent decades.

In contrast to this stand-alone overview chapter, the chapters in Part 1 reflect the usual concentration of the HER workshops on particular issues within the HE system of the host country, in this case Canada. The first of these chapters, by editors Walter Archer and Hans G. Schuetze, is a brief overview of the history and structure of the Canadian HE system, the nature of the students who participate in it, and some of the major issues currently facing these students. One of these issues is the participation of Indigenous Canadians in the HE system.

Participation in HE by the three categories of Indigenous Canadians is the subject of the second chapter, "Aboriginal Higher Education and Indigenous Students" by Michelle Pidgeon. The author describes the three groups of Canadian Indigenous peoples and discusses the impact of colonialism on them since European settlement of what is now Canada began almost five centuries ago. One major factor was the imposition of residential schools on Indigenous peoples during the nineteenth and twentieth centuries, whereby their children were taken away from their families to be educated in one of the two colonial (also the official) languages. It is only recently that Canadians have become aware of the cultural and psychological impact of these schools, and their detrimental effects on Indigenous people to this day. One of these long-lasting effects is a general lack of access to and success in the HE system, which is only recently beginning to be rectified.

Another chapter in Part 1 addresses issues faced by students with disabilities, and is written by an author Mahadeo A. Sukhai (with assistance from several collaborators) whose research is focused on this issue. This chapter discusses how various myths and misconceptions about students with disabilities who enter graduate school, as well as the dynamics of these students' relations with their supervisors, may affect their success. The insights raised in this chapter may also be applied to the experiences of disabled students in other contexts within HE.

The final Canada-focused chapter is titled "Student Affairs and Services in Canadian Higher Education." With a much broader focus than the previous two chapters, author Kyle D. Massey discusses how the provision of services that will support the learning of all students in the system has evolved as the HE system itself has evolved and is continuing to evolve to address emerging needs of students and their institutions.

Part 2 of this volume, consisting of seven chapters contributed by authors from different parts of the world, discusses various issues in different national or international contexts. Two of them focus on Mexico. The first, by Wietse de Vries, is titled "Reforms and Myths: University Graduates and the Labor Market in Mexico." The author suggests that there are many myths and much misinformation about graduates from Mexican universities. As a result, some government policies based on this faulty information are flawed and need to be reconsidered. Furthermore, the longer term solution to this problem lies in producing and making public more and better information about the Mexican HE system, which in turn will result in the making of better policies.

The chapter by Germán Álvarez Mendiola and Brenda Pérez Colunga focuses on "Policies for Adult Students in Mexican Higher Education and Motives for Returning to Study." The authors note that adult students have constituted a steadily growing proportion of the student body in recent years, but this has not yet been reflected in data gathering about adult students or in policies addressing their particular needs. This chapter attempts to fill part of this gap in knowledge, and set the stage for changes to HE policies designed with adult students in mind.

Moving outside of North America, the chapter by Shinichi Yamamoto describes a pattern of massification of HE that has taken a very different form in Japan, as compared to Mexico or most of the OECD countries. The Japanese HE system has very few adult students, and relatively few graduate students. The author discusses the particular features of the Japanese employment scene that have resulted in this apparent anomaly.

The next chapter in this section of the volume, by Maureen W. McClure, is titled "MOOCs, Students, Higher Education and Their Paradoxes." This chapter is not focused on any particular geographic area but rather on one aspect of HE systems throughout the world. The author begins by stating that MOOCs (Massive Open Online Courses), for all their exposure in the popular media, are still encrusted with a number of myths about their origins, nature, and possible futures. She details the continuing rapid evolution of this form of learning into a large number of new and different forms. She also comments on the multiple paradoxes in the relationship between MOOCs and HEIs, including a need for HEIs to revamp their thinking about students.

Massification of the HE system in Germany is described in the chapter by Andrä Wolter. The author recounts the various policy reforms that have greatly expanded and diversified the German HE system since the 1960s, and asks whether this expansion of the system has also tended to foster equality of opportunity. After analysis of the data, he concludes that, against the expectations of the policy makers, massification of the HE system has not, in fact, led to greater social inclusiveness nor social equity.

A more narrowly focused study related to just one aspect of the German HE system is titled "The Abolition of Tuition Fees in Germany: Student Protests and their Impact," by Dieter Timmermann. This chapter discusses the background for the introduction and then abolition of tuition fees in the HE systems of seven of the sixteen German states (Länder) between 2006 and 2015. The discussion is enlivened by the author's personal experience, while serving as rector of one of the affected universities, of the student actions that influenced the situation and helped to ensure the eventual abolition of tuition fees.

A rather different perspective on the HE systems of four different countries is provided by Jade Zhao, who describes her experiences and observations while an undergraduate and later graduate student in Canada, China, the UK, and France in her chapter titled "Conditions of Learning at High-Ranked Universities in Four Countries: An International Student's Perspective." She notes that, while an international student's host university may score well on national or international rankings, that does not guarantee that it will have competent teachers, good student services, and congenial local students – all matters of intense concern to international students. From her own experience, she reports that performance on these important (to students) factors varies widely even among top-ranked institutions. She concludes with some suggestions for reforms that would benefit international students, who are presumably the centre of the internationalization aspect of the "principal mission" of all HE systems.

Part 3 of this volume consists of three chapters. The first of these, "Student Policies and Protests: The Student Movements of the 1960s and the 2012 Canadian 'Maple Spring,'" compares the student protests of fifty years ago, their causes and patterns, with the recent protests in Quebec. In spite of different objectives, contexts, and environments, in this chapter author Hans G. Schuetze finds that there are a great number of commonalities.

Alexandre Beaupré-Lavallee and Olivier Bégin-Caouette, also focuses on the 2012 Quebec Maple Spring protests. In their chapter "Collective Student Action and Student Associations in Quebec," they analyze the roles that different types of student organizations can play – and have played in Quebec in 2012.

The final chapter, by Pavel Zgaga, "European Higher Education Reforms and the Role of Students," also discusses the role of students in influencing major changes that have affected the HE systems in the European Higher Education Area from even before the beginning of the Bologna Process in 1999, when student organizations became a part of the formal process of Europeanization of HE systems. They have since been instrumental in turning more attention onto the social dimension of the reform process, particularly related to groups of people generally underrepresented in HE.

Given the central place that students occupy in higher education it is remarkable how relatively little research has been done on the situation of this group. This is in contrast to the great research interest recently focused on the situation of the professoriate. Research on students is rather narrowly focused, primarily on financial issues such as student aid or debt and how they affect access and participation. The editors hope that this book will help to fill parts of that research gap and draw attention to the need for more policy relevant research on some of the neglected issues.

CHAPTER 1

How Central Is the "Principal Mission" of the University Today?

Chris Duke

Abstract

The author describes the distinct mission and situation of university education in England from his own students days to the present, arguing that the changing ways that students are perceived and treated today, in the United Kingdom and other countries, are becoming more similar due to the "globalization" of political economy and the "internationalization" of higher education. The focus on teaching and learning was then seen as more important than 'impact' such as graduate employment or the university's standing in international league tables. The author concludes that universities continue providing a moral compass for society, and that university engagement with the community should not be understood as a "third mission" but rather a integrative thread of research and teaching.

Keywords

higher education in United Kingdom – mission of universities – student experience – university engagement – teaching quality

Students in the "Good Old Days"

I remember when "mission" first crept into the education management language of modern UK higher education. As in other respects, the country was conservatively inclined but also favoured innovation in the post-War optimism and rising prosperity of the third quarter of the 20th century. Bustling, innovative and, as perceived in the UK, dubiously commercialised, the New World was both resented and admired as a model of freedom and success. Being well advanced, American universities would no doubt be up in such things as mission statements. In my own world of university adult education and extension

---

© KONINKLIJKE BRILL NV, LEIDEN, 2019 | DOI:10.1163/9789004393073_001

in particular, by the sixties the US cash register rang louder and more vulgar than the missionary liberalism of John Henry Newman. Extension courses were sold at what to us in the Workers' Educational Association (WEA) and liberal adult education tradition (Hughes & Brown, 1981; Wiltshire, Taylor, & Jennings, 1980) seemed appallingly high fees; the subject matter was often rather practical, but lucrative.

Meanwhile, in UK senior common rooms and Governing Council board rooms, academic staff joked about adopting the missionary position: a crudity that one might describe a few decades later as a truth too near to home. Looking not to the US but to the Old Continent of Europe, Rectors (to the British, Vice-Chancellors and now increasingly Presidents) were, as with UK Vice-Chancellors, habitually and emphatically *primus inter pares*, drawn from and belonging to the professoriate. Academic businessmen, where they existed, were more likely to be Deans – itself an illuminating term when you think about its religious connotation.

In the sixties Oxbridge spires still dreamed. Their (overwhelmingly male) student elite moved naturally from prestigious private schools to a world of privileged learning. They blended easily with the elite of Empire (British Commonwealth); internationalisation was older than Teaching Quality Assessment (TQA). They were joined, and fraternised while retaining social distance, with a few lower class boys and a few girls; local nurses and trainee teachers were the main female company. Students found a menu of outstanding lecture room performers, all erudite, many famous, some brilliant orators, others thoroughly boring. They chose which to follow as one might today follow a celebrity on LinkedIn, Facebook, or some other social media site. The individual tutorial was, at least for non-scientists,[1] a weekly climax: inspiration and dread.

Careers advice was absent or rudimentary. There were no indicators of employability or fussing over graduate unemployment. My tutor at Cambridge explained that university was a time out, a time of irresponsibility in discovery. His advice when I sought a branch of the Public Service was not to consider the worthy British Council but to go for the tough Foreign Office. When later I plumped for school-teaching he had fixed me up with fourth year paid tutoring of undergraduates – probably the most precious career asset I could then obtain. My Institute of Education tutor (applied social science kept at arms-length from the University's heartland) sent me to a top school for teaching practice, then to top private schools for interview. However, instead of taking a position at an elite school I returned to my cockney roots to teach at a London polytechnic.

How Was and Is the Primary Mission of the University Defined?

Students were at the heart of the Cambridge that I knew, as at Woolwich Polytechnic where teaching hours were long, but rewarding in the sense we now call challenging. At Cambridge young men, gowned for College dinner and in town in the evenings, swamped then vacated the city thrice annually: the sun-cycle around which City and Varsity [university] year rotated.

My College days were followed by experience of a wider higher education clientele: foreign undergraduates and local second chance return-to-learners at Woolwich, then the liberal adult education students of the northern industrial redbrick University of Leeds. Then we had the new "plate-glass" universities in Australia as in the UK. Here students were initially at the heart of sense of identity (or mission) and social life. The new universities were places more apart from than a part of their localities: city-fringe, residential, college-based, student and teaching centred. As ever more institutions were opened or reclassified as universities, size and total student numbers grew and changed. So too did the higher education profession, to the point that a great Oxford scholar A. H. Halsey wrote in 1992 of *The Decline of Donnish Dominion*, heralding a spate of doomsday books on the "crisis of the university" theme (see e.g., Readings, 1996; Reeves, 1988; Scott, 1984).

About this time also the idea took hold that students might study locally instead of going away to university: a hesitant step towards the student becoming a more normal part of ongoing community, locality and even working life. Thus the transition from elite to mass and now to nominally universal higher education, and in the new millennium the Knowledge Society. Today a university degree is supposedly an all-round good: for the competitive region within the global competitive knowledge economy; and for the individual graduated student, calculated in terms of enhanced lifetime earnings. It was until recently axiomatically an all but unquestionable benefit. The cultural epoch now called neo-liberal, ushered in by Reagan, Thatcher and their gurus, made each individual the master of his and increasingly mistress of her own destiny: Success or failure in higher education starts the road to life success or failure. It is your own fault or triumph, chosen or self-inflicted. So much for three "irresponsible years" of student learning.

This tells us three things. First, the expectations and requirements of most young people entering university came to be utterly transformed. Second, aspirations are socially and culturally conditioned, and all but determined by approximate birth years (as well as family of origin and social class), to the point that we label people by generational cohort: baby-boomers, Generation X or Y, and recent newer terms. Third, education is, in the old sociology, a dependent variable. We fail to understand the emergent and changing "university mission" if we ignore its determining world. Academics now seek promotion via reputably published research. The reality and the rhetoric of the "Knowledge Society" require new and applied knowledge. These pressures coming from outside the higher education system may collide with earlier, notably Humboldt's and Newman's, traditions of the university, demanding new statements of role and contribution in larger and more costly higher education systems. Similarly, national political-strategic interests override sensitivities about academic autonomy. Mission is an artefact of the broader social, political, economic, and above all cultural changes by which higher education is shaped and to which it responds.

"Cheques on Legs": A New Global Business Model

I have referred to universities as institutions, higher education systems, students themselves, and outside influences impacting the higher education sector. The term stakeholder confuses those involved in an area with those actually holding a stake in it. It is, however, useful when we consider the different ways that the principal stakeholders, students, are seen. This takes us in two different directions: to the local and specific; and to where the university sits in the bigger picture. To the general public and the media in many countries students are young, full-time, noisy, often tenants in lodging living away from home for the first time; to some, rowdy come-and-go intruders, even political trouble-makers. In Australia as in North America, different mixes of distance, self-directed, part-time and full-time study modes have long been common. With proportionately more and older people studying (compare Campbell, 1984), students are less of a breed apart. Many also work to earn money while studying. Students are less "different": now just younger versions of financially stressed and anxious grown-ups.

There is nothing new about students being disruptive. A loved and detested part at least of British university and civic traditions, they are more widely problematic and invasive when 50% rather than 5% of the age cohort become students. Their life is not carefree as once it was. Another main stakeholder is the institution itself, transformed under pressure from being primarily an academic community of experts and mentored juniors headed for the professions, including, for some of the brightest, academe itself. Now it is a business, often with an entrepreneurial Chief Executive. The language and priorities of business prevail. Business acumen and a strong management record can translate into status and market position;

a new leader is no longer necessarily from the academic world. Tenure may be brief and stormy: big rewards over a few short and turbulent years, before moving on.

The business interests of the wider community – is the university giving value for public money? – are expressed or imposed via the Governing Body of Council or Trustees. Since success coincides closely with status, which is much determined by research output, balance in the "dual mission" of the modern university has tipped from teaching and students towards research measured by income and outputs. As student numbers and institutional size have increased, students have drifted to the periphery of the ambitions of academies and academics alike. Little wonder that the key stakeholders after students, the University and its staff, are seen with some suspicion. Students may, however, be too busy and financially stressed to make much fuss. The expectations of those other main stakeholders, the employers of a year or two hence, may matter more than the dullness of the lecturer, the awkwardness of Administration, or the low number of teaching contact hours. Yet students and their unions notice and challenge where the university invests its funds, and how it takes to government intrusion into its life and broader curriculum: as agents, for instance, of the UK Border Agency over control of overstaying and therefore now illegal immigrants.

Students are described as clients, purchasers, customers of a business with a bottom line (and auditors). Yet the university may be a remote abstraction in students' own audited and fiscalised daily lives. The individual "student experience" in the core teaching-learning sense may be as varied and localised as contact with the values and behaviour of one or two teacher-scholars. For both learner and teacher, the space to manoeuvre and be themselves may be severely diminished by the new audit army.

Students among Other Stakeholders and Influences

What remains that is distinctive about the university student experience? Systems have grown massively to become "universal." Higher education and degrees are available in ever more modes through an ever wider range of institutions, many now called universities. Although private universities, for and not for profit, are still uncommon in Western Europe, Australia and New Zealand, they are a well-established part of the US system and a major part of many other newer systems as in The Philippines, Republic of Korea and Eastern Europe. Universities are increasingly subject to policies based in short-term electoral gain. Economic austerity has been at the centre of most

UK policy pronouncements since the 2008 financial crash. Neoliberal philosophy favours a small State and a dominant private sector. Higher education is still *more* obviously a sub-system of the economy: a source of workers for the labour market. For a while massive expansion of post-school education seemed to lead towards what would then be called an integrated tertiary system (Duke, 2005), somewhat on the lines of the renowned California system praised in UK policy circles: specialisation by sub-sector combined with easy movement between the parts.

But in England, at least, this has not happened purposefully, though piecemeal changes now drift in this direction. The non-university further education (FE) or college system is a disheartening product of where the education system under the Right-leaning socio-political establishment is moving. English FE colleges, nominally freed from local authorities, suffer a schizophrenic combination of central regulatory control, frequent experimental disruption, and financial deprivation. Scotland has deliberately chosen a more integrated approach. Readers outside England may be forgiven for underestimating and not comprehending the power of social class in shaping policy – for universities and students as for much else. Social class – the socio-cultural – is reflected in the high over-representation of high-status high-fee private school students in the most prestigious universities, underpinning the reproduction of social and economic wealth. Policies and institutional "good practice" between countries do not transfer well without the socio-cultural "packaging" that contains and constrains them. In the UK as elsewhere we need to consider "students as principal mission" also from this perspective.

"Quality," degree standards and stress on job readiness in a mass higher education marketplace blow away earlier sometimes idealised assumptions about the role of student and the wider, liberal in the older and liberating, sense of student development. Add the pressure to perform in research, and the importance given to competitive national and global league tables, and warm words about students as principal mission sound hollow. Seen thus, a new intrusive, centralising and probably standardising UK Teaching Excellence Framework (TEF) will fail to reinstate the interests of students and teaching at the heart of mission. Unpalatable as it may be, universities are increasingly a sub-system of a larger education industry which is itself subordinate to the labour market and the yet wider economic system. Look at the terms: learners, students, clients, consumers; university (as) business, income, the bottom line; learning, studying, teaching, inducting, coaching and mentoring; the university as a place of safety rather than for "irresponsible" learning and growth: a holding pen till a job, student placement or volunteering appears – the university as the Economy's waiting room.

Whether or not eligible to vote, all students are citizens, and ever more citizens are students or ex-students. Normal life for most citizens in most countries this decade means increased financial stress and greater inequalities. Students get caught up in oscillations between left and right; the campus becomes another battleground. The identity of students and their unions may be weakened: less sharply defined when universities are varied, complex and divided, and when those who oversee, part-finance and audit them intervene inconsistently: policy-makers mumbling through a fog of confusion.[2]

In the UK, competing assumptions about cost-sharing to earn a degree lead to ambiguous policy and governance. The department and minister charged with higher education has changed frequently, co-located with school education, then with different economic, business and labour market portfolios. This betrays uncertainty over what higher education is and how it should be managed. Distinct student interests and perspectives get lost. The sector is fragmented into groups and alliances of institutions, maybe unsettling student unionism, especially where rights and fees are concerned.

Meanwhile Scotland, in resisting "austerity" as a basis for policy generally, has continued to provide free higher education. Authorities like OECD and IMF praise the English high fee-high loan approach but less formally also express concern at how high fees have become. Continental European experience, diverse and fluid country by country, in general remains more "socialist" than England. We are, however, unwise to assume homogeneity in a bloc like the EU. In the UK the debate over fees retreated from principle to a financial calculus as to what proportion of a degree was private benefit and what a public good. This is an important issue country by country: a by-product of the transition from elite to mass to universal and legacy of what is called meritocratic aspiration.

Being the first in the family to enter higher education remains the route to success for many families in fast-changing nations. Discourse vacillates between "knowledge economy" for a high-skill workforce and "knowledge society" for an educated citizenry. Significantly (perhaps "functionally" in a sociological and economic sense) there are media plaudits for young billionaires who either never went to or dropped out of university. Yet policy-making for higher education is subject to ROI (return on investment) analysis and neoliberal fiscalisation. Which stakeholders control the curriculum, using what models of university education?

The UK Teaching and Research Debate

To raise the quality and global competitiveness of university research, the UK in the mid-eighties introduced a Research Assessment Exercise (RAE) that now costs many millions and is the dominant criterion of university standing. It was recently modified by adding an "impact" element to enhance University Engagement, a poor cousin "third mission" after Teaching and Research. Unintended consequences in turn attract sometimes perverse further consequences. There is nothing new about engagement with the locality, region, community or economy, although the terms have changed and "third mission" has crept in unhelpfully. From the mid-nineteenth century "service" was a favoured US term in the context of the land grant universities; the great redbrick universities mainly of northern industrial Britain were started by public-spirited and sharp-eyed industrialists who needed a local "knowledge economy" before that term was used, and funded subjects like textiles and mining. Engagement is a much newer term, still barely feeling its way globally beyond the "Anglo-club" of North America and the former British Empire. The fast-grown US-based Talloires Network is a 21st century vehicle for this. Books about engagement have multiplied (for example, Field, Schmidt-Hertha, & Waxenegger, 2016; Inman & Schuetze, 2010). The term encompasses many activities from student service and experience for "internal" students to the regional development leanings of the OECD and EU. At its best, "engagement" penetrates the whole institutional identity and mission, and the experience of all students as well. Failing such penetration it becomes a feel-good public relations add-on: or worse, an internal competitor for resources against teaching and research. There has been a continuing fracas over the high and ever-rising cost of research assessment, and criticism of gaming the Research Excellence Framework (REF) (Collini, 2016). Perverse consequences of research assessment include the distorting effect of ranking and league tables on mission, often contrary to wider public interest and good. More ruthless university CEOs seek to enhance research profile irrespective of student subject preference; some sacrifice whole disciplinary departments with low research ratings.

Teaching and Mission in the UK

In most of the UK, high tuition fees plus a loan-and-repayment system have replaced the free higher education that still obtains in Scotland, an example of "spend now pay later." First welcomed but perhaps now regretted, a consequence is to define students as purchasers of degree-and-job-getting opportunity. Market forces and competition for students seen as fee-paying "cheques on legs" mean that universities must adopt market practices and package their wares for sale. Student as consumers assess and judge the quality of their experience: Like trip advisers, they are unreliable in their motives and not well equipped to judge quality of product and service. Having given birth to this new notion of student, the government must now also judge the quality of student learning and university teaching, then pull levers in a nominally free market and decide whose teaching, like whose research, earns bonuses.

Before the dust in the UK had settled on the meaning, methodology and cash value of "Impact," the assessment of teaching was mooted by means of a Teaching Excellence Framework (TEF) alongside the RAE (now Research Excellence Framework or REF). Maybe intended to rebalance mission and mollify students, the TEF has dominated recent higher education policy discourse. It remains contested but will proceed, despite the certainty that unknown and unintended consequences will follow – a known-unknown. As a device, the TEF may hold back student and parental criticism and the litigation that might follow. It may also buy time to limit unintended consequences such as the much-feared threat that TEF assessment will undermine the international marketing proposition of the common high quality of UK degrees.

Given that students are supposedly central to the mission of the university, how far do student feedback on quality of experience and teaching surveys satisfy, please or help these students at the heart of the mission? Do students thus get what they want? Customer experience of choice and feedback in other nominally free markets such as energy raise doubts. TEF as companion to REF mimics a wider national culture and malaise.

In this philosophically divided "United" Kingdom four-nations house, students are part of the human resources production system rather than free-spirited learners. If the neo-liberal free market in education services is losing its hold, is a new post-neo-liberal student age cohort forming? Is this merely the familiar short radical transition phase from "being a student" to adulthood? Or does it challenge former UK Prime Minister Margaret Thatcher's claim to have built a new individualistic and competitive national culture as well as a new economy? Is a new culture being created, old student-hood having died on the altar of economic modernity, while university teaching is becoming less a sacred calling, more an income stream?

Student Experience and the Global Contest

The student is one of several main university stakeholders along with students' parents and families, staff within the institution, the institution itself, and external interests represented within the university in diverse ways. Beyond that, national and maybe regional (provincial; state) governments have an interest, stake, and often direct financial and economic interest. The funding source and mix of pressures vary from country to country; the UK could until recently surprise others by its free provision, still prevailing in Scotland, but England now surprises with its high fees. Continuing vigour of demand in the UK also surprises; it has probably stayed strong because the deferred repayment loan system puts off the cost till later. Living with large debt has become a national as well as individual cultural norm, and anxiety. The belief that a good degree (that is to say a degree from a prestigious university) is worth a lifetime of good income props up both global and local market.

Another external factor, powerful but not easily measured, pushes students to a less central position: the aggregated-criteria ranking of institutions, first nationally, now globally. It rank-orders universities so that according to different criteria many hundreds of institutions are ranked from "world best" down, the reach extending ever further into national systems. Leading and headline position is a powerful element in attracting students worldwide to one of the world's "top universities": the prestige of the university may rate higher than the class or subject of degree in most labour markets.

Competitive global ranking grew from the UK ranking of research from the 1980s. The periodic increasingly sophisticated and costly research assessment exercise continues as the REF (it might also be argued that the habit originated from within the competitive USA system). Institutional ranking, giving authority to more vulgar informal ranking from ancient to modern, new, regional or technical-technological university, grew out of research ratings. Research continues to dominate nationally and globally in status and influence. It has become a matter of national pride for poorly rated nations to get at least one institution well placed in global rankings, incidentally aiding the onward global march of the English language. The interests of students as well as regional communities and even in any direct sense the economy and exchequer, are subordinated to this, as resources are drained off from other institutions to build one flagship success.

This powerful new phenomenon is driven by institutional as well as national pride and business sense. It leads to business success measured as world-best students, staff, partners and benefactions. The experience of students plays at best a modest part, while the retribution for research "under-performance" can be extreme: Closure of departments and loss of subjects may relate little to student demand or regional need.

"International outlook" among global ranking criteria embraces very different things. In a business sense universities compete to attract bright young people, now including international students, by prestige and by offering things that students value and enjoy. How they are treated and how they feel is a business matter.

How Much Do Students Matter?

If the preparation and teaching of students really does matter, is this mainly to and within higher education, or mainly in the world beyond? Economically speaking, students matter a lot to most universities. A broad wider-world consensus would be that the university's main business is to prepare students for work, and perhaps also to be good citizens. Whatever private grumbling discourse may take place among academics about interrupting research, expansion to include so many in the population as present or past students means that they have to be taken seriously. Students must also be made to feel important, or the cheques will walk elsewhere. Not only that: Institutions are now free to sink or swim in entrepreneurial competition. Passionate and capable HE teachers remain; but in a neoliberal culture typical young students may be forgiven for sensing coolness about real membership of an "academic community" behind Public Relations razmataz.

Outside the university mass-produced students matter in diverse and perverse ways. Universities are haunted by graduate under- and unemployment indicators. Completion rates, value-adding, student satisfaction surveys join earlier gender, ethnic minority and social class access and widening participation measures, even before the TEF comes in. External pressures for quality-assured and oversighted curriculum "development" coincide with a UK government drive to free schools up as "academies." Confused policy-making, including student self-financing, displays ambiguity about what universities and students are, and how they are to live through austerity and a redefined role of the State. Inevitably, this means ever more administration. In perversely unsought ways students matter a lot to the character, life and work of the university.

The political behaviour of youth is uncertain and unsettling: They can be radical followers of third-age new socialists at the global heart of neoliberalism, but are less likely to vote than senior citizens. These generational phenomena are not limited to students, but students play a big part: by sheer numbers, and because campuses bring them together in energetic proximity. The new social media are important, and not only for serious campaigning. The spread of IT-enabled distance open learning systems known as MOOCs (see Maureen McClure's chapter in this volume) may be a welcome relief to some if it isolates students at home with their laptops instead of rallying on campus and taking to the streets.

This may seem irrelevant to teaching students as the university's primary mission: Look at it from another direction and you see this clientele paying high fees and accumulating debts in working life where costly degrees fail to protect them from insecurity. Meanwhile, UK government interest is laced with suspicion: treating universities as untrustworthy and imposing tasks that have nothing to do with student welfare and interests. It is surprising how little confrontational student activism about student life there is. What there was, when fees were being raised around 2002, was crushed in London by heavy police retaliation.

Taking a broader canvas and a longer view, however, comparison with the late sixties across many OECD countries shows how quiescent students in the UK normally are, but not because teaching has returned centre-stage or degrees now offer a better job prospect. We may have to look off-campus to the seismic shift from rising post-War mid-century prosperity, the fragmentation of eighties individualism, and the loss of economic confidence evident from the seventies and all-pervasive today. It may seem harder than ever to achieve real change for students whose future looks so much gloomier than for their predecessors.

Look beyond the OECD countries and we find students still playing a central part in politics, and in the life of the nation, whether or not activism to do with student life occurs on campuses. At the time of writing it happens to be India and South Africa, as well as Chile in recent years, where universities are in student turmoil (see Hans Schuetze's chapter in this volume). Students played a leading part in what proved to be the false dawn of the Arab Spring. Some are now seen in Britain as complicit in the "threat of terrorism." In Hong Kong they have played a central if so far unsuccessful part in trying to shape the character of that Special Administrative Region.

What Is Lost and What Follows?

Consider how different teaching arrangements relate to different purposes for students and the providers of education. Despite Tapper and Palfreyman's (2000) account of a dying collegiate tradition, tutorial teaching still lives on in Oxbridge colleges. A privileged and richly bestowed learning environment survives. Students can still be defined and choose whether to behave as junior colleagues, if no longer in an almost gated academic community.

For most in mass higher education, higher total system cost and a needy politically influential ageing population make undergraduate fees a vital income stream. Time-wise, students are a problem for research-focused staff, and cost-wise for labour-market-fixated governments. New information technology including MOOCs supports a management scenario proposed over many years of travelling light, off-loading costly infrastructure and treating students to Amazon-style home delivery, fundamentally negating the student-centred Oxbridge tradition.

With the diminution of student campus life and probable weakening of student unions, only a minority can now access the kind of student learning and lifestyle of which Oxbridge is the most obvious example. In line with emasculated "lifelong learning," being a student becomes just one dimension of personal and family life along with other work and non-work activity. The alternative is a heavily regulated and standardised shadow of university life tailored to what a diminished budget can afford – and then lifelong debt.

More optimistically, as befits early 21st century individualism, self-directed learning and personal responsibility may yet triumph. There are roots in the early 19th century London external degree for the staunch autodidact with the will to succeed. Another relic of those times is a tradition of hard-working solidarity along with self-improvement. This was the social and moral foundation of the UK Labour Party forbears. A mid-Victorian touchstone was Samuel Smiles, who wrote treatises like *Self Help* and *Thrift*. The vision of liberal optimist J. H. Newman, as in *The Idea of a University*, is a touchstone for the liberal adult education and wider university tradition cited and mourned in a more selfishly entrepreneurial era. These influences flowed into initiatives by and for the working class of entirely student-focused institutional providers with a keen sense of mission – but with what we now call non-traditional students: the Workers' Education Association (WEA) and the university Joint Tutorial Classes movement (Hughes & Brown, 1981; Wiltshire, Taylor, & Jennings, 1980). This separate sub-system of Oxbridge has direct contemporary lineage to what survives of distinct university adult or continuing education, now a minor sub-sector of mainstream higher education.

Starting with the experience of working people and with a clear focus on political education for action, such student-centred teaching continued to offer a more participatory alternative to the traditional more instructional approach. That approach is today seen as something East Asian, but it still colours teaching and academic authority in Britain. It is not clear where TEF quality assurance of teaching or the distance authoritative learning of MOOCs will take universities' central mission. It is however clear that "hard times" have moved policies and systems away from a culture of deliberately planned convergence between youth and adult higher education. The student remains to most minds a young person in a waiting room held outside the labour market who is being prepared, with whatever difficulty, for that market.

Moral Leadership and "Mission": Lifelong Learning and Engagement

Two final questions: If universities have in part forfeited a claim to moral leadership and as a main seat of public intellectuals in a more economy-and-wealth focused time, what takes their place in providing a moral compass? My experience in Australia and the UK suggests that the most socially responsible, thoughtful and longsighted internal university stakeholders are often not the Council, management or even professoriate, but student and staff unions. If universities are there mainly for young people and the public good, but threatened in their own viability, does moral authority in an ageing society not of necessity pass in part to long-living retired civic-minded senior citizens and to the civil sector, the older thus (re-)connecting with the young?

The second question returns to the theme of students, and the meaning and use of *mission*. It has been common at least in the UK to refer to engagement with local-regional society as the third mission of higher education: mainly economic-entrepreneurial or with wider and deeper resonance as "community." It may include student service, work experience, regional economic development, community development and civic leadership training; it may apply more to enterprises or more to individual learners (Inman & Schuetze, 2010). The effect of seeking to bring engagement and place-based relationships into "mission" has, however, proved perverse in two senses.

Coming third means taking bronze and not gold, being less important than internal enrolled students and research. In competitive, heavily scrutinised circumstances a poor research rating and soon perhaps a poor TEF teaching rating can cost an individual promotion or their post, a department its existence, and a university its income-drawing power and status. Engagement with an implication of public service to society is then off the chart of priorities.

The now familiar use of the term "mission" is also problematic. For most, despite the numbers taking degrees, adults learning is still an outsider's add-on despite decades of lifelong learning rhetoric: The earlier British and British Commonwealth term "extramural" haunts engagement by self-marginalisation[3]; it reproduces the universal, long-proscribed and ever reinvented error of managing by separating into compartments. Teaching students and engaging should be as institutionally all-pervasive in the life of the university as is learning in the social world beyond. Rather than only enabling youngsters to study there, universities should grasp what the modern university must be, and see engagement as an integrative thread, not a distinct mission. If society and its universities together comprehend what modern lifelong and life-wide learning and students really are, and what a knowledge

HOW CENTRAL IS THE "PRINCIPAL MISSION" OF THE UNIVERSITY TODAY?   15

society must mean, the fog of confusion about both students and mission may clear.

Notes

1   There was really no Social Science; my own tutor led a successful campaign to keep Sociology out of the University of Cambridge; Psychology belonged with the Humanities, and Economics tended to keep company with History and Politics. Yet already the crisis in the Humanities was being bewailed (see Plumb, 1963).
2   Yet Sir Peter Scott, no champion of modern managerialism, wrote in the *Guardian* (5 April 2016) that evidence-free Ministers have decided that standards are low and so management must improve: "Be on message or beware: targets and rankings are the way forward for universities."
3   In the United States the term "extension" rather than "extramural" prevailed, growing out of the land-grants' service sense of mission.

References

Campbell, D. (1984). *The new majority: Adult learners in the university*. Edmonton: University of Alberta Press.

Collini, S. (2016, January). Who are the spongers now? *London Review of Books, 38*(2), 33–36.

Department for Business, Innovation and Skills (DBES). (2015). *Fulfilling our potential: Teaching excellence, social mobility and student choice*. London: HMSO.

Duke, C. (Ed.). (2005). *The tertiary moment: What road to inclusive higher education?* Leicester: National Institute of Adult Continuing Education.

Field, J., Schmidt-Hertha, B., & Waxenegger, A. (Eds.). (2016). *Universities and engagement*. New York, NY: Routledge.

Freeman, H. (2016, April 19). Empowerment. *The Guardian*.

Halsey, A. H. (1992). *Decline of donnish dominion: The British academic professions in the twentieth century*. Oxford: Clarendon Press.

Hillman, N. (2015, October). *Students and the 2015 general election: Did they make a difference?* Oxford: Higher Education Policy Institute.

Hillman, N. (Ed.). (2015, November). *It's the finance, stupid! The decline of part-time higher education and what to do about it*. Oxford: Higher Education Policy Institute.

Hillman, N. (Ed.). (2016, January). *Response to the education green paper*. Oxford: Higher Education Policy Institute.

Hughes, H. D., & Brown, G. F. (1981). *The WEA education year book 1918*. Nottingham: University of Nottingham.

Inman, P., & Schuetze, H. G. (Eds.). (2010). *The community engagement and service mission of universities*. Leicester: National Institute of Adult Continuing Education.

Newman, J. H. (1852). *The idea of a university*. London: Dent.

Plumb, J. H. (Ed.). (1963). *Crisis in the humanities*. Harmondsworth: Penguin.

Readings, B. (1996). *The university in ruins*. Cambridge, MA: Harvard University Press.

Reeves, M. (1988). *The crisis in higher education*. Milton Keynes: Society for Research into Higher Education and Open University Press.

Schleicher, A. (2016, January). *Value-added: How do you measure whether universities are delivering for students? HEPI 2015 annual lecture*. Oxford: Higher Education Policy Institute.

Scott, P. (1984). *The crisis of the university*. London: Croom Helm.

Scott, P. (2016, April 5). Be on message or beware. *The Guardian*.

Tapper, T., & Palfreyman, D. (2000). *Oxford and the decline of collegiate tradition*. London: Woburn Press.

Wiltshire, H., Taylor, J., & Jennings, B. (Eds.). (1980). *The 1919 report*. Nottingham: University of Nottingham.

PART 1

Canada

..

CHAPTER 2

Access to and Participation in Higher Education in Canada

Hans G. Schuetze and Walter Archer

Abstract

After a general overview of the main features of the Canadian system of higher education, the authors focus on access to and participation in this system. Although Canada has one of the highest participation rates among OECD countries, there are several groups who are under-represented. Among these are members of the Indigenous population, partly for historical and political reasons, and partly because many of them share features with two other underrepresented groups, i.e. would-be students from rural and sparsely populated areas, and potential students from families with a low social-economic background. Discussing barriers to participation such as cost, affordability, student aid and graduate employment, the authors conclude with a call for reforms that will abolish or at least lower present obstacles to successful participation by these groups.

Keywords

higher education Canada – access to higher education – participation in higher education – barriers for indigenous students – barriers for rural populations – barriers for low income families – costs and affordability of higher education – student aid

Introduction

By most accounts Canada has a successful system of higher education (HE): It is widely accessible, generally affordable, and participation is almost universal, as two thirds of the school leaver cohort are enrolled in some form of HE.

Canadians have avoided some of the major divisions that characterize the US and some other countries: between public and highly selective private

© KONINKLIJKE BRILL NV, LEIDEN, 2019 | DOI:10.1163/9789004393073_002

"elite" institutions, between low-quality for-profit and "world class" research universities, many of which charge exorbitant tuition fees and are therefore unaffordable for people from average and low income families. In Canada the profile of HE graduates resembles the profile of the population as a whole, and Canadian HE does not serve as a means of reinforcing inequalities of income and status within the society (Usher, 2018a). In a way, Canadian HE is perceived as is the country itself: solid, equitable, accessible and hospitable, aware of and even thriving on ethnic and cultural diversity.

However, there are a few flaws hidden under this positive image. We discuss some of them, focusing mainly on access and participation. We begin by looking at the HE system generally and the profile and situation of its most important element, students.

History, Geography and the Structure and Nature of the Canadian HE System

While Indigenous people have lived in what is now Canada for many thousands of years, what we would recognize as higher education began only after the first French settlement was established in what is now the province of Quebec in 1608. The Roman Catholic church was in charge of all education in that settlement. A Jesuit college began offering advanced courses later in that century, but no degree granting institutions existed until the 18th century. By the time a number of British colonies were combined with Quebec into what was then called the Dominion of Canada in 1867, degree granting institutions (mostly church operated and supported) existed in all four of the original provinces – i.e., Ontario, Quebec, New Brunswick, and Nova Scotia. At that time these provinces had a total population of 3.46 million population but only about 1500 university students. Higher education was only for a few and HE in Canada in that era was an "elite" system,[1] even if the term "elite" did not indicate noble or upper class origin of students, as in Europe.

That began to change in the late 19th and early 20th centuries with the addition of the four western provinces (British Columbia, Alberta, Saskatchewan, and Manitoba) to the Dominion. Each of those provinces created a single public university modeled on the American land-grant institutions and designed to serve all the people of the province with programming that included strong agriculture and extension programs. While numbers were still relatively small compared to those today, the system was opening up to more students.

More rapid change set in at the end of the Second World War. As in many other OECD countries, the Canadian system grew rapidly both in number of students and number of institutions. Over the past 70 years, new types of institutions have been established, especially community colleges, for which the United States provided the model. This community college model, which included a broad range of vocational programs as well as the first two years of a university program, was followed most closely by the two western provinces of British Columbia and Alberta (Dennison, 1995; Jones, 2014).

Although the rate of growth slowed in the 1980s and 1990s. Canada has presently a higher education system that accommodates about two thirds of the school leaver cohort, more than most other industrialized countries. In Trow's classification (2007), Canada now has a "universal" system, with over two million students (see Table 2.1).

One of the major characteristic features of Canada's post-secondary education system is that, with the exception of a few theological colleges and the short program vocational training sector, virtually all HE in Canada is public (Schuetze, 2019). That does not mean that all HE costs are assumed by the public purse. Rather, students bear some – and an increasing percentage – of

TABLE 2.1   Area, population (2016), university and college enrolment (2015) by province and territory

Jurisdiction	Area km²	Population	University	College	Total HE enrolment
Newfoundland and Labrador	405,212	530,128	17,940	9,231	27,168
Prince Edward Island	5660	148,649	4,248	2,301	6,552
Nova Scotia	55,284	949,501	43,923	11,274	55,200
New Brunswick	72,908	756,780	20,733	7,584	28,320
Quebec	1,542,056	8,326,089	314,079	221,844	535,923
Ontario	1,076,395	13,982,984	516,672	305,793	822,465
Manitoba	647,797	1,318,128	46,092	15,837	61,926
Saskatchewan	651,036	1,150,632	35,829	20,733	56,565
Alberta	661,848	4,252,879	128,847	55,179	184,026
British Columbia	944,735	4,751,612	177,747	95,058	272,808
Nunavut, Yukon, & Northwest Territories combined	3,921,739	119,043	–	3,993	3,993
CANADA	9,984,670	36,286,425	1,306,110	748,833	2,054,943

SOURCE: AREA DATA FROM NATURAL RESOURCES CANADA. POPULATION DATA FOR 2016 FROM STATISTICS CANADA, CANSIM, TABLE 051-0042. ENROLMENT DATA FOR 2014/2015 FROM STATISTICS CANADA, CANSIM, TABLE 477-0019

the costs through tuition and other user fees. So do some other users of university and college services, such as university hospitals, laboratories used for joint projects with industry, etc. However, the public nature of universities and colleges has not only the effect that provincial governments exercise a certain degree of oversight and control but also that, compared to tuition in countries with larger and more important private post-secondary sectors, for example the US, tuition is affordable, at least for undergraduate education and non-professional programs (see below).

Another characteristic of Canadian higher education[2] is that there is no single Canadian HE "system" in the sense of a well-articulated and coordinated organization. Instead, the country's ten provinces and three territories are, in accordance with the constitution of 1867, responsible for education and, as a consequence, there are no national policies on matters such as international education, transferability of academic credits, or quality standards. Unlike the US or Germany which have federal ministries of education even if education is a responsibility of the regions (states and Länder), there is no Canadian federal ministry of education or higher education. While many principles and procedures in HE are similar across the country there are some variations that have developed over the course of time.

Nonetheless, the notion that Canadian HE is a "non-system" is incorrect, since the federal government has, like in the US and Germany, some major roles with regard to HE, namely financing academic research and research infrastructure, and student financial support. Thus, for example, the federal government does exercise considerable influence on HE by setting specific requirements for research and infrastructure funding as well as for student financial support.

In spite of responsibility for HE being located with the various provinces and territories, the structures and procedures of universities are remarkably homogenous – partly because of voluntary isomorphism among the larger research oriented universities which cooperate even if competing with each other, while smaller institutions often imitate larger, more prestigious institutions ("mimetic isomorphism"). This homogeneity is partly the effect of some pan-Canadian HE associations, especially Universities Canada[3] and the Canadian Association of University Teachers (CAUT), both providing non-binding but widely observed platforms for pan-Canadian standards and norms.

In the college and institute sector there is less homogeneity, as these institutions have less autonomy than the universities with regard to their structures and procedures and are more directly controlled by their provincial governments. The most distinctive college system exists in Quebec, where upper secondary school students graduate after grade eleven, as compared to grade twelve in all the other provinces and territories. This is followed by two years in a *Collège d'enseignement général et professionnel* (Cégep), which is compulsory for students wanting to enter university in Quebec. Since the standard undergraduate degree in Quebec requires only three years instead of the four as in the other provinces, the total time to university graduation from primary school to university graduation is the same – sixteen years. The Cégeps also offer vocational programs that are three years in length (Dennison, op. cit.).

Overall, in comparison with other industrialized countries Canada's postsecondary education looks impressive. Educational attainment of 25 to 34 olds in Canada ranks second (after South Korea) with 59% graduates. In comparison, the total in the US is 47%, and the OECD countries average 42%. Looking at a larger segment of the adult population, 55 % of Canadians aged 25 to 64 have completed some form of postsecondary education, well above the OECD average of 35% (OECD, 2016a).

Table 2.1 shows some important variations of participation in postsecondary education between the provinces and territories. This is due to several factors, some of which – Indigenous origin and remoteness from urban centres – will be further discussed below.

The Post-Secondary Students
Canada's post-secondary student body is increasingly diverse. A growing number of today's university students belong to the group that was called "nontraditional" only a generation ago because they differed in one way or another from the standard characteristics of being white, between 18 and 24 years of age, single, enrolling in higher education directly after completing high school and having the traditional access credentials, i.e., a high school diploma or an equivalent qualification (Schuetze, 2014; Slowey & Schuetze, 2012).

Finding accurate data on student characteristics is often a problem, but the Canadian University Survey Consortium (CUSC) has provided something like a longitudinal study of a large proportion of Canadian university students for more than twenty years. Selected data from the 2016 survey of first year undergraduate students are presented in Table 2.2. It should be noted that since this is a voluntary survey the results may not be a very accurate representation of the university sector of higher education in Canada, and the large non-university sector is not reflected in these data.

It is interesting that while the percentage of "visible minorities" stood at 25% in 2010 and at 36% in the 2013 CUSC survey, in the 2016 survey 40% said that they belong to a visible minority group. As it is completely unlikely that within six years the share of visible minority students has increased at such a rate it can be assumed that this growth is due, since the data were self-reporting, to these students' changing self-awareness of and pride in their ethnic origin.

Also, in the 2016 cohort of first-year university students 22% said they had a disability, as compared to 7% in 2010 and 9% in the 2013 survey (CUSC, 2013, p. 8). Of the disabilities mentioned, mental health issues ranked at the top of the list at 12% (as compared to 4% in 2013). Among those reporting a disability in 2016, almost one third, especially those with a learning disability, said their disability required some special accommodation. Even if the tripling of students with disabilities over just six years seems alarming it can also be interpreted as a sign of growing awareness and acceptance of their disabilities by the students (see the chapter by Sukhai in this volume).

International Students

International students are a significant and growing proportion of Canadian HE. They represented 10.9% of enrolments in Canadian postsecondary institutions in 2015/2016 (Statistics Canada, 2017). Of the 352,523 foreign students in Canada in 2016, about 118,000 were from China, 49,000 from India, and just

TABLE 2.2   The changing undergraduate student[a] profile

Gender[4]	Male	34
	Female	66
Average age		18.6
Family status	Single	77
	In a relationship	21
	Married or common law	2
With a child		1
	Canadian	88
Nationality	Permanent resident	5
	International	7
Visible minority (self-identified)[b]		40
Aboriginal (self-identified)		3
With a disability		22
Parents' education	High school or less	11
(highest level)	College	18
	University or professional degree	38
	Graduate degree	20

a 2016 cohort of first year undergraduate students, N=14,886. Data from CUSC (2016).
b "Visible minority" includes students who self-identified as belonging to a group other than "Aboriginal," "Inuit," "Métis," or "White" (CUSC, 2016).

under 20,000 from South Korea. Together the students from these three countries account for 53% of foreign students while the just over 12,000 students from the US represent only about 3.5 % (Immigration, Refugees and Citizenship Canada, 2016).

Until recently, Canada was thought to be disadvantaged in competition for international students because of a lack of a national policy and concerted effort regarding international students – provinces, as well as institutions were working independently, in contrast with competing countries such as Australia and the UK where the national governments took the lead. However, in 2011 the provinces and territories adopted an International Education Marketing Plan and the federal government created an advisory panel on international education that held consultations with the various agents and stakeholders, including some in the private sector. The result was *Canada's International Education Strategy* of 2014 (Global Affairs Canada, 2014). In this document the federal government clearly stated that one important objective of the policy was to attract international students as a source of immigration to fill the workplace gaps left by an aging population; foreign students are well positioned to immigrate to Canada as they have typically obtained Canadian credentials, are proficient in at least one of Canada's official languages and often have relevant Canadian work experience. Indeed, according to the Canadian Bureau of International Education, 51% of them do intend to apply to become permanent residents (CBIE, 2017b).

Outbound international study provides a very different picture; only 3% of Canadian full-time university students and only 1.1% of full time college students go abroad for part of their education, and this figure has been static for several years. There are a number of reasons for this, including cost, inability to fit the experience abroad into the structure of their program by transferring credits, family responsibilities, and a number of others. In response to the paucity of Canadians willing and able to study abroad, a number of institutions are providing aid and incentives of various types, and urging the federal government to provide financial support as well (Academica Group, 2017; Association of Universities and Colleges Canada (AUCC), 2014; CBIE, 2017a; Johnson, 2016). (For a personal account by a Canadian student who did study abroad in four different countries, see the chapter in this volume by Jade Zhao.)

Groups Under-Represented in the Canadian HE System

Since Canada has one of the highest rates of participation in postsecondary education, one could conclude that access and participation are no longer pertinent issues. In particular, the high degree of differentiation in the HE sector and hence the great variety of institutions and programs, as well as the flexibility of a system of portable course credits, make access to HE a realistic option for most young people. This is generally true unless (a) they are Indigenous, especially those living on reserves; (b) they live in rural or remote areas with no proximity to postsecondary institutions; or (c) they are from a low socioeconomic family background. In the following sections we discuss these three groups in turn.

Indigenous Students

Indigenous people,[5] particularly those whose families live on reserves[6] (especially reserves that are remote from population centres) are still clearly underrepresented in HE – in spite of various recent efforts to address this issue. (For a detailed discussion see the chapter by Pidgeon in this volume).

This issue has partly to do with the dramatically low graduation rate of Canadian Indigenous people from high school (upper secondary school). In recent years, 40% of First Nations students have not graduated from high school, and this failure rate is substantially higher for youth living on reserves where 58% fail to graduate. This compares to 10% of the non-indigenous population who do not graduate (Statistics Canada, 2013b).

While Indigenous people have become increasingly urbanized in recent decades, they are still more likely to reside in rural areas (often but not always on reserves) than is the non-Indigenous population. And when they relocate to urban areas for the purpose of attending HE they are more likely than non-Indigenous students to experience culture shock, which can negatively affect their academic performance.

The substantial gap in the rate of completion of high school greatly reduces the proportion of Indigenous youth who are eligible to enroll in postsecondary studies. This gap is decreasing, although slowly (Richards, 2014) as HE insti-

TABLE 2.3   Highest post-secondary credential earned by NHS 2011 respondents

	Aboriginal	Non-Aboriginal
Trades	14.4	12.0
College diploma	20.6	21.3
University certificate/diploma	3.5	4.9
University degree	9.8	26.5

SOURCE: STATISTICS CANADA 'NATIONAL HOUSEHOLD SURVEY' (2013)

tutions have begun to offer courses and programs that cater to Indigenous students and are relevant to their culture and traditions. So far, this has primarily been the case at colleges and technical institutes and in the vocational training sector, but not university degree programs, as shown in Table 2.3.

The proportion of Indigenous people holding a trades or college credential is roughly equal to that of the non-Indigenous population. The major discrepancy between Indigenous and non-Indigenous people is in completion of a university degree, the credential that has the greatest effect on employment possibilities and income.

The overall education gap between Indigenous and non-Indigenous people is often attributed to the operation of Indian Residential Schools, which many Indigenous youth were forced to attend well into the 20th century (see the chapter in this volume by Pidgeon). To fully assess the damage inflicted on Canada's Indigenous population by these schools the national government, which is responsible for the education of Indigenous people, set up a Truth and Reconciliation Commission (TRC) which began its work in 2008 and published its findings and recommendations in 2015 (Truth and Reconciliation Commission of Canada, 2015). The new Liberal government that was formed after the general election in the fall of 2015 promised to enact and fund all the recommendations made by the TRC.

Three sections of the TRC report that are particularly relevant to higher education are those in which the TRC calls for:

1. the federal government to provide adequate funding to end the backlog of First Nations (Indigenous) students seeking a postsecondary education;
2. post-secondary institutions to create university and college degree and diploma programs in Indigenous languages; and
3. provision of necessary funding to post-secondary institutions to educate teachers on how to integrate Indigenous knowledge and teaching methods into classrooms.

In response, many universities have begun to put specific programs and targeted support services in place. According to a Universities Canada directory, universities collectively offer 233 undergraduate and 62 graduate-level programs focusing on Indigenous issues or specifically designed for Indigenous students (Universities Canada, 2015a, 2015b). Some universities are going beyond such special programs and measures for Indigenous students by requiring that all undergraduate students also take at least one course from these programs. HE institutions have also increasingly started to appoint Indigenous professors, artists and administrators familiar with Indigenous culture who can serve as role models for Indigenous students (MacDonald, 2016).

Students from Rural and Sparsely Populated Areas

Canada's population (currently about 36.5 million) is relatively small compared to its large geographic area (the second largest of the world, after Russia) and it is very unequally distributed. Most Canadians now live in urban areas located quite close to the US-Canadian border, whereas the remainder of the country is very sparsely populated (see data re population vs. geographic area of the different provinces and territories in Table 2.1). There are few PSE institutions in these large, sparsely populated areas. Colleges (often small branch campuses) are sometimes located in smaller population centres, but universities are mainly found in the large cities. According to Statistics Canada (2008), 20% of high school students live beyond commuting range (80 km) of the nearest university, while only 3% live beyond commuting range of a college. Therefore, young people in rural areas who want to attend a university often face the necessity of leaving home and spending money for travel and accommodation, in addition to tuition, books, etc.

This issue of the added cost of having to relocate in order to attend a HEI is more likely to affect the decisions of potential students coming from low-income families. Of potential students living more than 80 km from a university, those in the top third in terms of income were six times as likely to enroll as those from the bottom third (Statistics Canada, 2008). There is also a gender factor. Among high school graduates living within commuting range of a university females are considerably more likely to enroll than males, but beyond commuting range this gender disparity disappears. Overall, young people living in rural areas are 10% less likely to participate in PSE of any kind, as compared to young people living in larger population centres (Wickham, 2017, p. 16).

A possible solution to this access issue experienced by students and potential students in rural areas is access to postsecondary education via distance delivery. Athabasca University, which offers distance delivered programs in English, and the Télé Université du Quebec (Téluq), which offers programs in French, are the two specialized university-level providers of distance programs in Canada, although many other universities also offer a smaller number of programs.

These distance programs are offered mainly via the Internet. Since Internet connections are inadequate in remote and rural areas, Internet-based HE is not always a satisfactory alternative. Besides this infrastructure problem, students in remote regions often experience feelings of isolation and an over-reliance on text-based learning, factors which contribute to the chronically high attrition rates in distance delivered courses and programs (Parkes, Gregory, Fletcher, Adlington, & Gromik, 2015, p. 67). It is quite possible for determined students to overcome these problems, but, as noted by Brindley (2014, p. 287), "... studying at a distance requires maturity, a high level of motivation, capacity to multi-task, goal-directedness, and the ability to work independently and cooperatively."

Given the extra problems faced by distance students as compared to those studying on-campus, "[i]t is essential to give attention to the context, characteristics, motivation, abilities, prior knowledge, experience, and so forth of the learners to design appropriate and successful learning opportunities and to avoid failure and drop-out" (Stöter, Bullen, Zawacki-Richter, & von Prümmer, 2014, p. 424).

Massive Open Online Courses (MOOC) do not address the access problem for rural residents, for two reasons: First, the majority of MOOCs do not lead to a degree, i.e. a recognized credential of value in the labour market, and second, few course offerings are tailored for students in remote area (see the chapter on MOOCs by Maureen McClure in this volume). Blended learning, another form of distance education and learning, does not really address the particular problems of rural residents either, since blended learning does require some face-to-face attendance at a HE institution, which is difficult for students beyond commuting range of that institution.

Remoteness is, therefore, often in combination with other factors, a significant barrier to participation in HE in Canada (Frenette, 2002, 2003; Poulin & Straut, 2017; Statistics Canada, 2008; Usher, 2018b; Usher & Pelletier, 2017).

Students from Families with Low Socio-Economic Background

International research shows a strong correlation between a background of lower socio-economic status (SES) and low levels of participation in HE. Conditions in Canada at one time seemed, however, more favourable, given the generally low cost of tuition and the availability of student aid. This situation began to change in the 1990s, when tuition was significantly increased – a result of cuts in public funding. Even when tuition increases were offset by eligibility for higher public student loans, an increased gap in enrolment of students from lower and higher income families developed. Although additional factors such as high school marks and test scores play a role in the decision not to enrol in HE, a major factor seems to be the reluctance of low income families to incur debt by taking out student loans, especially when these families are not fully aware of the benefits of attending university (Junor & Usher, 2004, p. 109).

In their study of why young adult Canadians from predominantly lower-income backgrounds do or do not undertake postsecondary education, Junor and Usher (2004) found that academic barriers account for just for about 10%, financial barriers for 20–33%, and motivational and information barriers for about 50% of the reasons for non-attendance. These data show that finances, paucity of information, and lack of motivation are the most pervasive barriers to participation in higher education. Policies in Canada (with regard to student loans) and in several provinces have tried to lower the former two barriers but the third one, motivation, is more difficult to affect with public policy. As many studies of participation in HE have shown, family background is a powerful determinant. In particular, parental education is a strong predictor of participation in postsecondary education, particularly university education (Junor & Usher, 2004, pp. 109–112). This relation is confirmed by Table 2.2: just 11% of university students are first-generation while the rest had parents with at least some PSE background.

Similar to motivational barriers, financial barriers are complex and inter-related with other factors. We turn now to these financial barriers.

Affordability

Tuition

Although the cost of tuition is only a part of entire cost of participation in HE, it is the focus of most discussions of affordability and accessibility. In many countries, including recently in Canada, tuition increases have triggered student protests and unrest. (See chapters by Schuetze, as well as Beaupré-Lavallée & Bégin-Caouette, in this volume.)

Two factors make it difficult to calculate tuition rates in Canada with any precision. First, tuition rates vary both by province and by institution; second, the real net cost to the student, as opposed to the nominal or "sticker" price, depends on various forms of student financial assistance programs which diminish the actual net cost to the student, again varying from province to

TABLE 2.4   Weighted average undergraduate tuition fees for Canadian full-time students, by province, 2016/2017

Canada	6,373
Newfoundland and Labrador	2,759
Prince Edward Island	6,288
Nova Scotia	7,218
New Brunswick	6,682
Quebec	2,851
Ontario	8,114
Manitoba	4,058
Saskatchewan	7,177
Alberta	5,750
British Columbia	5,534

SOURCE: STATISTICS CANADA (2016B), CANSIM TABLE 477-0077

ACCESS TO AND PARTICIPATION IN HIGHER EDUCATION IN CANADA 31

province and depending on academic achievement and socio-economic status.

An overview is provided by Table 2.4. Average undergraduate tuition in 2016–2017 was $6,372, with huge variations between the provinces, ranging from a high of $8,114 in Ontario down to $2,759 in Newfoundland and Labrador (Statistics Canada, 2016b).

Tuition fees shown in Table 2.4 are an average; they differ depending on fields of study, with medicine, dentistry, law and legal professions at the top of the list while education comes last. Table 2.5 shows the average undergraduate tuition fees by subject.

TABLE 2.5 Weighted average undergraduate tuition fees for Canadian full-time students, by field of study, 2016/2017

All fields of study	6,373
Education	4,580
Visual and performing arts, and communications technologies	5,640
Humanities	5,482
Social and behavioural sciences	5,566
Law, legal professions and studies	11,385
Business, management and public administration	6,776
Physical and life sciences and technologies	6,048
Mathematics, computer and information sciences	6,978
Engineering	7,825
Architecture and related technologies	6,581
Agriculture, natural resources and conservation	5,651
Dentistry	21,012
Medicine	13,858
Nursing	5,527
Pharmacy	9,738
Veterinary medicine	7,419
Other health, parks, recreation and fitness	6,135

SOURCE: STATISTICS CANADA (2016B), CANSIM TABLES 477-0021 AND 477-0077, DATE MODIFIED: 2016-09-07

In addition to tuition there are some mandatory fees which, for example, include the cost of public transportation passes, athletics fees, student health services and student associations. The average amount is $873 in Canada, again with variations between the provinces and according to field of study (Statistics Canada, 2016b).

A few European countries, for example Germany (see chapter by Timmermann in this volume), offer PSE free of charge to their own citizens and students from other EU countries. In Canada, PSE institutions traditionally do charge tuition even though there are occasional demands from student groups for free tuition (see the chapter by Beaupré-Lavallée & Bégin-Caouette in this volume). Critics counter that free tuition would help mostly the rich, and neither reduce intergenerational inequality nor inequality of access. Even worse, free tuition would take money away from other policy priorities, many of which (e.g., First Nations' health and sanitation) are of higher political importance (Usher, October 28, 2016).

In 2016 two provinces (Ontario and New Brunswick) announced policies of "free tuition" for *low-income* students, with "low income" defined as below $50,000 (Ontario) or below $60,000 (New Brunswick). As for instituting a policy of free tuition for all (rather than for only lower income students), this type of "free tuition" would be quite different from what student associations demand, namely targeted financial assistance to students from low income households.

Student Financial Assistance

The federal government and the various provinces all offer various types of subsidies to students in the form of grants, bursaries, interest free loans and the ability to deduct tuition and other costs of education from income tax. The result of this very complex system is that in some cases the "net tuition" (tuition paid to the HE institution, minus subsidies received from provincial and federal governments) is zero or less – i.e., the value of the subsidies received by some students exceeds the amount of tuition they pay (Usher, Lambert, & Mirzazadeh, 2014). Canadian student assistance is poorly packaged and advertised and therefore, for many, especially for first generation would-be students, a confusing mystery, especially the mix of back-end money (i.e., remission and tax credits) and front-end money (i.e., grants). Usher (2014a) has compiled a list of the most important types of student financial support from various public sources (federal government, provincial governments and HE institutions). Together they amounted to approximately 10.6 billion dollars in 2011. Table 2.6 breaks this figure down into various categories.

It can be safely assumed that the overall amount of student aid has increased over the last few years since Usher did the calculation from the budgets of the various aid actors. It is also apparent, however, that the system of student aid has not been simplified since then.

Student Debt

The amount of student debt is a recurrent theme in discussions of access to and affordability of HE. Recently, tuition fees in Canada have been rising

TABLE 2.6   Sources of post-secondary student financial assistance (2011)

Type	Amount (in millions)	Provided by	Remarks
Student loans	4,000	Fed government and provinces	Of which 500 is forgiven through loan remissions
Up-front grants	1,300	Fed government and provinces	
Tax credits for actual HE students and/or their families	2,300	Fed government (2/3) and provinces (1/3)	For tuition and related costs
Taxes forgone for Education Saving Grants and Learning Bonds for future HE students	700	Fed government	
Merit grants and scholarships	350	Fed government and provinces	
Educational transfers to First Nations	350	Fed government	
Scholarships	1,500	HE institutions	
TOTAL	10,500		7,000 of this is non-repayable

SOURCE: USHER (2014A, APRIL 21)

but, somewhat counter-intuitively, student debt has gone down. According to Usher (2014b) the number of students graduating with debt has decreased between 2012 and 2015 (from 59,000 to 50,000). Of the three types of sources from which students borrowed money, average debt owed to governments has slightly increased (from $25,000 to almost $27,000) among students who have incurred that kind of debt. Debts owed to banks have stayed more or less the same ($15,000) whereas family debt has substantially decreased (from about $14,000 to about $10,000). Usher concludes that data over the last ten years indicate a continuous trend, namely that average debt is slightly rising but that debt incidence is falling.

Graduate Employment and Income
A major concern of students everywhere is the transition from education to the labour market – in other words, finding an adequate job upon graduation.

Higher levels of education reduce the risk of unemployment. This is clearly true for Canada, where the employment rate of individuals with bachelor's (or equivalent) qualifications is 83% as compared to 71% of people with upper secondary (high school) education. Despite the substantial advantage in finding and maintaining employment conferred by a bachelor's degree, in Canada the advantage in earnings conferred by a degree is only 39%, as compared to the OECD average of 55% (OECD, 2016b).

According to the National Graduate Survey (NGS), conducted by Statistics Canada every five years, the employment rate of graduates has been relatively constant over the ten-year time span of the last two surveys. Employment levels of college and university graduates have been fairly constant, with 90% or more employed – which is particularly remarkable, given that the data are from both before and after the financial crisis of 2008 (Statistics Canada, 2014).

For university graduates, between 84% and 86% have been in full-time employment, while between 6% and 8% worked part-time. The unemployment rate for all HE graduates at this early stage in their careers was 5%, which compares favourably with that of people without secondary school completion (13.9%), those with only secondary school completion (8.3%), and the overall population (6.9%) (Statistics Canada, 2016a). Table 2.7

TABLE 2.7　Median cumulative (1991–2010) earnings by sex, level of education, and field of study

	Men		Women	
	Bachelor's degree	College certificate	Bachelor's degree	College certificate
Education	1,290,400	996,600	1,044,600	513,500
Fine and Applied Arts	843,900	807,200	652,100	437,300
Humanities	1,144,600	827,500	808,200	555,900
Social Sciences	1,358,900	1,241,500	824,300	563,800
Business Administration	1,619,400	1,099,500	1,169,100	625,100
Life Sciences	1,334,700	753,500	844,900	502,300
Engineering	1,845,000	1,244,200	972,600	718,800
Health	1,627,600	1,089,700	1,094,000	812,800
Mathematics and Physical Sciences	1,607,500	1,128,000	1,148,700	793,800
All fields of study	1,517,200	1,137,000	972,500	643,200

Note: High school diploma only: men 882,300, women 458,900
SOURCE: OSTROVSKY AND FRENETTE (2014, P. 2)

indicates how earnings are affected by level of education achieved, as well as field of study.

Most importantly, in terms of HE outcomes and the general principle of equality, the data reveal a shocking difference of income between men and women. The gap between men's and women's earnings in Canada is larger than it is, on average, among other industrialized countries (OECD, 2016b). It is little consolation that the gender gap in earnings narrows with increasing educational attainment.

Women in Canada with a bachelor's degree earned (1991–2010) a cumulative amount of \$972,500 (about 2.1 times as much as high school graduates), whereas those with a college certificate earned \$643,200 (about 1.4 times as much as high school graduates). In international comparison, Canadian women with less than upper secondary education earned just 61% of what males with the same education earned while on OECD average that percentage was 76%. Canadian women with higher education degrees still earned less than Canadian men, namely just 72% of what their male colleagues with the same credentials earned, yet this was comparable to the OECD average (73%).

This is not the place to explore the reasons for this huge gender pay equality gap when it comes to graduate earnings. Girls and women who are now enrolled in HE in greater numbers than in the past and are no longer a minority group or "non-traditional students." However, they still earn less than three-quarters of what their male co-workers earn; this shows that gender discrimination is alive and well in Canada.

Summary and Outlook

In raising issues of access to and participation in higher (postsecondary) education in Canada we wanted to provide some introduction and context for other chapters dealing with Canadian topics, but also to show that reforms are needed to make HE in Canada more accessible and fairer for Canadians who presently face specific barriers.

Some of these barriers, such as those experienced by Indigenous students, are the subject of policy changes at the national level. However, because of the decentralization of HE in Canada, policy change is also required at the level of the province or territory, or within individual HE institutions. Reforms at these levels have some advantages, as successful new policies are likely to be imitated by other provinces or institutions, while those that are unsuccessful are not imitated, thereby limiting the damage. The overall effect is a rate of change that is slow but usually positive, thereby preserving the generally high quality of Canadian higher education.

Looking forward, some trends that are already manifest will require significant change in the present Canadian system. The expansion of tertiary education, the diversification of provision, increasingly heterogeneous student bodies, new forms of institutional governance, and a greater emphasis on outcomes and accountability will become more important. Likewise, the diversification of funding sources, performance-based funding, and competitive procedures for obtaining public funding are trends observed in many other industrialized countries.

The changing world of internationalization of higher education is already, as we have shown, causing great changes in traditional structures and processes. Internationalization no longer concerns just "recruiting" foreign students, exchange programs, or agreements on double degree programs; it is developing into a new system of cross-border design and delivery of academic programs. Associated with this is the expansion of partnerships, franchises, off-shore satellite campuses as well as the privatization, corporatization and commercialization of a new and fast growing part of the HE system. A host of new providers (for example media companies, multinational companies and corporate universities) and new delivery methods are the most conspicuous characteristics of this development. These providers and their new programs and qualifications require new types of quality assurance and accreditation.

All these changes will have an impact on the issues discussed in this chapter: access, participation, affordability and outcomes. While arguably the entire PSE system will move further towards a model where market mechanisms play a more important role that up to now, public policy and public institutions will not become less important. On the contrary, policy will need to define the rules of the game and the responsibilities of the various actors. Postsecondary education is, as is all education, a public good and must remain under the control of the public.

Notes

1 In terms of the classification developed by Martin Trow, who distinguished "elite", "mass" and "universal" systems of HE (Trow, 2007).

2 The terminology used in Canada to refer to education that follows secondary school is somewhat confusing. While the term "higher education" is prevalent, provincial government departments with responsibility for this level of education usually use the term "postsecondary education" (PSE). Under the PSE label all forms of study after secondary school are subsumed – i.e., organized and systematic learning at universities, community colleges and technical institutes,

ACCESS TO AND PARTICIPATION IN HIGHER EDUCATION IN CANADA

private training organizations and on-line programs. PSE means simply students who have completed (upper) secondary school or holding equivalent alternative qualifications.

3 Until 2016 called Association of Universities and Colleges of Canada, or AUCC, http://www.univcan.ca/

4 The figure showing 66% female students given in this table is almost certainly misleading due to a higher proportion of female students responding to this voluntary survey, as compared to males. Census data for all postsecondary education, not just universities (Statistics Canada, 2017), indicate that women represented 56.3% of enrolments in programs that could lead to a credential, a proportion that has remained relatively stable since 1992. It is interesting to note that despite an increase in the *number* of women enrolled in a program leading to a degree in science, technology, engineering, mathematics and computer sciences (STEM), the *percentage* of female enrolment in these programs has remained stable since 2010/2011 at around 39%. By contrast, women represented the majority of enrolments in degree programs in most fields of study in 2015/2016, especially in education (76.0%) and health and related fields (72.9%) (Statistics Canada, 2017).

5 The two terms "Indigenous" and "Aboriginal" are used interchangeably to refer to people whose ancestors (or at least some of them) lived in North America prior to European settlement.

6 Of the 1.4 million (self-identified) Aboriginal people in Canada, 325,000 live on reserves.

References

Academica Group. (2017). *Why don't more Canadian students study abroad?* Retrieved from https://forum.academica.ca/forum/why-dont-more-canadian-students-study-abroad

Association of Universities and Colleges of Canada (AUCC). (2014). *Canada's universities in the world: AUCC internationalization survey.* Retrieved from http://www.univcan.ca/media-room/publications/canadas-universities-in-the-world-survey/

Brindley, J. E. (2014). Learner support in online distance education: Essential and evolving. In O. Zawacki-Richter & T. Anderson (Eds.), *Online distance education: Towards a research agenda* (pp. 287–310). Athabasca: Athabasca University Press.

Canadian Bureau for International Education (CBIE). (2017a, February 23). *The Canadian Bureau for International Education (CBIE) launches learning beyond borders initiative.* Retrieved from http://cbie.ca/canadian-bureau-international-education-cbie-launches-learning-beyond-borders-initiative/

Canadian Bureau for International Education (CBIE). (2017b). *Facts and figures.* Retrieved from http://cbie.ca/media/facts-and-figures/

Canadian Information Centre for International Credentials (CICIC). (2017). *Quality assurance in postsecondary education in Canada.* Retrieved from https://www.cicic.ca/1264/an-overview.canada

Canadian University Survey Consortium (2010, 2013, 2013). *First-year university student survey: Master report.* Retrieved from http://www.cusc-ccreu.ca/new/publications.html

Council of Ministers of Education Canada (CMEC). (2007). *Ministerial statement on quality assurance of degree education in Canada.* Retrieved from http://www.cmec.ca/postsec/qa/QA-Statement-2007.en.pdf

Cross, K. P. (1981). *Adults as learners.* San Francisco, CA: Jossey-Bass.

Dennison, J. D. (Ed.). (1995). *Challenge and opportunity: Canada's community colleges at the crossroads.* Vancouver: UBC Press.

Fisher, D., Rubenson, K., Bernatchez, J., Clift, R., Jones, G., Lee, J., MacIvor, M., Meredith, J., Shanahan, T., and Trottier, C. (2006). *Canadian federal policy and post-secondary education.* Vancouver: The Centre for Policy Studies in Higher Education & Training (CHET).

Frenette, M. (2002). *Too far to go on? Distance to school and university participation* (Analytical Studies Branch Research Paper Series, No. 191). Ottawa: Statistics Canada. Retrieved from http://www.publications.gc.ca/Collection/Statcan/11F0019MIE/11F0019MIE2002191.pdf

Frenette, M. (2003). *Access to college and university: Does distance matter?* (Analytical Studies Branch Research Paper Series, No. 201). Ottawa: Statistics Canada. Retrieved from http://www5.statcan.gc.ca/olc-cel/olc.action?objId=11F0019M2003201&objType=46&lang=en&limit=0

Global Affairs Canada. (2014). *Canada's international education strategy: Harnessing our knowledge advantage to drive innovation and prosperity.* Retrieved from http://www.international.gc.ca/education/strategy-strategie.aspx?lang=eng

Immigration, Refugees and Citizenship Canada. (2016). *Canada – International students with a valid permit on december 31st by country of citizenship (2015 ranking), 2006–2015.* Retrieved from http://open.canada.ca/data/en/dataset/052642bb-3fd9-4828-b608-c81dff7e539c

Johnson, T. (2016, May 25). Why do so many Canadian students refuse to study abroad? *University Affairs.* Retrieved from http://www.universityaffairs.ca/features/feature-article/staying-home-study-abroad/

Jones, G. A. (2014). An introduction to higher education in Canada. In K. M. Joshi & S. Paivandi (Eds.), *Higher education across nations* (Vol. 1, pp. 1–38). Delhi: B. R. Publishing.

Junor, S., & Usher, A. (2004). *The price of knowledge 2004: Access and student finance in Canada* (Canada Millennium Scholarship Foundation Research Series). Ogdensburg, NY: Renouf.

MacDonald, M. (2016, April 6). Indigenizing the academy: What some universities are doing to weave indigenous peoples, cultures and knowledge into the fabric of their campuses. *University Affairs.*

OECD. (2016a). *Education at a glance.* Retrieved from http://www.oecd-ilibrary.org/education/education-at-a-glance-2016_eag-2016-en;jsessionid=32vtf69tc9avq.x-oecd-live-03)

OECD. (2016b). *Education at a glance: Country note Canada.* Retrieved from http://www.keepeek.com/Digital-Asset-Management/oecd/education/education-at-a-glance-2016/canada_eag-2016-45-en#.WKtv-hD8HaU#page1

Ostrovsky, Y., & Frenette, M. (2014). *The cumulative earnings of postsecondary graduates over 20 years: Results by field of study.* Ottawa: Statistics Canada. Retrieved from http://www.statcan.gc.ca/pub/11-626-x/11-626-x2014040-eng.htm

Parkes, M., Gregory, S., Fletcher, P., Adlington, R., & Gromik, N. (2015). Bringing people together while learning apart: Creating online learning environments to support the needs of rural and remote students. *Australian and International Journal of Rural Education, 25*(1), 66–78.

Poulin, R., & Straut, T. (2017). *WCET distance education price and cost report.* Boulder, CO: WICHE Cooperative for Educational Technologies (WCET).

Richards, J. (2014). *Are we making progress? New evidence on aboriginal outcomes in provincial and reserve schools.* Retrieved from https://www.cdhowe.org/are-we-making-progress-new-evidence-aboriginal-education-outcomes-provincial-and-reserve-schools

Schuetze, H. G. (2014). From adults to non-traditional students to lifelong learners in higher education: Changing contexts and perspectives. *Journal of Adult and Continuing Education, 20*(2), 37–55.

Schuetze, H. G. (2019). Private higher education in Canada and the United States: Development, reform, and likely futures. In P. Zgaga, U. Teichler, H. G. Schuetze, & A. Wolter (Eds.), *Higher education reform: Looking back – looking forward* (2nd ed., pp. 293–309). Frankfurt: Peter Lang.

Slowey, M., & Schuetze, H. G. (Eds.). (2012). *Global perspectives on higher education and lifelong learners.* New York, NY: Routledge.

Statistics Canada. (2008). *Distance as a postsecondary access issue.* Ottawa: Author. Retrieved from http://www.statcan.gc.ca/pub/81-004-x/200404/6854-eng.htm

Statistics Canada. (2013). *The educational attainment of aboriginal peoples. The National Household Survey (NHS) 2011.* Ottawa: Statistics Canada. Retrieved from http://www12.statcan.gc.ca/nhs-enm/2011/as-sa/99-012-x/99-012-x2011003_3-eng.pdf

Statistics Canada. (2014). *National graduates survey, labour force activity of graduates, by province of study, level of study and sex, every 5 years*. Retrieved from http://www23.statcan.gc.ca/imdb/p2SV.pl?Function=getSurvey&SDDS=5012

Statistics Canada. (2016a). *Postsecondary enrolments, by student status, country of citizenship and sex*. Retrieved from http://www5.statcan.gc.ca/cansim/a26?lang=eng& retrLang=eng&id=4770031&tabMode=dataTable&srchLan=-1&p1=-1&p2=9

Statistics Canada. (2016b). *Tuition fees for degree programs, 2016/2017*. Retrieved from http://www.statcan.gc.ca/daily-quotidien/160907/cg-a001-eng.htm

Statistics Canada. (2017, December 7). *Canadian postsecondary enrolments and graduates, 2015/2016*. Retrieved from http://www.statcan.gc.ca/daily-quotidien/171207/dq171207c-eng.htm

Stöter, J., Bullen, M., Zawacki-Richter, O., & von Prümmer, C. (2014). From the back door into the mainstream: The characteristics of lifelong learners. In O. Zawacki-Richter & T. Anderson (Eds.), *Online distance education: Towards a research agenda* (pp. 421–457). Athabasca: Athabasca University Press.

Trow, M. (2007). Reflections on the transition from elite to mass to universal access: Forms and phases of higher education in modern societies since WWII. In J. J. F. Forest & P. G. Altbach (Eds.), *International handbook of higher education* (pp. 243–280). Dordrecht: Springer.

Truth and Reconciliation Commission of Canada. (2015). *Honouring the truth, reconciling for the future: Summary of the final report of the truth and reconciliation commission of Canada*. Ottawa: Author. Retrieved from http://www.trc.ca/ websites/trcinstitution/File/2015/Honouring_the_Truth_Reconciling_for_the_ Future_July_23_2015.pdf

Universities Canada. (2015a). *Principles on indigenous education*. Retrieved from http://www.univcan.ca/media-room/media-releases/universities-canada-principles-on-Indigenous-education/

Universities Canada. (2015b). *Indigenous programs and services directory*. Retrieved from http://www.universitystudy.ca/Indigenous-programs-and-services-directory/

Usher, A. (2014a, April 21). *Canada's annual student assistance bill: $10 billion, most of it non-repayable* [Web log post]. Retrieved from http://higheredstrategy.com/ canadas-annual-student-assistance-bill-10-billion-most-of-it-non-repayable/

Usher, A. (2014b, May 23). *New data on student debt: The 2010 national graduates survey* [Web log post]. Retrieved from http://higheredstrategy.com/new-data-on-student-debt-the-2010-national-graduates-survey/

Usher, A. (2015, July 16). *Student debt in Canada: Sorry, still no crisis* [Web log post]. Retrieved from http://higheredstrategy.com/student-debt-in-canada-sorry-still-no-crisis/

Usher, A. (2016, October 28). Priorities [Web log post]. Retrieved from http://higheredstrategy.com/priorities/

Usher, A. (2018a, January 22). *Canada's secret weapon against inequality* [Web log post]. Retrieved from http://higheredstrategy.com/canadas-secret-weapon-inequality/

Usher, A. (2018b, March 22). *A challenge and an opportunity in college education* [Web log post]. Retrieved from http://higheredstrategy.com/a-challenge-and-an-opportunity-in-college-education/

Usher, A., Lambert, J., & Mirzazadeh, C. (2014). *The many prices of knowledge: How tuition and subsidies interact in Canadian higher education.* Toronto: Higher Education Strategy Associates.

Usher, A., & Pelletier, Y. Y. (2017). *Government of Manitoba: Manitoba college review – System-wide report.* Toronto: Higher Education Strategy Associates.

Wickham, D. (2017). Canada – access at the crossroads. In G. Atherton (Ed.), *Access to higher education: Understanding global inequalities* (pp. 13–28). London: Palgrave.

CHAPTER 3

Aboriginal Higher Education and Indigenous Students

Michelle Pidgeon

Abstract

Higher Education in Canada began in the late 1700s with the establishment of the first universities in Quebec and New Brunswick (Jones, 2014). While these institutions were often built upon unceded Aboriginal lands, Aboriginal peoples' participation in higher education did not begin until the late 1960s. There were a few early participants (e.g., post WWII) but participation at that time meant giving up one's status as a First Nations person. This act of assimilation occurred in Canada throughout its educational systems' policies and practices (e.g., residential schools and day schools for K-12). The participation shift that took hold in the late 1960s and 1970s was due to several factors including: development of Aboriginal specific programs and services; establishment of Aboriginal post-secondary funding programs; and increased high school completion rates. The purpose of this chapter is to describe the policy, program, and practice changes that have resulted in slowly transforming Canada's higher education system from a tool of assimilation to one of Indigenous empowerment and decolonization. The chapter will explore ideas of what the purpose of higher education is in relation to Indigenous understandings of life, work, and civic engagement.

Keywords

Aboriginal education – indigeneity – Indigenous students – higher education – student affairs & services – decolonization

Introduction

Higher Education in Canada began in the late 1700s with the establishment of the first universities in Quebec and New Brunswick (Jones, 2014). While these

© KONINKLIJKE BRILL NV, LEIDEN, 2019 | DOI:10.1163/9789004393073_003

institutions were often built upon unceded[1] Aboriginal lands, that is, lands they had not relinquished their ownership or rights to, Aboriginal peoples' participation in higher education did not begin until the late 1960s. This chapter provides a brief historical overview of the policy, program, and practice changes, notably the role of Indigenous empowerment in influencing Canada's education systems to be more responsible, respectful, reciprocal, and relevant to Canada's Indigenous peoples (Kirkness & Barnhardt, 1991).

Indigenous Peoples of Canada

Indigenous peoples are the fastest growing population in Canada, according to Statistics Canada (Statistics Canada, 2013b). In the 2011 National Household Survey (NHS) there are 1,400,685 people self-identified as having an Aboriginal identity, representing 4.3% of the total Canadian population, an increase from 3.8% in the 2006 Census (Statistics Canada, 2013b). Within the body of this chapter, I use the terms Indigenous and Aboriginal interchangeably to refer inclusively to the first peoples of Canada, including First Nations, Métis, and Inuit peoples and, where appropriate, I use more specific terms that speak to how groups self-identify (e.g., Mi'kmaq, Cree, Sto'lo, Inuit).

From a decolonizing perspective, respecting the diversity of over 60 different Indigenous nations, which represent as many cultures and languages, is critical to counter the colonially imposed government defined parameters and terms. One such term is "First Nations," which results from the Indian Act of 1876. While several amendments have been made over time, the essence of the document has remained the same since 1876.[2] The Act oversees those who are considered status and registered members of a First Nation. Many First Nations people live "on-reserve" (i.e., on parcels of land defined by the Indian Act) and these reserves are governed by the elected council of the "Band," who are registered members under the Act, and the Canadian government department currently known as "Indigenous and Northern Affairs Canada."

However, not every Aboriginal group in Canada is "covered" under this Indian Act; the Royal Commission on Aboriginal Peoples (RCAP) (1996b) describes the historical contexts that have led to Canada's three unique Aboriginal groups: First Nations, Métis, and Inuit. For example, separate treaties were negotiated with different Aboriginal nations that have specific relationships with provincial and federal governments and these treaties may (or may not) be associated with land reserves, and there are others who choose to self-identify as belonging to a specific nation but do not have either status through the Indian Act or treaty recognition (RCAP, 1996b). The Métis are a unique cultural group who have First Nations and European ancestry, their own language and cultural practices, and are recognized as one of three Aboriginal groups within Canada in the 1982 Canadian Charter of Rights and Freedoms.[3] The third group, the Inuit, are Indigenous peoples who live in the Arctic and northern regions of Canada.

There are others who do not fit neatly into one of the three recognized groups of Indigenous people. There are those who come to learn of their Aboriginal ancestry later in life – e.g., as a result of being adopted out into non-Aboriginal families, particularly during "the 60s scoop," a period when Aboriginal children were taken into foster care and adopted out (RCAP, 1996). This could also result from a family's decision to not disclose their Aboriginal identities to their descendants. The history of colonization, government policy, and politics regarding who is defined as Indigenous and by whom (e.g., community, federal government) has had profound impacts on Indigenous individuals, families, communities, and nations that continue across society today, most recently documented by the Truth and Reconciliation Commission (TRC) (RCAP, 1996; TRC, 2015a, 2015b).

The Education Gap: A Concern for All

The 2012 Aboriginal Peoples Survey found that "72% of First Nations people living off reserve, 42% of Inuit and 77% of Métis aged 18 to 44 had a high school diploma or equivalent ("completers"). The 2011 National Household Survey data showed that the figure for the non-Aboriginal population was 89%"(Statistics Canada, 2013a, p. 1). Table 3.1 shows that among the 671,400 Aboriginal participants who responded to the 2011 NHS the disparity of university attainment between Aboriginal and non-Aboriginal peoples remains wide (e.g., approximately 10% to 26%) (Statistics Canada, 2013b).

Further analysis and commentary on the NHS 2011 data set for on-reserve First Nations shows a higher rate of non-completion of high school at 58%, compared to 10.1% of non-Aboriginal Canadians (Richards, 2013). These statistics should also raise concern, as lower high school completion rates directly influence future post-secondary participation. Richards (2013) also pointed out the important provincial variations in these statistics that are hidden when we look solely at national trends, given the mobility of Aboriginal families between rural, reserve, and urban centres. For example, high school completion rates were higher in the provinces of British Columbia and Ontario, whereas Manitoba had a non-completion rate 12.3 points higher than the national average.

While these credential holders represent 48% of Aboriginal respondents to the NHS survey, when we look at the non-Aboriginal population of the same

TABLE 3.1   Highest post-secondary credential earned by NHS 2011 respondents[4]

	Aboriginal	Non-Aboriginal
Trades	14.4	12.0
College diploma	20.6	21.3
University certificate/diploma	3.5	4.9
University degree	9.8	26.5

survey, their total post-secondary education (PSE) completion rate is 67%, with the main difference between the Aboriginal and non-Aboriginal populations being in the proportion of university graduates (approximately 10% Aboriginal compared to 26% non-Aboriginal) (Statistics Canada, 2013b). The educational attainment differences are even more pronounced when we look at national census data, where "Aboriginal people are still much less likely to have a university degree than non-Aboriginal peoples in 2006 (8% compared to 23%). This gap is larger than what it was in 2001 (6% compared to 20%)" (Statistics Canada, 2008, p. 19).[5]

The disparity of educational attainment, particularly university degrees, is a core issue facing Canadian society with broad implications not only for Indigenous peoples and communities but also for the entire country, socially, politically, economically, and even ethically.

Responsibility & Contestation

The politics of who is responsible for Aboriginal post-secondary education and even the educational disparity between Aboriginal and non-Aboriginal Canadians directly connects to Canada's assimilationist policies from the late 1800s to the present. Systemic barriers across the post-secondary system still remain prevalent despite clear policy changes (e.g., in admissions, housing, funding) and program development (e.g., Indigenous content, courses, and programs) (Pidgeon, 2014, 2016b). Unlike many other countries, Canada does not have a national higher education system – education, both K-12 and post-secondary, by constitutional law is the legal jurisdiction of the provincial/territorial governments. The federal government plays a role in post-secondary education through a system of transfer payments to the provinces and territories. However, the federal government is responsible and has "jurisdiction" over Aboriginal peoples' education through the Indian Act – which that government interprets as a legal responsibility for K-12 education only (Battiste & Barman, 1995).

Contestation over who is responsible for Aboriginal higher education is clearly evident in Canadian policy and legislation where there is "fundamental policy disagreement ... between First Nations and the federal government over whether higher education is a treaty and Aboriginal right obtained in return for sharing of lands" (Stonechild, 2006, p. 1). The federal government does not see post-secondary education of First Nations as a legal or constitutional responsibility; it views higher education as a social responsibility based on the idea that post-secondary attainment helps the economic viability of the nation. The Indian Act, as a policy document, clearly outlines the legal responsibility of the federal government for K-12 education while higher education is not mentioned. Thus, the relationship between federal and provincial/territorial governments in identifying First Nations students attending public schools at the K-12 level results in transfer of funds from the one government to another; at the post-secondary level there are no similar transfer agreements for Aboriginal students attending college or university.

Indigenous nations, however, see the federal role for higher education as a legal responsibility. In a detailed analysis of the treaties and associated documents of the time, Stonechild (2006) recounted the history of the negotiation of Treaty 8 in 1899,[6] where the commissioner, representing the Crown, reported:

> They [meaning the First Nations leaders] seemed desirous of having educational advantages for their children, but stipulated that in the matter of schools there should be no interference with their religious beliefs, suggesting that education should respect Indian culture. Such understandings also imply that the Indians who signed the treaties believed they were entitled to all forms of education, including higher education, as part of the spirit and intent of the treaties. (p. 16)

Therefore, higher education from the Indigenous point of view is inherently part of the life-learning journey and interconnected to work (e.g., relevant and respectful career and employment opportunities) and civic engagement (e.g., responsibility and reciprocity to community). In discussing Aboriginal higher education in Canada, one has to acknowledge and discuss the legacy of residential schools, and the impact of these schools on Aboriginal families, communities, and, pertinent to this discussion, Aboriginal post-secondary aspirations and attainment.

Residential School Era & Relationship to PSE
Residential schools (i.e., boarding schools) and Indian day schools were primarily operated from the early 1800s to 1996 across Canada by various religious orders with the aim of assimilation and removing the "Indian" from the

child (e.g., no Aboriginal language or cultural practices were allowed). The Truth and Reconciliation Commission (TRC) (2010–2015) sought to witness and document the intergenerational trauma from residential schools. It had the mandate

> to learn the truth about what happened in the residential schools and to inform all Canadians about what happened in the schools. ... Reconciliation is an ongoing individual and collective process, and will require commitment from all those affected including First Nations, Inuit and Métis former Indian Residential School (IRS) students, their families, communities, religious entities, former school employees, government and the people of Canada. (TRC, 2015a, pp. 3–4)

This commission documented the stories of survivors of residential schools, hearing more than 6,750 testimonies and collecting documents, pictures, and other artifacts along the way. The TRC final reports spanning 10 volumes document the notable atrocities such as physical, emotional, and sexual abuse, death in care, and the intergenerational trauma that resulted from children being taken away from their families, their cultures, and their homes (TRC, 2015a).

The Calls to Action speak directly to the responsibility that education has in reconciliation (TRC, 2015b). It is evident that work is needed at the post-secondary level to reconcile the roles universities and colleges played in residential schools. For example, post-secondary institutions educated the teachers, administrators, social workers, and other professionals who worked in residential schools or within government offices that sanctioned these schools. The President of the University of Manitoba released a statement of apology for the role that the University had in the residential school legacy in which he stated that "Our institution failed to recognize or challenge the forced assimilation of Aboriginal peoples and the subsequent loss of their language, culture, and traditions" (Barnard, 2011, p. 8).

Upon the closure of these schools, some universities and colleges repurposed former residential schools as part of contemporary university culture without addressing the systemic harm these schools perpetuated on Aboriginal peoples and their families, nor recognizing the impact that returning to these buildings has on residential school survivors and their families, and not understanding why Aboriginal families did not feel safe in sending their children to these institutions. The journey to reconciliation has been paved with much turmoil and pain for Aboriginal peoples, and as Justice Sinclair reminds us, it will not be done by taking short cuts; reconciliation will take time, and post-secondary institutions have key responsibilities in educating Aboriginal and non-Aboriginal peoples while moving our nation forward.

Aboriginal Relationship with PSE: Politics, Policy, and Agency

The relationship between Aboriginal peoples and higher education has changed over time and can be best described through three major periods: 1800s through 1950s, 1960s through 1990s, and 2000s to present. These periods demonstrate the shifts from little to no participation to increased growth in participation, from assimilationist policies to Indigenization of policy, programs, and practices.

1800s through 1950s

The beginning of the 1800s through the 1950s is generally seen as the assimilationist era, with policies aimed at assimilating Indigenous peoples into Canadian culture and society, namely through residential schools, and with little focus on post-secondary aspirations or attainment outside of the preparation of Indigenous peoples to do low skilled jobs (e.g., housekeeper, farmer, etc.) (Battiste & Barman, 1995; RCAP, 1996; TRC, 2015b).

In fact, this period of history saw little to no progress in the actualization of the higher education aspirations of Indigenous peoples in Canada. University completion for Aboriginal peoples was rare, and only nine by 1902 had completed degrees, "three from Quebec, five from Ontario, and one from the Northwest Territories [the part that is now the province of Alberta]." (Stonechild, 2004, cited in Fisher et al., 2006, p. 11). Pursuing higher education at this time was primarily through private educational opportunities established by religious orders to train Aboriginal catechists, teachers, and interpreters (Fisher et al., 2006; Stonechild, 2006). For example, in 1879 Emmanuel College was opened by Right Reverend John McLean in Prince Albert, Saskatchewan, and later became part of the University of Saskatchewan (Fisher et al., 2006; Stonechild, 2006).

Aboriginal persons who did pursue their university degrees (or became ministers of religion, thus educated) and were under the jurisdiction of the *Indian Act of 1876* lost their federal status as First Nations persons, which had intergenerational repercussions for their descendants (Furi & Wherrett, 1996, February). Amendments to the Indian Act in 1951 and Bill C-31 in 1985 sought to rectify such "acts" that had resulted in disenfranchisement (loss of Aboriginal status) and to align the outdated policy with the Canadian Charter of Rights and Freedoms:

The amendments were intended to remove discrimination, restore status and membership rights, and increase control by bands over their affairs. The federal government continues to maintain control over who is registered as an Indian and the rights that flow from registration. The bill represented a compromise between the positions of Aboriginal women and non-status Indian groups, and the national status Indian organization, the AFN. (Furi & Wherrett, 1996, February, p. 4)

However, the legacy of disenfranchisement still has lasting impact on many Indigenous families who were directly affected by these policies.

Post World War II saw a dramatic shift in the Canadian higher education landscape; not only were there thousands of returning veterans to provide programs and services for (e.g., career advising, accommodation services, and counseling), but also the latter part of this era saw increased participation in higher education by women and non-traditional learners (e.g., students older than 21, students with disabilities, and ethnic minority students) (Hardy Cox & Strange, 2010). During the latter part of the 1950s and into the 1960s, more Aboriginal communities and organizations (e.g., the National Indian Brotherhood, now the Assembly of First Nations) became influential across several areas including education, policy, and legal advocacy. This signaled that important political, social, and cultural change was coming for Indigenous peoples.

1960s through the 1990s

During the late 1960s and early 1970s, specific Aboriginal programs and services, such as Native Teacher Education and Native Studies, and Aboriginal support services were established in response to the growing numbers of Aboriginal students graduating from high school and seeking relevant post-secondary credentials (Pidgeon, 2005; Pidgeon & Hardy Cox, 2005). The first Native Student Centres were established in the early 1970s at the University of Calgary and the University of Alberta in response to the need to have culturally relevant support services on campus for the Aboriginal students attending Native-focused academic programs. It wasn't until the 1990s that, through provincial grants, other institutions followed suit in establishing Aboriginal Student Services (Pidgeon, 2005; Pidgeon & Hardy Cox, 2005). Based on a revisiting and updating of the data from Pidgeon (2001) from publically available online sources, today over 95% of universities and colleges now offer some form of Aboriginal student support services.

In 1969, the Minister of Indian Affairs, Jean Chrétien, presented a discussion document entitled *Statement of the Government of Canada on Indian Policy*;

this document is commonly referred to as the White Paper (Chrétien, 1969). This document aimed to set out a new relationship between Aboriginal nations and the federal government. The challenge was that this document did not include Indigenous perspectives on their own futures; in response to this document, in 1972 the Canadian National Indian Brotherhood (now Assembly of First Nations) released the document entitled *Indian Control over Indian Education* to outline an Indigenous vision for education of their peoples which spoke to: parental responsibility; programs, curriculum, and values; teachers and counselors; facilities and services; and research (National Indian Brotherhood, 1972; Pidgeon, Muñoz, Kirkness, & Archibald, 2013).

The National Indian Brotherhood (1972) clearly stated, "We want education to give our children the knowledge to understand and be proud of themselves and the knowledge to understand the world around them" (p. 1). This position has not changed since the 1970s; in a recent statement regarding the constitutional right of Indigenous peoples to education across the life span, the Assembly of First Nations (2012) stated:

> Section 35 (1) of the Constitution Act of 1982 recognizes Aboriginal and Treaty rights and affirms First Nations inherent right to self-government including the creation of laws and systems for the provision of lifelong learning for First Nations populations. First Nations expect the Crown, not only to recognize their jurisdiction to lifelong learning, but also to "fulfill their Constitutional, Treaty and international obligations to First Nations peoples by supporting the design and implementation of First Nations comprehensive learning systems with adequate and sustainable resourcing. (p. 5)

Hence, when we enter into discussions of higher education we can clearly see how different world views require us to understand how the ways in which such policies articulate positions and how these policies are interpreted have impacted Indigenous communities across this country. In this period, "the role of Aboriginal post-secondary education has evolved from a tool of assimilation to an instrument of empowerment. There has been a succession of policy phases proceeding from assimilation and integration to the recognition of Aboriginal rights and the struggle for self-government" (Stonechild, 2006, p. 2).

The RCAP (1996a) provides the historical and contemporary launching point where we can enter into the conversation for contemporary Indigenous persons' experiences with Canadian higher education. The Commission was established in 1991 to better understand Aboriginal and non-Aboriginal historical and contemporary relations through national consultation and research. The RCAP resulted in a five volume report with recommendations regarding Aboriginal governance, land and economy, social and cultural issues, and response and legacy.[7]

The RCAP report dedicates one entire volume to the educational experiences of Canada's First Nations, from assimilationist policies and practices (e.g., residential schools), the Aboriginal post-secondary funding program and the impacts that such limited funding opportunities have had had on post-secondary educational attainment, and the establishment of specific Aboriginal programs, services, and even institutions (Fisher et al., 2006; RCAP, 1996a, 1996b).

The federal governments' Postsecondary Student Support Program (PSSP) aims to support First Nations and eligible Inuit people who wish to attend university or college, but is not available to Métis students.[8] The funding program, which began in 1977, has increased access for some Indigenous students, yet there has also been controversy due to the inadequate funding of the program (Fisher et al., 2006; RCAP, 1996a; Usher, 2009). For example, the funding levels per student have been capped since 1996, while tuition, living costs, and inflation have continued to rise. This program shortfall results in many First Nations students being put on wait-lists for funding; finding alternative funding sources has been problematic and many choose not to pursue higher education as a result (Human Capital Strategies, 2005; Malatest & Associates Ltd., 2004). For those who do get funding, the full costs of their education and living expenses are not covered, requiring students to take fewer courses, which extends their degree completion time or jeopardizes their ability to be eligible for further funding. Other Aboriginal students balance going to school, working part-time, and caring for their families, while others stop out to save funds, or not complete their program at all (Human Capital Strategies, 2005; Malatest & Associates Ltd., 2004).

Given the structure of higher education in Canada and provincial/territorial jurisdiction, the decisions for Aboriginal policies, programs, and services at the public university and college level are at the discretion of the institutions themselves (Stonechild, 2006). This is an important distinction to make within the Canadian higher education landscape, because it is this institutional responsibility that is often "initiated" either by grassroots Aboriginal and non-Aboriginal staff and faculty establishing a program or service, or when the provincial governments provide specific and strategic (and often short-term) funding opportunities for Indigenous initiatives (Pidgeon, 2014).

Utilizing provincial grants and infrastructure initiatives, Canadian universities and colleges began developing more relevant programs and services for

Aboriginal students in the late 1990s to 2000s, supporting White et al.'s (2009) argument for systemic change because

> [W]e can not simply push forward on the same path and expect things to be get better. We argue that there is a need to confront this current situation [i.e., educational disparity between Aboriginal and non-Aboriginal Canadians] based on the evidence, and not turn away from the difficult decisions. Thinking outside the box will mean raising issues that some people do not want raised, such as viability of certain communities and certain social, economic, and bureaucratic structures. (pp. 7–8)

The 1990s and early 2000s can be seen as a period of growth in the development of culturally relevant programs, services, and institutions due to federal and provincial policy initiatives aimed at increasing Aboriginal participation. More importantly, Aboriginal communities, organizations, and leaders valuing post-secondary education have made significant policy, program, and advocacy changes towards that goal. Many universities and colleges are also now operating in partnership with local Aboriginal communities through Aboriginal advisory councils. Other institutions have established formal Indigenous leadership positions within their governance models, such as Special Advisor to the President, Director of Aboriginal Initiatives, or an Associate Dean within a faculty. Another policy development that is noteworthy is institution-wide Aboriginal strategic planning which aims to connect institutional mission and goals with specific goals and initiatives focusing on Indigenous policy, programs, and services in addition to the recruitment of Indigenous peoples to the institution.

2000s to Present

In the 2000s Indigenous higher education continues to evolve and transform Canada's public post-secondary system. There is more diversity of program offerings across many academic disciplines, specialized degree or diploma options for Indigenous students (e.g., Forestry, Child and Youth Care Services), and also more targeted recruitment and retention initiatives aimed at increasing the number of Aboriginal students in particular fields – for example, Science, Technology, Engineering, and Mathematics (STEM), health, and law. We see more Indigenous peoples pursuing graduate education and taking their place within the professoriate at universities and colleges and in other key leadership roles within the higher education system.

Stonechild (2006) argues that higher education "to be truly the 'new buffalo' that will ensure a strong and prosperous future for First Nations" (p. 1) must be recognized as a legal right. He further argues one must also critically look at institutional capacity to address higher education needs that are relevant to First Nations communities in that the education received has direct benefit to the communities' economic, social, and cultural empowerment. He further points out that the difference of perspective between the federal, provincial, and Aboriginal governments on whose responsibility (e.g., in whose jurisdiction) Aboriginal higher education is creates policy and practice fractures within our higher education system that are still evident today (Stonechild, 2006).

Statistics and research reports continue to demonstrate that the system's fractures are still not all healed. There is still much work to be done at the policy and practice levels to create a higher education system that supports Indigenous learners and their communities with respectful, relevant, reciprocal, and responsible education (Kirkness & Barnhardt, 1991). As a society we are still dealing with: the educational attainment gap between Aboriginal and non-Aboriginal peoples (White, Beavon, Peters, & Spence, 2009); the intergenerational trauma of residential schools; systemic, overt, and covert forms of racism in educational policies and practices (RCAP, 1996a); and chronic underfunding at the K-12 and PSE systems for infrastructure, positions, and scholarships (Howe, 2004; Malatest & Associates Ltd., 2004; Usher, 2009).

As well, identity politics continues to play out in higher education in a variety of ways, from those First Nations, Métis, and Inuit students who choose not to disclose their Indigenous identity in their application, to those who have to provide "proof of identity" to be eligible for Aboriginal-specific funding, programs and services, and to those who during their academic journey come to understand more of who they are as Indigenous peoples (Archibald et al., 1995; Human Capital Strategies, 2005; Malatest & Associates Ltd., 2004; Pidgeon, 2008a; Restoule, 2011). For example, Restoule's (2011) study asked administrators specifically how they used the "self-identification" information on students' applications; they stated that this information had no bearing on student admissions and was simply shared with Aboriginal student services units as a means of providing access to relevant support. However, Restoule (2011) learned from some Aboriginal students that they did not disclose their identity due to either "their distrust of government, their concerns over being assessed on their individual merit instead of their cultural heritage, and a need for privacy" (p. 54). For those students who choose to self-disclose, or are singled out due to their physical representation of "being Aboriginal," their identities come into question in several ways as they are asked to speak for all Aboriginal peoples or on Aboriginal issues; they also encounter the overt and covert forms of racism in and outside the classroom that are systemic in our universities and colleges (Pidgeon, 2014; Restoule, 2011; TeHennepe, 1993).

There has been a steady increase in the high school completion rates of Aboriginal youth, with more and more being "post-secondary ready" – i.e., prepared to enter college or university upon graduation. The challenge is that within this growth, there is clear differentiation of completion rates between on- and off-reserve schools, with on-reserve high school completion rates still remaining low across each province and territory (Richards, 2013). High school completion rates impact readiness of this group to enter into university or college, and for the non-completers it directly influences when they may choose to pursue further education (e.g., waiting until they are older than 21 to enter as mature students).[9] Such choices then impact how post-secondary institutions respond to this particular student group. For example, recognizing the need for more transition support, many universities and colleges have begun offering academic bridging programs to increase the academic readiness of Aboriginal students with culturally-relevant pedagogies and curriculums to support their success in their chosen education path.

Approaching support services from a strengths- or gifts-based approach honors the cultural integrity of the Indigenous student. In the past, students' poor academic achievement was often blamed on the student for not conforming or performing; moving away from the deficit model has also been an active way of decolonizing the institutional programs and policies (Pidgeon, 2016a; Pidgeon, Archibald, & Hawkey, 2014). Within this discussion there is recognition that barriers exist, whether structural, social, economic, etc., that hinder Aboriginal student success.

One must also consider the connection between the transition from K-12 to higher education, and how Aboriginal students are being prepared to be ready for higher education. Within the K-12 system across the country there have been concerted efforts to make K-12 a better place for Aboriginal students, with the aim of increasing high school graduation rates. For example, British Columbia's Ministry of Education has been articulating policies with its school districts and Aboriginal communities called "Aboriginal Education Enhancement Agreements" (AEEA) (see http://www.bced.gov.bc.ca/abed/agreements/).

As of June, 2015, 58 school districts in BC have some form of AEEA, most of which are 5-year agreements.[10] What is interesting to note is that only two school districts are working under their fourth agreement, while another three districts are now working with their third EA so have completed at least 10 years of this work within their districts. In looking at these agreements using a post-secondary lens, there is a lost opportunity to support the successful transition of Aboriginal K-12 learners onto a post-secondary pathway. Of these 58 agreements, only a few specifically mention supporting Aboriginal learners transitioning to post-secondary education (e.g., through scholarships, fostering post-secondary aspirations, or having representatives of post-secondary institutions visit the schools) (Kitchenham, Fraser, Pidgeon, & Ragoonaden, 2016). In some ways this connects back to the governance issues discussed earlier in this chapter as British Columbia Aboriginal post-secondary education is under the jurisdiction of the Ministry of Advanced Education and Training, while Aboriginal K-12 is seen as the responsibility of the Ministry of Education.

It is important to recognize that Aboriginal peoples have always known and articulated their visions for post-secondary education. Across the higher education landscape in Canada one must recognize the work of Indigenous institutions, which may be universities such as First Nations University of Canada in Saskatchewan, or colleges like Blue Quills College in Alberta, or institutes such as First Nations Technical Institute in Ontario. Within British Columbia, the Indigenous Adult and Higher Learning Association (IAHLA) represents 38 Indigenous-based institutions. The IAHLA mission is "to support quality post-secondary educational institutes that leverage Indigenous language, culture and knowledge to create adaptable, competent, skilled citizens who are able to contribute to local, provincial, and national advancement" (The Indigenous Adult & Higher Learning Association, 2013, p. 3). Such institutions have played a vital role in the post-secondary journeys of many Aboriginal peoples. In providing culturally-relevant programs and services in close proximity to Indigenous communities, such Indigenous institutions provide gateways of access and success, partnering with colleges and universities to offer degree programs, apprenticeship programs, certificate programs, and diplomas (The Aboriginal Institutes' Consortium, 2005).

Some key events occurring within Canadian society aimed at addressing systemic issues in Canadian society that have hindered Aboriginal empowerment and self-determination bring us to a contemporary conversation of Indigenous higher education and also an envisioning of an aspirational future for Indigenous learners. The TRC (2015a) brought national attention to the residential school legacy for Aboriginal and non-Aboriginal Canadians. The TRC actively engaged universities and colleges to be part of the witnessing of the testimonials given by residential school survivors and their families. Today, universities and colleges across the country are taking up the call to actions in examining their policies, programs, and practices regarding reconciliation. Witnessing is an important Aboriginal value and cultural practice, and it is not only occurring as part of the TRC process, but also as more Indigenous college and university students and professors are sharing through research and teaching within academic contexts about Indigenous ways of knowing and being, languages, and cultures.

Today's Challenges & Opportunities

Who Are Our Aboriginal PSE Students Today?

In setting up the historical journey of Indigenous higher education in Canada, it is now important to contextualize who are our First Nations, Métis, and Inuit post-secondary learners today. Aboriginal learners take multiple pathways through higher education to obtain their goals; some may first start out at a local community college close to their home and support networks, and others decide to relocate to a more urban centre to attend university or college. In our classrooms today, we see a range of ages from direct entry (directly from high school) to older adults returning to college or university. As older learners, the latter group bring a wealth of lived and professional experiences; they often have families of their own, and have to maintain a balance between working and attending school. Students also range in their cultural identities and backgrounds, for reasons explained earlier in this chapter, and come from diverse contexts (e.g., urban, rural, reserve). Nationally, Aboriginal students still represent only 3% of the Canadian post-secondary student population, but provincial and geographical differences exist based on Aboriginal population demographics and mobility. For example, the student body of some remote or northern institutions is predominately Aboriginal (e.g., over 90% of students enrolled in Yukon College's Carcross campus are Indigenous) and some urban institutions have considerably higher than the national average Aboriginal student population (e.g., 10% of the University of Northern British Columbia student population is Aboriginal). It continues to be difficult to provide specific enrollment and graduation numbers, as many Indigenous students choose to not identity as such to their institution whether for political or personal reasons.

Research on Aboriginal student experience demonstrates that their conceptions of success are multiple and often differ from the institutional definitions of success based on GPA and graduation (Pidgeon, 2008b; Pidgeon et al., 2014; Shotton, Lowe, & Waterman, 2013). The reasons they attend post-secondary also extend beyond the individual aspiration of completing a credential and getting a job; this is, of course, important, but students often speak about their goals in connection to their family and community – being a role model for others, and making a difference in Indigenous people's lives. Aboriginal students attend higher education for all these reasons as well as for their own personal dreams for themselves. It is also important that these students speak of the role of their cultural identity and being, in these conversations about success; it is not about assimilating into another culture. They choose to attend and complete post-secondary with their own cultural integrity intact, empowered in who they are as Indigenous peoples, and educated balancing both worlds of Indigenous and non-Indigenous (Huffman, 2008, 2010; Pidgeon, 2016a; Shotton et al., 2013; Tierney, 1995; Tierney & Jun, 2001). Hence the Indigenizing the Academy movement is critical to supporting Indigenous learners and their communities.

Indigenizing the Academy

"Indigenizing the academy" (Alfred, 2004; Justice, 2004; Mihesuah & Wilson, 2004; Pidgeon, 2016b) is a movement that spans institutional policy and practices to ensure Indigenous ways of knowing and being are part of the institutional framework, moving education from a tool of colonization to one of empowerment and decolonization (Battiste, Bell, & Findlay, 2002; Kuokkanen, 2007; Mihesuah & Wilson, 2004). This movement has arisen largely due to the fact that the educational system in Canada remains slow to change and the educational disparity remains between Aboriginal and non-Aboriginal Canadians. The ramifications of this disparity are not just about education attainment: According to White et al. (2009) the actual crisis is the fact that despite the enormous resources directed at "the problem" the situation is not improving and the recent report by Richards (2013) further demonstrates that the gap is becoming a chasm in educational attainment between on- and off-reserve Aboriginal peoples, and even more between Aboriginal and non-Aboriginal Canadians.

There is a common misconception that all Aboriginal peoples receive full funding for higher education. However, research demonstrates the opposite; for example, fewer than 50% of the Aboriginal students in Restoule's (2011) study had received band funding for their education, so had to rely on other forms of financial sources for their education (e.g., student loans, working part-time, family support). There are still many financial barriers for Aboriginal students seeking to pursue university or college education – lack of funding, inadequate resourcing, and cumbersome procedural policies between funding groups – e.g., First Nations bands (who are administrators of a reserve community and transfer payments from the federal government), other outside funders (e.g., businesses, private scholarships), educational institutions, and students themselves (Human Capital Strategies, 2005; Malatest & Associates Ltd., 2010; Millennium Scholarship Foundation, 2006).

Our institutions still have overt and covert forms of racism in-class and on-campus. Within the academy there is still some resistance, in some academic disciplines, to include Indigenous ways of knowing and being into their curriculum and programs. So while there are pockets of presence of Indigenous knowledge(s) in some disciplines, it is not institution-wide. This is where Indigenizing the academy has emerged as a point of decolonizing the academy to have it become a more successful place for Indigenous peoples, involving respect, relevance, reciprocity, and responsible relationships (Kirkness & Barnhardt, 1991; Pidgeon, 2014, 2016b).

Conclusions

This chapter has attempted to tell the story of Aboriginal higher education in Canada. I hope it has also illuminated for readers the ongoing systemic problems within the Canadian education systems and society that continue to hinder the educational success of the Aboriginal peoples of this country. There is still so much to be done to have policies and practices that are inclusive and respectful of Indigenous learners' needs. It is the hope that future generations will be able to experience a different post-secondary system than the one that those in the late 1800s encountered. Indigenizing the academy is not one strategy, or one policy change, and there are no short cuts to be taken – it is a culminating and complex living movement that aims to see our university and college campuses empower Aboriginal peoples' cultural integrity through respectful and relevant policies, programs, and services. It will take time, and it will be an ongoing process, and it is time for all of us to further support Indigenous empowerment and self-determination.

Notes

1   In the founding of Canada as a British Colony, Aboriginal peoples residing in what is now Canada were not seen as equal nations. Instead, the land was seen by Europeans as a terra nullius (nobody's land) and free for the taking. Over time, this relationship between European settlers and documents such as the Royal Proclamation of 1783 and the Indian Act 1876 (and its subsequent amendments which are binding to this day), set out the relationship between the Crown and Aboriginal peoples. The term "unceded territories" acknowledges the fact that the land that is known as Canada was occupied prior to colonization and Aboriginal peoples did not relinquish their rights to these lands through treaty or other means. Aboriginal peoples did not legally give up their territories and lands; they were dislocated from their lands through policy and practices of colonization in what we now refer to as Canada (Royal Commission on Aboriginal Peoples (RCAP), 1996) (also see https://www.aadnc-aandc.gc.ca/eng/1100100013778/1100100013779).

2 For more information on the Indian Act see http://laws-lois.justice.gc.ca/eng/acts/i-5/

3 For more information on the Métis nation see http://www.metisnation.ca/index.php/who-are-the-metis/citizenship

4 According to the 2011 National Household Survey, the proportion of First Nations with such credentials was higher among those without registered Indian status (52.1%) than those with status (42.3%). Those First Nations people living off-reserve were more likely to have post-secondary education (21.2% had a college diploma and 10.9% had a university degree) than those on-reserve (14.8% and 4.7% respectively) (Statistics Canada, 2013b). From this same survey, 35.6% of Inuit, and 54.8% of Métis had a completed post-secondary education (PSE) credential (from certificate to graduate level) (Statistics Canada, 2013b).

5 At the time of writing this chapter, the most recent census was not available. This data will be released in October, 2017. Please see http://www12.statcan.gc.ca/census-recensement/index-eng.cfm

6 "The Government of Canada and the courts understand treaties between the Crown and Aboriginal people to be solemn agreements that set out promises, obligations and benefits for both parties. Starting in 1701, in what was to eventually become Canada, the British Crown entered into solemn treaties to encourage peaceful relations between First Nations and non-Aboriginal people. Over the next several centuries, treaties were signed to define, among other things, the respective rights of Aboriginal people and governments to use and enjoy lands that Aboriginal people traditionally occupied. Treaties include historic treaties made between 1701 and 1923 and modern-day treaties known as comprehensive land claim settlements. Treaty rights already in existence in 1982 (the year the *Constitution Act* was passed), and those that came afterwards, are recognized and affirmed by Canada's Constitution" (Indian and Northern Affairs Canada, 2010, pp. 1–4).

7 http://www.thecanadianencyclopedia.ca/en/article/royal-commission-on-aboriginal-peoples/

8 See website for current information on the PSSP https://www.aadnc-aandc.gc.ca/eng/1100100033682/1100100033683

9 The common conception is a mature learner is someone who is over 21 years of age. See Ryerson, University of Western Ontario, and Memorial University for examples: http://www.ryerson.ca/undergraduate/admission/admissions/mature.html; http://welcome.uwo.ca/admissions/admission_requirements/mature_and_senior_applicants.html; http://www.mun.ca/regoff/calendar/sectionNo=REGS-0289. Other institutions, like Simon Fraser University, see mature learners as 23 or older, e.g., https://www.sfu.ca/students/admission-requirements/profile-mature.html

10 See https://www.bced.gov.bc.ca/abed/agreements/status_report.pdf At the time of writing this chapter, no further updates were available.

References

Alfred, T. (2004). Warrior scholarship: Seeing the university as a ground of contention. In D. A. Mihesuah & A. C. Wilson (Eds.), *Indigenizing the academy* (pp. 88–99). Lincoln, NE: University of Nebraska.

Archibald, J., Selkirk Bowman, S., Pepper, F., Urion, C., Mirenhouse, G., & Shortt, R. (1995). Honoring what they say: Post-secondary experiences of First Nations graduates. *Canadian Journal of Native Education, 21*(1), 1–247.

Assembly of First Nations. (2012). *A portrait of First Nations and education.* Retrieved from http://www.afn.ca/uploads/files/events/fact_sheet-ccoe-3.pdf

Barnard, D. T. (2011). *University of Manitoba statement of apology and reconciliation to Indian residential school survivors.* Retrieved from https://umanitoba.ca/about/media/StatementOfApology.pdf

Battiste, M., & Barman, J. (Eds.). (1995). *First Nations education in Canada: The circle unfolds.* Vancouver: University of British Columbia Press.

Battiste, M., Bell, L., & Findlay, L. M. (2002). Decolonizing education in Canadian universities: An interdisciplinary, international, Indigenous research project. *Canadian Journal of Native Education, 26*(2), 82–95.

Chrétien, J. (1969). *Statement of the government of Canada on Indian policy.* Retrieved from http://www.aadnc-aandc.gc.ca/eng/1100100010189/1100100010191

Fisher, D., Rubenson, K., Bernatchez, J., Clift, R., Jones, G., Lee, J., ... Trottier, C. (2006). *Canadian federal policy and postsecondary education.* Vancouver: The Centre for Policy Studies in Higher Education & Training (CHET).

Furi, M., & Wherrett, J. (1996, February). *Indian status and band membership issues.* Ottawa: Library of Parliament. Retrieved from http://www.parl.gc.ca/content/lop/researchpublications/bp410-e.pdf

Hardy Cox, D., & Strange, C. (Eds.). (2010). *Achieving student success: Effective student services in Canadian higher education.* Montreal: McGill University Press.

Howe, E. (2004). Education and lifetime income for Aboriginal people in Saskatchewan. In J. P. White, P. S. Maxim, & D. Beavon (Eds.), *Aboriginal policy research: Setting the agenda for change* (Vol. 1, pp. 175–192). Toronto: Thompson.

Huffman, T. E. (2008). *American Indian higher educational experiences: Cultural visions and personal journeys.* New York, NY: Peter Lang.

Huffman, T. E. (2010). *Theoretical perspectives on American Indian education: Taking a new look at academic success and the achievement gap.* Lanham, MD: AltaMira Press.

Human Capital Strategies. (2005). *Review of Aboriginal post-secondary education programs, services, and strategies/best practices and Aboriginal Special Projects Funding (ASPF) program.* Retrieved from http://www.aved.gov.bc.ca/aboriginal/docs/educator-resources/2005-Jothen-Report.pdf

Indian and Northern Affairs Canada. (2010). *Treaties with Aboriginal people in Canada.* Retrieved from http://www.aadnc-aandc.gc.ca/eng/1100100032291/1100100032292

ABORIGINAL HIGHER EDUCATION AND INDIGENOUS STUDENTS 61

Jones, G. A. (2014). An introduction to higher education in Canada. In K. M. Joshi & S. Paivandi (Eds.), *Higher education across nations* (Vol. 1, pp. 1–38). Delhi: B. R. Publishing.

Justice, D. H. (2004). Seeing (and reading) red. In D. A. Mihesuah & A. C. Wilson (Eds.), *Indigenizing the academy: Transforming scholarship and empowering communities* (pp. 100–123). Lincoln, NE: University of Nebraska Press.

Kirkness, V. J., & Barnhardt, R. (1991). First Nations and higher education: The four R's-respect, relevance, reciprocity, responsibility. *Journal of American Indian Education, 30*(3), 1–15. Retrieved from http://www.jstor.org/stable/24397980

Kitchenham, A., Fraser, T. N., Pidgeon, M., & Ragoonaden, K. (2016). *Aboriginal education enhancement agreements: Complicated conversations as pathways to success.* Retrieved from http://www.bced.gov.bc.ca/abed/research/AEEA-Final_Report_June_2016.pdf

Kuokkanen, R. (2007). *Reshaping the university: Responsibility, Indigenous epistemes and the logic of the gift.* Vancouver: UBC Press.

Malatest, R. A., & Associates Ltd. (2004). *Aboriginal peoples and post-secondary education: What educators have learned.* Retrieved from http://www.millenniumscholarships.ca

Malatest, R. A., & Associates Ltd. (2010). *Promising practices: Increasing and supporting participation for Aboriginal students in Ontario.* Retrieved from http://www.afn.ca/uploads/files/education2/promising_practices_increasing_and_supporting_participation_for_aboriginal_students_in_ontario-_2010.pdf

Mihesuah, D. A., & Wilson, A. C. (Eds.). (2004). *Indigenizing the academy: Transforming scholarship and empowering communities.* Lincoln, NE: University of Nebraska Press.

Millennium Scholarship Foundation. (2006). *Changing course: Improving Aboriginal access to post-secondary education in Canada.* Retrieved from http://www.millenniumscholarships.ca/images/Publications/mrn-changing-course-en.pdf

National Indian Brotherhood. (1972). *Indian control of Indian education.* Ottawa: Author.

Pidgeon, M. (2005). Weaving the story of Aboriginal student services in Canadian unviersities. *Communique, 5*(3), 27–29.

Pidgeon, M. (2008a). *It takes more than good intentions: Institutional accountability and responsibility to Indigenous higher education* (PhD dissertation). University of British Columbia, Vancouver. Retrieved from https://open.library.ubc.ca/cIRcle/collections/ubctheses/24/items/1.0066636

Pidgeon, M. (2008b). Pushing against the margins: Indigenous theorizing of "success" and retention in higher education. *Journal of College Student Retention: Research, Theory & Practice, 10*(3), 339–360. doi:10.2190/CS.10.3.e

Pidgeon, M. (2014). Moving beyond good intentions: Indigenizing higher education in British Columbia universities through institutional responsiblity and accountability. *Journal of American Indian Education, 53*(2), 7–28.

Pidgeon, M. (2016a). Aboriginal student success & Aboriginal student services. In D. Hardy Cox & C. Strange (Eds.), *Serving diverse students in Canadian higher education: Models and practices for success* (pp. 25–39). Montreal: McGill University Press.

Pidgeon, M. (2016b). More than a checklist: Meaningful Indigenous inclusion in higher education. *Social Inclusion, 4*(1), 77–91. Retrieved from http://dx.doi.org/10.17645/si.v4i1.436

Pidgeon, M., Archibald, J., & Hawkey, C. (2014). Relationships matter: Supporting Aboriginal graduate students in British Columbia, Canada. *Canadian Journal of Higher Education, 40*(1), 1–21.

Pidgeon, M., & Hardy Cox, D. (2005). Perspectives of Aboriginal student services professionals: Aboriginal student services in Canadian universities. *Journal of Australian & New Zealand Student Services, 25*, 3–30.

Pidgeon, M., Muñoz, M., Kirkness, V. J., & Archibald, J.-a. (2013). Indigenous control of Indian education: Reflections and envisioning the next 40 years. *Canadian Journal of Native Education, 36*(1), 5–35.

Restoule, J.-P. (2011). Looking for a way in: Aboriginal youth talk about access to university in Ontario. *The Canadian Journal of Native Studies, 31*(2), 47–62.

Richards, J. (2013). *Are we making progress? New evidence on Aboriginal outcomes in provincial and reserve schools.* Retrieved from https://www.cdhowe.org/are-we-making-progress-new-evidence-aboriginal-education-outcomes-provincial-and-reserve-schools

Royal Commission on Aboriginal Peoples (RCAP). (1996a). *Gathering of strength, report of the Royal Commission on Aboriginal Peoples (RCAP)* (Vol. 3). Ottawa: Minister of Supply and Services.

Royal Commission on Aboriginal Peoples (RCAP). (1996b). *Report of the Royal Commission on Aboriginal Peoples.* Ottawa: Minister of Supply and Services.

Shotton, H., Lowe, S. C., & Waterman, S. J. (Eds.). (2013). *Beyond the asterisk: Understanding native students in higher education.* Sterling, VA: Stylus.

Statistics Canada. (2008). *Educational portrait of Canada, 2006 census.* Retrieved from http://www12.statcan.ca/census-recensement/2006/as-sa/97-560/pdf/97-560-XIE2006001.pdf

Statistics Canada. (2013a). *The education and employment experiences of First Nations people living off reserve, Inuit, and Métis: Selected findings from the 2012 Aboriginal peoples survey.* Retrieved from http://www.statcan.gc.ca/pub/89-653-x/89-653-x2013001-eng.htm

Statistics Canada. (2013b). *The educational attainment of Aboriginal peoples. The National Household Survey (NHS) 2011.* Ottawa: Statistics Canada. Retrieved from http://www12.statcan.gc.ca/nhs-enm/2011/as-sa/99-012-x/99-012-x2011003_3-eng.pdf

Stonechild, B. (2006). *The new buffalo: The struggle for Aboriginal post-secondary education in Canada.* Winnipeg: University of Manitoba Press.

TeHennepe, S. (1993). Issues of respect: Reflections of First Nations students' experiences in post-secondary anthropology classrooms. *Canadian Journal of Native Education, 20*(2), 193–260.

The Aboriginal Institutes' Consortium. (2005). *Aboriginal institutions of higher education: A struggle for the education of Aboriginal students, control of Indigenous knowledge, and recognition of Aboriginal institutions.* Retrieved from http://caid.ca/AboHigEdu2005.pdf

The Indigenous Adult & Higher Learning Association. (2013). *About IAHLA.* Retrieved from http://iahla.ca/about-iahla

Tierney, W. G. (1995). Addressing failure: Factors affecting Native American college student retention. *Journal of Navajo Education, 13*(1), 3–7.

Tierney, W. G., & Jun, A. (2001). A university helps prepare low income youth for college: Tracking school success. *The Journal of Higher Education, 72*(2), 205–225.

Truth and Reconciliation Commission of Canada (TRC). (2015a). *Honoring the truth, reconciling for the future: Summary of the final report of the Truth and Reconciliation Commission of Canada.* Retrieved from http://www.trc.ca/websites/trcinstitution/File/2015/Honouring_the_Truth_Reconciling_for_the_Future_July_23_2015.pdf

Truth and Reconciliation Commission of Canada (TRC). (2015b). *The Truth and Reconciliation Commission of Canada: Calls to action.* Retrieved from http://www.trc.ca/websites/trcinstitution/File/2015/Findings/Calls_to_Action_English2.pdf

Usher, A. (2009). *The post-secondary student support program: An examination of alternative delivery mechanisms.* Retrieved from http://www.educationalpolicy.org/publications/pubpdf/INAC.pdf

White, J. P., Beavon, D., Peters, J., & Spence, N. D. (Eds.). (2009). *Aboriginal education: Current crisis and future alternatives.* Toronto: Thompson Educational Publishing.

CHAPTER 4

Minding the Gap: Perspectives on Graduate Education for Students with Disabilities

Mahadeo A. Sukhai

Abstract

In 2012, the National Educational Association of Disabled Students (NEADS), which is based in Canada, established the National Taskforce on the Experiences of Graduate Students with Disabilities to address a critical lack of understanding of the issues faced by graduate students with disabilities. Based on the taskforce's research, this chapter examines how myths and misconceptions, as well as student-supervisor dynamics, may impact students with disabilities in graduate school. Specifically, our findings suggest that while student-supervisor relationships are largely positive, myths and misconceptions can have a detrimental effect on supervisors' expectations. Additionally, ineffective communication may fuel the disparity which exists between students and supervisors in their respective understandings of academic rigor and academic integrity. The research reveals uncertainty among students, faculties and departments around the concept of "necessary competencies." The centrality of the student-supervisor relationship is further underscored by its role in mediating students' access to accommodations. An analysis of the data indicates the need for increased research, education and collaboration in enriching the graduate school experiences of students with disabilities.

Keywords

graduate school – graduate education; disabilities – myths and misconceptions – student-supervisor relationship – policies towards students with disabilities – policy reforms

Introduction

Education at all levels in Canada is regulated by the provinces and territories rather than the federal government, and there has been no recent system-wide

© KONINKLIJKE BRILL NV, LEIDEN, 2019 | DOI:10.1163/9789004393073_004

reform to postsecondary education in Canada. As the number of students with disabilities entering graduate education in Canada continues to increase, disability service providers, financial aid administrators, student life professionals, students themselves, graduate departments, deans and student services directors, and universities as a whole must develop new strategies to facilitate the success of graduate students with disabilities. This effort is also driven in part by the need to be responsive to new and evolving provincial legislation in Canada. There is, to date, a critical lack of knowledge surrounding the issues faced by graduate students with disabilities; therefore, higher education institutions are basing policy and practice guidelines on limited, anecdotal and/or local experience. No significant research on this population has been undertaken within Canada, and demographic data sets are lacking. In this environment, a number of myths and misperceptions arise which can evolve policy and practice in potentially inappropriate directions. Therefore, there is a significant requirement to have a detailed understanding of the experiences of students with disabilities in graduate studies.

This chapter will focus on the major myths and perceptions surrounding the academic experience of graduate students with disabilities, identified through our research efforts. These include issues concerning: expected vs. actual times to program completion; the disconnect between student training in academic integrity issues, and institutional perceptions of the impact of accommodations on academic integrity; the ability to achieve the "necessary competencies" of graduate programs and disciplines; the nature and cost of academic accommodations and undue hardship; the differences between the accommodation requirements of undergraduate and graduate programs of study; and, the importance of faculty education in understanding the complexities of the interface between disability issues and graduate education. The student-supervisor relationship will also be explored as an important component of the graduate student experience.

Current Knowledge

It is recognized that there are multiple barriers for students in graduate education; however, these barriers are increased for students who have a disability (Teichman, 2010). These students encounter obstacles throughout the course of their education; these range from negative attitudes of educators, to difficulties in accessing material (for example, obtaining course readings and other lecture notes electronically or in Braille if the student is unable to read standard print) to financial constraints. While these barriers continue to exist at the graduate level, there are unique challenges that exist for students with disabilities pursuing graduate work (Teichman, 2010). In this section, we will discuss the current knowledge on unique barriers to graduate education faced by these students.

The literature on graduate students with disabilities is limited in scope, and much of it consists of individualized accounts of graduate education based on a specific disability type (Perez, 2013; Teichman, 2010). This "auto-ethnographic" research seeks to describe and systematically analyze personal experience in order to understand cultural experience. Additionally, most literature focuses on undergraduate/college or professional program accommodations and student experience. This lack of research on barriers and conditions for completing graduate work for students with disabilities highlights the critical need for a comprehensive research project aimed at educating faculty and service providers working with students with disabilities.

Barriers to Graduate Education

Universities and colleges report dramatic increases in the number of requests for accommodation by graduate students with disabilities and in the complexity of the accommodation issues needing to be addressed (Rose, 2010). For our purposes, we define accommodation as: an alteration of environment, curriculum format, or equipment that allows an individual with a disability to gain access to content and/or complete assigned tasks. The range of accommodation requests by students with disabilities has broadened. Disability offices routinely field accommodation requests from students with disabilities that are visible (e.g., visual impairments, physical disabilities) or invisible (e.g., mental health and learning disabilities). Many of the latter are particularly challenging in terms of accommodation, because they tend to be "situational" (temporary state imposed by a person's current environment that results in an accessibility issue), or "episodic" (long-term conditions that are characterized by periods of good health interrupted by periods of illness or disability), requiring different strategies at different times as students move through their program of study. As well, significant disabilities that have been accommodated at the undergraduate level may need to continue to be addressed at the graduate level, but using different methods of accommodation, given the complexity of graduate education (Rose, 2010).

Accessibility of Materials

Graduate education requires students to independently conduct and synthesize research. One of the challenges for students with print disabilities (e.g., sight loss and learning disabilities) is how to retrieve information when so many of the resources required are not readily available in an accessible format. An accessible format requires printed material to be converted into electronic format to be read with screen-reading software. The biggest problem faced by graduate students with print disabilities is gaining access to the reading materials required for coursework (Perez, 2013). Graduate students often are required to rely on volunteer and paid readers to convert the print information into an accessible format. This process is time-intensive, and can result in additional expenses for the student that are not covered by the institution (Galdi, 2007; Gilmore & Bose, 2005). Although students with print disabilities face barriers to accessing information at the undergraduate level, these barriers are more significant at the graduate level, as there is an increased expectation to complete independent research using multiple sources of information (e.g., books in printed format, journal articles that are not available electronically, archived material, etc.). Review of materials that exist only in an inaccessible format may be necessary for the research methodology the student has chosen to inform their research topic.

Attitudinal Barriers

Joshi (2006) interviewed 19 graduate students with visual disabilities who were enrolled in or had recently completed clinical psychology or master's level counseling programs. Participants were asked about their experiences with the admissions process, internships and practice, and access to classroom materials. Professors who possessed negative attitudes towards accommodating a student with a disability were identified as a significant barrier. Students also referred to prejudicial attitudes from clinical supervisors for their practicums and internships. The students considered peers a positive part of their lives. They felt that peers were helpful both with class work and with helping to lessen their feelings of social isolation. Many of the participants in this study wished to have more disability awareness activities implemented in the curriculum of their graduate programs to address the attitudinal barriers they had encountered.

Financial Barriers

Chambers, Bolton, and Sukhai (2013) conducted a study reviewing the impact of educational debt and financial barriers for students with disabilities in Ontario post-secondary institutions. Governments at the federal and provincial levels have developed several programs (student loans, grants, scholarships) to address the financial needs of Canadian students. Despite these efforts, students with disabilities continue to experience significant financial barriers when attending post-secondary education (Chambers, Bolton, &

Sukhai, 2013). Many of the expenses students with disabilities accrue are the result of costly accommodations, testing to diagnose a disability, and assistive technology. For those students who are unsuccessful at acquiring scholarships and funding from part-time work, or whose funding is not enough to cover the costs associated with their disability, many of these expenses come in the form of student loans, which serves as a barrier to the student's education (Sukhai, Bolton, & Chambers, 2013). Students with disabilities are often required to take reduced course loads in order to meet the needs of their accommodation plan. This extended enrollment forces students to incur greater debt, as they are enrolled on average longer than students without disabilities (Sukhai, Bolton, & Chambers, 2013).

Our Research

To address the knowledge gap that exists about graduate students with disabilities, the National Educational Association of Disabled Students (NEADS) established the National Taskforce on the Experience of Graduate Students with Disabilities, populated with subject matter experts drawn from sectors across the Canadian post-secondary landscape. The Taskforce, after consideration of the issues, chose to undertake a multi-pronged approach, including a comprehensive online national survey of graduate students with disabilities; institutional surveys; focus groups of professionals involved in addressing the issues faced by graduate students with disabilities; key informant interviews with subject matter experts; data mining of existing surveys on higher education and disability; and a detailed national and international literature review.

Our overall goals were to: (1) review and discuss the academic experience of graduate students with disabilities, through exploration of graduate students' experiences in the context of the last twenty years' advancement in technology, attitudes, and legislation; (2) develop a "snapshot" of the current system issues faced by graduate students with disabilities; and, (3) develop testable and implementable recommendations for the continued improvement of graduate experience of students with disabilities.

Many myths and misperceptions were identified in the course of our project. These misconceptions were expressed by students, faculty and service provider/student life professionals, yet are *not* supported by our data. These myths and misperceptions can greatly impact a student's experience and reveal the nature of gaps which exist in graduate education for students with disabilities. The key findings of the research undertaken by the Taskforce may contribute to the questioning of widespread misconceptions about graduate education.

Myths and Misperceptions

Actual and Expected Time to Completion

Our analyses of the project data indicated a range of different experiences regarding time to completion. Based on student comments, it became evident that disability type and accommodations requirements were key factors in determining students' degree completion times.

Although there exists a perception that students with disabilities will take longer to complete their degrees than their nondisabled counterparts, this is not always true. As a consequence of having specific course requirements and prerequisites, students in professional programs reported taking longer to complete them. The shorter the program and less flexible the requirements, the more likely it was that these students reported expecting and experiencing longer times to completion. It is also true that students in research stream programs – particularly at the doctoral level – do not have to manage large course loads compared to the length and complexity of their programs of study. Consequently, the effects of course prerequisites and workload issues due to classroom accommodations on their times to completion were less.

While students with disabilities in research stream programs may identify as taking longer to complete their programs than expected, the delay was caused by progression of the research project. This issue also applies to the broader graduate student population, and may be discipline and/or field-specific. However, students with chronic medical conditions and/or mental health disabilities reported that their time to completion was affected by their disability – for example, needing medical leave or a reduced course load. Whether and how students' accommodation needs impacted their time to completion depended on what alternatives the students, their supervisors, and disability services offices were able to implement. Taken together, these data argue against a "one size fits all" approach to thinking about and accommodating disability in graduate education.

We strongly suggest that the expectation of longer times to completion for graduate students with disabilities needs to be evaluated on a case by case basis. In researching the issue of undergraduate time to completion as an analogy to the graduate data, it was difficult for us to ascertain the root cause underlying the expectation of longer time to completion at the undergraduate level. It is true that as higher education continues to evolve in Canada and its cost spirals, students generally are turning to different modes of completion in order to make ends meet. Among the general population, many students are themselves completing their undergraduate programs while registered as full time students, but with a reduced course load, in order to continue working and fund their education. It is possible that the notion of longer times to completion for students with disabilities generally needs to be re-evaluated against our changing expectations of, and experience with, the general student population.

Impact of Disability Accommodations on Academic Rigor

A prior publication, developed in response to the Customer Services Standard of the *Accessibility for Ontarians with Disabilities Act* (2005), describes the possibility that granting students with disabilities academic accommodations may weaken the academic rigor of graduate programs and disciplines (Rose, 2010). The term academic rigor refers to the quality and reputation of a program or discipline. It is easy to envision this argument, if one accepts the premise that academic accommodations for students with disabilities are synonymous with "getting help" or "not doing things on your own." There is also a belief in academia that graduate education – particularly in the research stream – involves a student exerting effort on their project in isolation, and relating to their supervisor and thesis advisory committee only. The project consultations and students' survey responses showed that the vast majority of academic accommodations do not fall within the category of "getting help" – and that, even when they do, many supervisors and disability services offices would not perceive them as weakening the program's academic reputation. Creativity around designing effective and successful accommodation solutions in the context of academic rigor and essential requirements is often necessary, as evidenced by responses from faculty and Disability Service Offices (DSOs) in the project.

It is important to note here that as the nature of research itself evolves – particularly in the sciences – graduate students generally now often find themselves part of large, complex, multi-disciplinary research teams, making it harder to design entirely independent student projects. Regarding graduate theses, in the sciences in particular (where each chapter of data is a separate, often collaborative, manuscript), the idea that students must work on their projects independently is being challenged. That is, students, in a variety of programs, are working in a more collaborative manner, with each other as well as with other collaborators locally, regionally, nationally and even internationally. In the context of academic accommodation, one can envision an "acknowledgement of contribution" for technical or editorial aid, in much the same way as collaborative contributions are now described in students' theses.

It should be noted that there are situations in which the provision of academic accommodations could reduce the rigor of a discipline or program (particularly in professional-stream programs, where requirements are more fixed than in research-stream programs). The responsibility here is on the university to demonstrate that it has taken action to fully assess the accommodation being proposed. Students must also always be involved in discussions around alternatives and next steps.

Academic Integrity versus Academic Rigor

As previously mentioned, the term "academic rigor" relates to the quality and reputation of a graduate program or discipline. Our research showed some confusion and variation in the meaning of the term "academic integrity." It was clear from Rose (2010), and our own consultations with faculty and deans of graduate studies that the term academic integrity referred to the concepts of academic rigor and essential requirements. Essential requirements refer to the skills and knowledge that student must develop and demonstrate in order to successfully complete their program (Roberts, 2013). However, it was equally apparent that students apply the term academic integrity in the context of academic integrity training, which many first year graduate students undergo, as well as to plagiarism and cheating. When examining this disparity further, we determined that faculty and deans were in fact equating academic rigor and integrity with responsible conduct of research, intellectual property and authorship. In this context, academic authorship is considered to be the process through which academics promote their research.

It is worthwhile to note the following points, which serve to highlight the separate paths this issue has taken in the minds of students and faculty. Firstly, students are trained by their institution or department on both intellectual property and responsible conduct of research practices but students do not report receiving this training as frequently as they do academic integrity training. Moreover, the training around responsible research, intellectual property and authorship often happens fairly early in the student's program, either during orientation or as part of a research methods course. A small number of students state that they have had authorship issues and intellectual property challenges associated with their disability during their graduate program, despite receiving training in these areas. While faculty and administrators may have genuine concerns around the impact of disability accommodation on academic rigor, these were not being discussed at any point during students' programs. This was also true for the issues of responsible research conduct and intellectual property. If such discussions were to occur, they could be integrated into the disability disclosure and accommodation processes.

Ability to Achieve the "Necessary Competencies" of Graduate Programs and Disciplines

Our research revealed a perception that students with disabilities are often not able to complete the "necessary competencies" (or essential requirements of their program) in the same way as students without disability. This perception was most widespread among faculty. There existed a belief that completion of these necessary competencies unaided by anything or anyone was a crucial part of graduate education. There appears to be confusion across disciplines about what constitutes "necessary competencies," as well as the different types of competencies that might be deemed necessary, and the means necessary to complete these tasks. Many students who participated in the project reported that, with the proper supports and understanding, they were able to complete the "necessary competencies" of their program. Our work, therefore, illuminated the need for greater understanding, among both students and faculties or departments, of "necessary competencies." Collaboration is also integral to ensuring that students are able to demonstrate a certain competency, even if it varies from traditional displays of that competency.

Nature and Cost of Academic Accommodations and Undue Hardship

Our research revealed that faculty and departments often believed the cost of academic accommodations could be prohibitive and potentially cause undue hardship for their university. Consequently, faculty and departments were reported to be reluctant to provide certain accommodations to graduate students with disabilities. Students reported feeling either discouraged from asking for them or that doing so would cause more issues, including being labeled as difficult or needy. Students with accommodation needs mentioned that supervisors either would not include them on grant applications or would give money promised to them to other students with no special accommodation needs.

In reality, the cost of approximately 90% of accommodations is less than $500 throughout the course of a given student's studies (Fredeen, Martin, Birch, & Wafer, 2013), with many having no actual monetary cost. These accommodations simply occur through trial and error and willingness to be flexible. For example, supervisors are willing to communicate with their students through webcam using Skype or Google Hangouts when a student is unable to attend in person due to illness.

Differences between the Accommodation Requirements of Undergraduate and Graduate Programs of Study

When asked about the difference in their accommodation requirements between undergraduate and graduate programs of study, many students reported that their needs varied, depending on the type of program and its progression. Due to the decrease in course work in graduate school, classroom accommodations such as note-takers and extended times for exams, although still needed, were not as important. In comparison, field or research assistants became much more important. Graduate students also needed accommodations that included editors and assistive technologies.

Many students discussed not being prepared for graduate education, or being unaware that they can request accommodations at this level. They also did not appear to know the role of DSOs in graduate education, which is to assist students with disabilities in securing the supports and services they need to complete their studies. The overall perception among students was that many DSOs are not aware of graduate education policies and practices.

Importance of Faculty Education in Understanding the Complexities of the Interface between Disability Issues and Graduate Education

Students with disabilities face the same problems as the general graduate student population, but also encounter additional challenges related to disability. These challenges are often not well understood, which is partly a consequence of the competitive environment and also an outcome of the expectation that everyone be able to complete graduate programs in the same way. The tensions highlighted underscore the necessity of faculty being educated on how to effectively support students with disabilities. The next section explores the importance of the student-supervisor relationship for graduate students with disabilities, which was found to be a central aspect of their overall experience.

The Importance of the Student-Supervisor Relationship

The student-supervisor relationship is experienced on a continuum from very poor to very effective, with most relationships realized between the two extremes: good in some ways, fair or poor in others. Our research showed that the relationship between student and supervisor is critical to the overall experience of the student. However, the relationship status was not always directly related to students' respective disabilities. That is, students with disabilities face issues specifically pertaining to their disability, such as trying to obtain needed accommodations, but also face issues that all students face, such as personality conflicts with their supervisor.

Our findings indicate that most graduate students with disabilities have solid and functional – even strong – personal and professional relationships with their supervisors. Additionally, their supervisors were, for the most part, understanding of disability and accommodation issues. There were some broad categories of scenario where the student-supervisor relationship had the potential to break down. Situations where disability impacted the student-supervisor relationship significantly included: the definition and clarification of expectations around productivity and accommodation; student non-disclosure, fear of stigma and the evolution of potential crisis situations; and attitudinal barriers on the part of the supervisor.

Some students reported that their supervisor was unable or unwilling to help with the accommodation process. For example, a supervisor being unwilling to write costs for accommodations into grant applications, or simply not acknowledging the disability exists, therefore creating an added barrier for the student. This was often due to a lack of understanding and communication regarding expectations. Students being excluded from their supervisors' grant applications was largely due to beliefs that the student may have added expenses or be unable to produce the caliber of work needed.

Students with invisible disabilities reported a fear of disclosing their disability to their supervisor for fear of stigma. Moreover, many students reported wanting to be seen for their abilities, rather than disabilities, and felt that disclosing would shift the balance. For example, many students reported not disclosing their disability due to the competitive nature of graduate education. Some also reported a change in attitude from their supervisor after they disclosed, in particular becoming more distant and not as willing to talk about future goals. The choice to disclose can be taken away from the student if the disability manifests suddenly (e.g., a mental health crisis).

Students with all forms of disability also reported that their supervisors presented a range of attitudinal barriers. These included lowered expectations and concerns that students with disabilities might undermine a program's academic rigor. Students felt the need to work harder to prove that they were able to compete on the same level as their peers.

Our findings are consistent with that of previous studies, which show that high quality relationships between students and their thesis advisors (supervisors) are associated with benefits for the university, the supervisor and the student. These benefits include timeliness and rates of degree completion (Girves & Wemmerus, 1988; Lovitts, 2001), lower rates of attrition (Golde, 2005; Lovitts, 2001) and successful socialization into the department and discipline. Since supervisors often provide career advice, letters of reference to potential employers, and/or further mentoring after graduation, the student-supervisor relationship is one of the most defining elements of students' success and their careers.

In positive student-supervisor relationships, the qualities of an effective advisor include high levels of interaction – accessibility, frequent informal interactions, and connections with many faculty members and purposefully helping the student progress in a timely manner (Lovitts, 2001). Students also note flexibility, respect, and strong communication skills to be important characteristics of effective supervisors (Skarakis-Doyle & McIntyre, 2008).

A shared understanding of expectations around the roles and responsibilities of both the student and the supervisor in the student's graduate program is also important to the relationship. It is necessary to clarify such expectations, since considerable variation exists pertaining to the roles of both supervisor and student. The roles of both supervisor and student are negotiated around topics such as: funding; graduate student employment; the frequency of meetings; timelines; the type, nature and frequency of feedback provided on written work; authorship and intellectual property; responsibility for thesis topic development and methodology; and the role of other committee members and co-supervisors (Skarakis-Doyle & McIntyre, 2008). Supervisors may also differ in how differences of ideology or opinion are handled and communicated to graduate students (Skarakis-Doyle & McIntyre, 2008), which may be a reflection of their own experience of being supervised.

The variation of roles and responsibilities is likely related to differences in disciplinary cultures and the position of the supervisor. For example, the culture of the discipline or department may determine the format of the dissertation, how the thesis topic(s) are chosen, how the research is conducted, how funds are allocated, and how students and faculty interact (Zhao, Golde, & McCormick, 2007). In addition, variation among institutions in the requirements of different graduate programs, different roles of graduate officers, and policies around the role of the supervisory committee also dictate expectations that must be considered in the student-supervisor relationship.

The quality of the student-supervisor relationship declines when expectations are either unclear to supervisor or student or both, or not mutually agreed upon. When the student has a disability, there is a greater risk of miscommunication and misunderstood expectations in the student-supervisor relationship arising from the disparate perspectives already mentioned.

Overall, many of the issues identified which can negatively affect the student-supervisor relationship align with the myths and misperceptions explored in the previous section. As a result, faculty, DSOs and students must work together to ensure supervisors and other faculty members are properly supported and understand how to work with graduate students with disabilities.

Conclusion

There is very little research and, therefore, understanding of the issues graduate students with disabilities face. Our study shows that advancing graduate education for students with disabilities cannot occur without strong commitment, persistence and continuous cross-collaboration. As more students with disabilities enter graduate education, it is important for the various parties involved to work together to understand the issues and the best practices going forward.

For graduate students with disabilities, the damage caused by misconceptions can adversely impact their educational experience, and their credibility as developing professionals. This may in turn influence their preparedness and willingness to complete their studies. Entrenched myths and misconceptions potentially undermine the position of students with disabilities in graduate school. In particular, understanding the student-supervisor relationship is crucial, as it can make or break the student's experience and success. Moreover, by providing suggestions and recommendations we hope to enrich the graduate student experience for people with disabilities.

Understanding the issues faced by graduate students with disabilities is an ongoing process through which students, faculty, departments, DSOs and others associated with the students' education must work together to understand and design creative solutions to ensure graduate education is not just accepting students with disabilities but is also helping them to complete their studies and make a successful transition to employment and professional careers.

Acknowledgement

This chapter benefited from the author's collaboration with Emily M. Duffett, Ainsley R. Latour, Chelsea E. Mohler, Christine Nieder and Anuya Pai.

References

Accessibility for Ontarians with Disabilities Act. (2005). Retrieved from http://www.aoda.ca

Chambers, T., Bolton, M., & Sukhai, M. A. (2013). Financial barriers for students with non-apparent disabilities within Canadian postsecondary education. *Journal of Postsecondary Education and Disability, 26*(1), 53–66.

Fredeen, K. J., Martin, K., Birch, G., & Wafer, M. (2013). *Rethinking disability in the private sector.* Ottawa: Public Service Commission of Canada.

Galdi, L. L. (2007). *Factors that enable graduate students with visual disabilities to succeed in their educational pursuits* (Doctoral dissertation). Fordham University, New York, NY.

Gilmore, D., & Bose, J. (2005). Trends in postsecondary education: Participation within the vocational rehabilitation system. *Journal of Vocational Rehabilitation, 22*, 33–40.

Girves, J. E., & Wemmerus, V. (1988). Developing models of graduate student degree progress. *Journal of Higher Education, 59*(2), 163–189.

Golde, C. M. (2005). The role of the department and discipline in doctoral student attrition: Lessons from four departments. *Journal of Higher Education, 76*(6), 669–700.

Joshi, H. (2006). *Reducing barriers to training of blind graduate students in psychology* (Doctoral dissertation). Available from ProQuest Dissertation and Theses database (UMI No. 3215379)

Lovitts, B. E. (2001). *Leaving the ivory tower: The causes and consequences of departure from doctoral study.* New York, NY: Rowman & Littlefield Publishers.

Perez, L. (2013). *The perspectives of graduate students with visual disabilities: A heuristic case study* (Doctoral dissertation). Retrieved from http://scholarcommons.usf.edu/cgi/viewcontent.cgi?article=5757&context=etd

Roberts, B. (2013). *A lifeline for disability accommodation planning: How models of disability and human rights principles inform accommodation and accessibility planning.* Kingston: Queen's University.

Rose, M. (2010). *Accommodating graduate students with disabilities.* Toronto: Council of Ontario Universities.

Skarakis-Doyle, E., & McIntyre, G. (2008). *Western guide to graduate supervision.* London: The University of Western Ontario Teaching Support Centre.

Teichman, S. (2010). *The expert knowledge of university graduate students with learning disabilities: A policy and service analysis* (Master of Social Work dissertation). McMaster University, Hamilton, Ontario.

Zhao, C.-M., Golde, C. M., & McCormick, A. C. (2007). More than a signature: How advisor choice and advisor behaviour affect doctoral student satisfaction. *Journal of Further and Higher Education, 31,* 263–281.

CHAPTER 5

Student Affairs and Services in Canadian Higher Education

Kyle D. Massey

Abstract

Student services provided in Canadian higher education are as distinctive as its institutions. Services for students attending higher education institutions are continuing to evolve to meet the changing expectations, needs, and issues faced by their students. This chapter will provide an overview of how Canadian higher education institutions use principles of good practice, policy, and programs to support students' learning, growth, and development.

Keywords

student services – best practices – higher education

Introduction

Student affairs and services divisions are involved in an array of programs, services, and advisory capacities that influence student success, the campus environment, and institutional policies and decision-making. This profession within higher education is referred to by several different names: student affairs; student personnel; student development; student services; and student life, for example. Many argue that student affairs is the term that best encompasses all the work that these professionals are engaged in, while the term student services is too limiting and indicates an outdated philosophical approach. Throughout this chapter, we use the phrase *student affairs and services* since both terms are used within the Canadian context (Seifert, 2014; Seifert, Arnold, Burrow, & Brown, 2011).

© KONINKLIJKE BRILL NV, LEIDEN, 2019 | DOI:10.1163/9789004393073_005

Student Affairs and Services Administration

Higher education institutions in Canada have designated officials, offices, infrastructure, and budgets to support students. According to the latest data analyzed by Maclean's magazine as part of their 2018 university rankings, student affairs and services accounts for 6.5% of institutional budgets (Dwyer, 2017). This figure matches that found by Maclean's each year since their 2014 rankings (Dwyer, 2013, 2014, 2015, 2016), signaling some stability in the student affairs and services proportion of budget allocation. While variations depend on institutional factors, the programs and services offered by student affairs and services divisions on Canadian campuses may include: health, counselling, career development, Aboriginal services, international services, housing/conference and food services, disability services, bookstores, and chaplaincy services. Typically, a senior administrative leader is assigned institutional authority and responsibility for services to students. While the job title may differ depending upon the institution, commonly held titles of this senior student affairs and services officer position include "Dean of Students," "Vice-President Student Affairs," and "Associate Vice-President of Students." This institutional leadership position is responsible for meeting the multifaceted needs of students and the various student affairs services offices and departments across the institution (Hernandez & Hernandez, 2014). Sullivan's (2010) in-depth review of his leadership role in both the college and university systems in Canada provides a window into its complexity and challenges. Among other managing processes highlighted, Sullivan points to the crucial role of intentional and ongoing assessment in the managing of student services. As has been repeated by many leaders and scholars in the field (e.g., Schuh & Gansemer-Topf, 2010; Upcraft, 2003), assessment has become one of the hottest issues in student affairs and services due to its utility in improving the quality of services and programs. Strong leadership is needed to advocate for the important role of assessment in student affairs and services, to attract and recruit staff members who can engage in ongoing assessment, and to protect assessment resources in times of budget constraints. Developing and implementing a collaborative assessment plan framed around defined learning outcomes is an important indicator of a well-managed student affairs and services portfolio.

Canadian student affairs and services professionals are best described as practitioner-scholars or scholar-practitioners. The nature of their work often challenges the notion that scholarship and practice are separate entities – innovative student affairs and services professionals acknowledge scholarship is needed to undergird practice and practice is needed to undergird scholarship.

These practitioner-scholars are often in the best position to test the theories about what really works for postsecondary students to have access, persist, and graduate. Through their daily interactions with students, they develop the grounding for theories and strategies to improve the higher education experience. These ideas, theories, and models are advanced through scholarship, with student affairs and services professionals presenting at conferences, writing and contributing articles to publications, and engaging in the debates this work stimulates. An advanced degree in student affairs and services currently remains a rare credential in Canada, unlike in the United States, where there are numerous graduate programs aimed at preparing future student affairs and services professionals by providing specialized advanced studies in foundational theories along with supervised practice. Historically, the majority of the focused professional preparation and development of student affairs and services practitioners in Canada has been delivered through the national professional organization, the Canadian Association of College and University Student Services (CACUSS), and through regional organizations such as the Atlantic Association of College and University Student Services (AACUSS). However, higher education as a field of scholarship in Canada has grown considerably in the twenty-first century (Jones, 2012), and this has meant that relevant graduate programs have emerged, signaling promise for a new and larger generation of practitioner-scholars in higher education generally, including student affairs and services.

Principles of Good Practice

A Canadian collection edited by Hardy Cox and Strange (2010), *Achieving Student Success: Effective Student Services in Canadian Higher Education*, identified eight "best practices" in shaping student services. These best practices focus on understanding how students grow, learn, and develop. One of the most important of these is student-centeredness. Student-centered learning tends to involve an emphasis on active learning, student empowerment and responsibility, communication and collaboration, and curricular flexibility to suit the students' needs. A student-centered approach to student affairs and services invites students to relate their prior knowledge and life experiences to the learning at hand, reflect on their perspectives as they expand their viewpoints, and apply new understandings to their own lives. A commitment to active learning in student affairs and services provides students with opportunities for experimentation through high-impact experiential learning experiences such as student government, internships, peer instruction, community service projects, international study, and resident advising. The success of services and programs offered on a student-centered campus is measured in terms of their impact on the student. That is, the key is to focus on the student – on his or her learning and development, well-being, and retention – such that all programs and services are delivered in ways that are demonstrably in the students' best interests.

Secondly, institutions should expect individual differences and be poised to cater to a variety of student needs. Students arrive on campus with varying degrees of preparedness, not only in terms of academic ability, but also with respect to social/cultural competence, self-awareness, personal agency, and a myriad of the other competencies and skills that student affairs and services professionals work to develop in all students. Recognizing and accepting the diversity of student needs is crucial to avoid the "one size fits all" approach to managing student services, which may offer cost savings but ultimately serves no one well.

Student learning occurs best in communities that value diversity, promote social responsibility, encourage discussion and debate, recognize accomplishments, and foster a sense of belonging among their members. One group of students who regularly report feeling isolated on university campuses are international students (Andrade, 2006; Lyakhovetska, 2004); thus, it is clear that institutions must do more to support their successful adjustment. Colleges and universities can provide training for their faculty on inclusive teaching techniques, and student affairs and services professionals can work to increase opportunities for international students' socialization in the community. Targeted orientations, outreach support groups, homestay programs, and intensive English language programs are examples of supportive initiatives that international students in Canada have reported as helpful (Lee & Wesche, 2000). A growing body of research has suggested that study abroad programs, and the homestay experience specifically, do not automatically provide students the sustained interaction required to socialize them through language and into the language (e.g., Rivers, 1998; Tanaka, 2007; Wilkinson, 2002). This research has demonstrated that all aspects of the students' experience abroad, including the homestay experience, must be strategically orchestrated by program administration and integrated into the study abroad program's curriculum if the experience is to live up to its promise (Shiri, 2015). Student affairs and services units often work in partnerships with their institution's international office and off-campus partners to offer international students, visiting scholars, post-doctoral fellows, and their families a range of specialized services including advice on immigration matters, health insurance plans, mentorships, trips and social activities, and liaison services with sponsoring agencies, foreign governments, consulates, and embassies. For example, support for international students at Thompson Rivers University in British Columbia includes personal counseling services with one of their eight International Student Advisors. These specialized advisors work with international students both before their arrival in Canada and during the extent of their program, and, at last count, offer their services in eleven different languages (Thompson Rivers University, 2016).

Crucially, rather than simply increasing the number of foreign students present, in order to truly internationalize a campus, institutions must foster increased cultural competence of all members of the university community. As stated by an internationalization consultant at Thompson Rivers University "There's a bit of a mythology that just by bringing ... diversity to our campuses, everyone's going to become globally and interculturally competent" (as cited in Smith, 2015, p. 3). Institutions have recognized that a holistic approach to internationalization is certainly a complex process which requires flexible and responsive internal structures. The Internationalization Task Force at McMaster University, for example, pointed to limitations of their institution's approach to internationalization, including idiosyncratic structures and limited infrastructure to support international initiatives (Baumann et al., 2012). Owing largely to this task force's recommendations, McMaster University has moved forward with initiatives to support their internationalization goals, including the creation of the International Strategy Advisory Group to oversee the coordination and planning of international activities, working in conjunction with a newly restructured Office of International Affairs (McMaster University, 2016). Other prominent examples of institutional emphasis on international and global affairs include the Balsillie School of International Affairs, which is an equal collaboration between the University of Waterloo, Wilfrid Laurier University, and the Centre for International Governance Innovation. The teaching, learning, curriculum, and research housed in institutes and centres such as these represent significant efforts to foster comprehensive global learning.

Another recent example of meeting the diverse needs of students is the provision of gender-neutral washrooms in university spaces. While studies have shown that levels of homophobia and transphobia are tempered on university campuses, as compared to the overall Canadian society (Bellhouse-King, Bacon, Standing, & Stout, 2008; Schellenberg, Hirt, & Sears, 1999), institutions of higher education in Canada can still be daunting places for students who identify as lesbian, gay, bisexual, transgender, queer, or questioning where the issue of disclosing one's sexual orientation and/or gender can be fraught with anxiety and, in some cases, danger. Research by Perry (2011) has confirmed that Canadian college and university campuses are sites where students are victimized by hate crimes, including hate crimes based on gender and sexual identities. For some students, restrooms are sites where confrontations are common, and therefore some genderqueer and transgender students, as well as other gender-nonconforming individuals who do not fit dominant society's gender expectations of physical appearance, choose to avoid sex-specified restrooms, including foregoing using any restroom, to avoid these difficulties. A positive recent trend at colleges and universities across Canada has been the creation of gender-inclusive, also known as multi-gender or gender-neutral washrooms, often as a result of student activism. The University of Regina, University of Winnipeg, Queen's University, McGill University, Memorial University, and Dalhousie University, among others, have all provided washrooms open to all students regardless of gender identity, equipped with appropriate signage with open and inclusive language. In other cases, these facilities are single-stall washrooms created by changing the door sign on disabled accessible washrooms. Further, some institutions provide multi-user gender-neutral washrooms, such as those found in the Student Union Building at the University of Victoria.

Third, institutions of higher education must employ flexible and adaptive approaches in order to continue to meet changing student needs. As research on organizational design has suggested, fluidity and adaptability are necessary for modern organizations (Bolman & Deal, 2003; Kellog, Orlikowski, & Yates, 2006), and there's no reason to think this does not apply to student affairs and services. While maintaining the highest academic standards and requirements, institutions must challenge and change the learning structures of the past. Colleges and universities should work strategically to continue to create dynamic and flexible opportunities for learning within and beyond the classroom, online and face-to-face, across full-time and part-time programs. While codes of conduct, legal guidelines, and institutional regulations must be adhered to, effectively supporting student success into the future demands that practitioners question past practices and advance new ways of thinking about how to best serve students. The strategic thinking that is needed in all areas of higher education, including in student affairs and services, requires adaptive thinking that goes well beyond "the way we've always done things." The current dominant approach of siloed units and functionally fixed processes may not be the most effective way to organize student affairs and services for the future. The institutional mission and strategic goals, as well as the institutional context, should impact the organizational design of student affairs and services. For example, urban institutions may need different structures than more rural institutions, and residential campuses may require a different structure than an organization designed to serve more commuter students. Also, as student needs change and demographic dimensions of the student body shift, the structure of student affairs and services must adapt to effectively meet new needs (Kuk, 2009). Rather than simply adding additional programs or services directed at distinct populations, a strategy requiring new allocations, a more efficient response may be to restructure existing resources according to new conditions.

The fourth principle of good practice identified by Hardy Cox and Strange is for institutions to respond to needs appropriately and in a timely manner. This principle intersects with each of the others, highlighting the overarching concern of responding to all student needs with care and attention. Collaborations and partnerships among institutional departments and units often aid in providing coordinated responses to complex challenges. Also, integrating new technology into student services processes and monitoring systems may assist in keeping response times short despite the growing demand from students. For example, research has shown that student affairs and services professionals can employ social media to improve students' adjustment to campus (DeAndrea, Ellison, LaRose, Steinfield, & Fiore, 2012). Research such as this has pointed to possible applications of technology to assist in building connections among students and lowering barriers to communication. For instance, DeAndrea and colleagues suggest asynchronous chat could help students develop relationships with a more diverse network of people on campus and receive support from a variety of resources including employment and health services and tutoring, while also facilitating more mentoring relationships among newer and older students. Many student affairs and services professionals may be hesitant in using technology to interact with students in areas where they are used to face-to-face contact. Indeed, a cultural shift within institutions is needed to realize the benefits that technology can bring to the services and programs provided to students.

Fifth is the principle of anticipating needs rather than simply reacting to them. With respect to supporting student needs, many institutions tend to be reactive in the assistance they provide to students, for example, in responding to their learning difficulties. The support provided within this model is often remedial and focuses on "fixing" problems or improving inadequate skills. While faculty may refer students for assistance, they often consider the support services as unrelated to, and disconnected from, the teaching and learning within their classrooms. This approach and conceptualization of student affairs and services is characteristic of the "student services" emphasis of the 1950s and 60s, in which learning was seen as a process of providing for students and treating them simply as receptacles for knowledge (Evans & Reason, 2001). Rather than a strictly reactive model, more colleges and universities could benefit by adopting a proactive and holistic approach to student affairs and services, in which the focus is on enhancing and advancing students' academic development grounded in students' experiences, in partnership with student affairs and services staff, faculty, and the students themselves. To more intentionally and effectively encourage student independence and self-directedness, faculty and student affairs and services practitioners must work as partners to integrate and embed learning into the curriculum. Proven partnerships include first-year experience programs, living-learning communities, and service learning initiatives. For example, at Trent University an Experiential Education Coordinator, while housed within Student Transitions and Careers, works in partnership with the Centre for Teaching and Learning and faculty across the campus to identify, develop, and facilitate diverse opportunities for experiential education such as community-based research, service-learning, practica, and internships. A growing number of Canadian universities offer living-learning communities (LLCs), in which students with a similar interest live in a common residence hall or on the same floor of a residence hall. For example, at the University of Manitoba, Residence Life works in partnership with the Faculty of Engineering to facilitate their Engineering Living Learning Community. In this LLC, students have access to supplemental instruction sessions, study groups and other related activities facilitated by their Residence Advisor, an upper-year Engineering student. A themed residence community with integrated academic support and activities such as this fosters strong community connections, in both residence and the academic community, and helps students adjust to the challenges of university life (Inkelas, Daver, Vogt, & Leonard, 2007; Stassen, 2003).

Additionally, institutions should take care in the design of campus buildings, infrastructure, policies, and services such that they support student learning rather than create a difficult-to-navigate web of obstacles. For example, at Memorial University there is an appropriately named desk, the ASK Desk, located in a centralized, high traffic location which provides a one stop shop for all questions related to student services and student life. Rather than having to seek out individual department offices to get critical information and specific questions answered, students can walk up to the ASK desk for all of their inquiries.

Sixth, institutions should apply resources sustainably and efficiently. All units have responsibility as stewards of their institutions' financial and human resources. For example, the engagement of students in energy savings is as simple as reminding students to turn off the lights in their class and study rooms. Such reminders trigger not only a sense of ownership and shared responsibility for their place of study but have the potential to demonstrate how such energy savings can contribute to resources to acquire a new learning technology in their classrooms. Principles of organizational planning should be employed to create and improve learning environments throughout the campus that emphasize institutions' desired educational outcomes for students. The institutional mission and strategic plan are essential foundations to guide efficiency in an institution and create a platform for meaningful collaborations which can be sustained. Because the most important resources for learning are human resources, it is imperative to ensure the right personnel are in positions to translate into practice guiding theories and research from areas such as human development, learning and cognition, communication, leadership, and program design and implementation. As elaborated on further in this chapter, the policy, programs and professionalization of student services are central to supporting resource sustainability and efficiency.

Seventh, student affairs and services should focus on outcomes and results. Good practice in the provision of student services demands that co-curricular educators and service providers ask, "What are students learning from our programs and services, and how can their learning be enhanced?" Student affairs and services practitioners often rely on anecdotal evidence when asked to demonstrate their contributions to the campus community, but increasingly, in this time of assessment and accountability, they are being required to be more data-based and outcomes-oriented. Thus, a recent trend in student affairs and services divisions at universities and colleges across Canada has been the development of committees to steer assessment efforts. Like the Student Affairs Assessment Committee at McMaster University, for example, these committees support purpose driven assessment within their division, guiding each divisional unit in the development of learning outcomes and accompanying assessment strategies. Like all other areas within higher education, student affairs and services departments must demonstrate that their services, programs, and initiatives bring value to the learning experience of students. The trend of establishing divisional assessment committees has granted student affairs and services professionals the "capacity to develop, implement, assess, and report student learning outcomes" (McMaster University, 2012, p. 12). Knowledge of and ability to analyze research about students and their learning are critical components of good student affairs and services practice. Without data about the effectiveness of programs and services, student affairs and services personnel cannot determine whether their efforts are having the desired effect. The most successful student services practitioners engage in reflective and improvement-oriented processes of assessment, and effectively apply the acquired information to guide change strategies which enhance institutional and student achievement.

The eighth and final principle of good practice in student affairs and services identified by Hardy Cox and Strange is to design and implement integrative services. Universities and colleges are, at their best, complex and multifaceted institutions which should design and implement integrative services to provide their students with the most robust and comprehensive services and programs. It is good practice in student affairs and services to initiate educational partnerships and develop structures that support collaboration. Partners in learning include students, faculty, academic administrators and others inside and outside the institution such as alumni, support staff, employers and professional associations. For example, carpentry and technical workshops on campuses have created unique items to support the learning environment for persons with disabilities such as customized modified desks. Alumni are very important partners in the educational enterprise, not only with supporting the career development of students but also fundraising for state of the art resources for the campus learning community. Collaboration involves all parts of the institution's community in the development and implementation of institutional goals, and reminds participants of their common commitment to students and their learning. Relationships forged across departments and divisions demonstrate a healthy institutional approach to learning by fostering inclusiveness, bringing multiple perspectives to bear on problems, and affirming shared educational values.

It is sometimes suggested in academia that there is a growing sense of disconnection and division among faculty and administrators. Some faculty members may believe that administrators are more likely to interact with external stakeholders than with them, and are more likely to be aware of and receptive to external aspirations for higher education. Among faculty, concerns may exist about the ability of campus administrators to effectively write policies and implement initiatives in the best interest of the academic mission. The extent to which such a disconnect between faculty and administrators exists will differ by institution, but even a slight disconnect is cause for concern. Administrators' and faculty recognition of their mutual support role in designing and implementing programs and services aimed at supporting student success is critical. A lack of synergy between faculty and administrators serves only to weaken the ability to work collectively in students' interests, and speaks to the need for institutions to foster a culture in which faculty and administrators regularly collaborate in curricular and co-curricular initiatives to support students.

Policy

In addition to these best practices, policy is also of great importance when it comes to student issues. For instance, many colleges and universities across the country have established a dedicated admissions process for Indigenous applicants as part of their commitment to improve access to higher education for this segment of the population and to enrich their student bodies with Indigenous students. All 17 Canadian medical schools, for example, have developed enhanced admission policies for Indigenous applicants in response to the recognized undersupply of Indigenous physicians and the continued underrepresentation of First Nations, Inuit, and Metis students in medical schools (Hanson, Moineau, Kulasegaram, & Hammond, 2016). Models such as this, most common in professional programs such as medicine, nursing, social work, and law, help to ensure diversity in these programs and are aimed at addressing systemic inequities.

Universities and colleges often have a *code of conduct* or community code, which moves the focus from the institution to the community at large. For example, St. Francis Xavier University has a Community Code which outlines behaviors that are reflective of the University's goals, and is meant to balance the rights and responsibilities of the students with campus safety and security. Many Canadian institutions frame their approach to dealing with conduct issues on principles of restorative justice. Such an approach to conflict management involves all parties and focuses on the needs of both victims and offenders, as well as the involved community. These means of resolution are designed to allow for a learning opportunity that would not necessarily take place within more traditional and formal adjudication proceedings.

Programs

Universities and colleges can also implement programs to respond to students. Student success programs have been designed to support student success from recruitment through orientation and graduation processes. Student affairs and services practitioners across the country collaborate with a variety of campus partners to plan and execute what is often the year's largest and more extensive student program, first-year orientation. While orientation programs go by varying names – *Head Start* at the University of Windsor, *Welcome Week* at Saint Mary's University, and *Frosh Week* at Cape Breton University, for example – the common distinctive challenge faced by student affairs and services practitioners charged with orientation programming is to create transition programs designed to strike the balance between meeting the formative needs of their first-time students and equipping them with the tools needed to successfully negotiate their new educational environment. The days at the beginning of the year set aside for new student orientation are an exciting and high-energy time, both for the students and the faculty/staff who participate and lead events. Common features of orientation programs include activities such as campus tours, pep rallies, and induction ceremonies. All across Canada, student affairs and services professionals intentionally design a schedule of activities and events during new students' first week on campus to help familiarize them with their new campus home while building community and setting the stage for their entire undergraduate experience.

While orientation week is often the largest single programmatic undertaking for student affairs and services staff each year, these professionals work tirelessly the year around offering programs to support a wide diversity of student needs. For example, wellness initiatives and mental health strategies to support healthy campuses are becoming increasingly common. According to Statistics Canada, teenagers and young adults aged 15–24 experience the highest incidence of mental disorders of any age group in Canada (Youth Mental Health, 2016). The education environment, and perhaps especially the transition into college or university, poses distinct challenges. It is expected that by 2020, mental health issues are going to be the leading cause of disability at Canadian universities (Hanlon, 2012). With understanding and cooperation on the part of administrators, professors, student services personnel, students, and their peers, a student's higher education journey does not have to be derailed by a mental illness or mental health problem. Universities and student affairs and services are beginning to take a pro-active approach to this growing epidemic in order to maintain the health and well-being of their students. Providing targeted mental health training to student affairs and services staff is a recent, promising trend at Canadian post-secondary institutions. The results of a study by Massey, Brooks, and Burrow (2014) conducted on a Canadian university campus have shown that providing Mental Health First Aid training to student affairs and services staff can be effective in increasing knowledge of mental health, enhancing sensitivity, and raising confidence to intervene and assist individuals experiencing a mental health issue. Another example of a pro-active initiative is the peer mental health mentoring program at Queen's University in Ontario. This peer mentoring initiative offers students, who may not feel professional counselling is right for them, a safe and secure communication outlet in the form a trained mentor. Research is currently underway to evaluate the effectiveness of this program and to develop a resource package that can be shared with other universities and colleges.

Many universities across Canada have recognized the need for intentional and coordinated student leadership development programs (LDPs). These leadership programs have become popular options for college and university students looking to build their resumes and develop a stronger connection to their campus. These LDPs are typically managed by student affairs and services staff and coordinated in conjunction with a variety of academic and student services units. The specific emphases of these programs vary, and are often aligned with the mission of the institution. The Allies in Equity program at Carleton University is focused around building intercultural awareness, understanding, and acceptance. This is accomplished through critical exploration of issues such as gender, race, class, and ethnicity on both an individual and collective level. The Impact Leadership Program at Trent University uses social, political, and public policy issues to educate individuals in being collaborative leaders as well as participatory followers. A major component of the Certificate in Innovative Leadership at Simon Fraser University is student volunteering in community service organizations. These experiences have a focus on self-initiated and self-sustained learning intended to lead students to discover what leadership means and learn to help others through self-directed community- or agency-initiated efforts. Beyond the goal of supporting academic achievement, student affairs and services practitioners design and implement student leadership development programs to provide students with positive social outcomes while building important skills that are relevant to life after graduation.

Some institutions, including Wilfred Laurier University in Ontario and Memorial University in Newfoundland and Labrador, have a *co-curricular record program*, which recognizes student accomplishments and experiential learning outside of the classroom and in the community. Co-curricular records chronicle students' engagement and leadership development activities, tracking their positions in clubs and organizations, for example, as well as the learning outcomes associated with those experiences. Other universities, such as the University of Waterloo, utilize an e-*portfolio* for students, which enables learners to build and maintain a digital repository of artifacts, which they can use to demonstrate competence and reflect on their learning. These are excellent examples of integration between student services, administration, academic units, and the community to support a student's learning while also providing a credential to document and showcase the student's experiential and volunteer leadership experiences for both personal and employment opportunities.

Colleges and universities across Canada offer career services programming to their students, and these efforts are typically aimed at preparing students to manage their career transitions to work and further education. Programming and resources in support of this mission typically take two forms, career education and employer development. Career education is offered through workshops, career counselling, and on-campus career events, while employer development typically involves bringing employers to the campus, either literally or virtually, to recruit students for new graduate positions, summer jobs, and internships. Some universities have *employment guarantee programs*, such as the University of Regina Guarantee, which implements many programs and services throughout a student's degree program, and guarantees employment upon graduation. If a student fails to obtain a career related to their degree within 6 months, they are eligible for a tuition voucher to take additional classes for free. Particularly at universities in mid-sized regional towns and cities, career services programming and strategic plans are being implemented in partnership with the municipality and local community industry stakeholders in an effort to entice graduates to remain in the locality to live and work after graduation. These university-city partnerships include collaborative programming such as leadership development programs, experiential, community, and work-integrated learning, as well as professional practice based internships and volunteer programs. Massey, Field, and Chan (2014) have demonstrated that the student-community links established and strengthened by such programming lead to positive town-gown relations. These co-curricular initiatives designed and managed by student affairs and services professionals are pivotal experiences that positively influence students' perceptions of their community, and the positive town-gown relations that result emerge as a "pull-factor" enticing students to stay.

Professionalism of Student Affairs and Services

In recent years there has been a move towards more professionalization of the student affairs and services field in Canada. The field has not historically been as defined in Canada as it is in the United States (Fenske, 1980; Saddlemire, 1980). Originally, faculty members, in addition to teaching and research, provided individual support to students both academically and personally. When postsecondary education in the United States began to expand in the nineteenth century, more specialized positions to support students began to develop; these included academically appointed staff such as Deans of Men and Deans of Women, whose roles could include housing, financial aid, athletics, and student groups (Hamrick, Evans, & Shuh, 2002; Sandeen, 1991). These roles largely took an in *loco parentis* ("in place of parents") approach and included an element of enforcing moral standards (Barr & Albright, 1990). In the twentieth century, student affairs and services in the U.S. reflected social changes, including an active student movement related to civil rights and anti-war demonstrations, which entailed student affairs and services officers dealing with campus disruption, and assisting in communication between student activists and institutional administrators (Laliberte, 2003). Towards the end of the twentieth century student affairs and services began to take on a more formalized role in American institutions, including having chief student affairs officers appointed at the vice-presidential level, an expectation of graduate preparation for student affairs practice, the expansion of professional associations, and a great deal of formal research in the field. The development of student affairs and services in Canada appears to have been similar, evolving from an initially paternalistic approach focused on monitoring and controlling student behavior to a more holistic approach with a host of programs and services to support the increasingly diverse student body in attaining educational goals (Hardy Cox & Strange, 2010). As one of the participants in Robinson's (2011) study on values in Canadian student affairs and services remarked about the development of the profession in Canada, "we're in our adolescence" (p. 145). Other comments by participants in Robinson's study described student affairs and services as not well articulated and lacking the constructs that are typical of professions, such as standardized credentials, a code of ethics, and a specific higher education program. In discussing the differences of the profession in Canada and the USA, Tony Chambers, a professor of education at the Ontario Institute for Studies in Education, commented, "The field is quite old in the U.S." but in Canada, student affairs is a comparatively young discipline and traditionally has been seen "as something that is a bit auxiliary to the central mission of the institution" (Tamburri, 2011, p. 3).

The Canadian Association of College and University Student Services (CACUSS), has led the way in professionalizing the field across the country. CACUSS offers a suite of professional development opportunities, including a national conference and a professional magazine, and has recently spearheaded the development of a Student Affairs and Services Competency Model (Fernandez, Fitzgerald, Hambler, & Mason-Innes, 2016). This model, designed to guide professional development in the field, addresses the skills, knowledge, and attitudes required across all areas of the profession in Canada. The competency areas defined in the model include: (a) communication; (b) emotional and interpersonal intelligence; (c) intercultural fluency; (d) Indigenous cultural awareness; (e) post-secondary acumen; (f) equity, diversity, and inclusion; (g) leadership, management, and administration; (h) strategic planning, research, and assessment; (i) student advising, support, and advocacy; (j) student learning and development; and (k) technology and digital engagement (Fernandez et al., 2016).

Unlike the United States, where there have been graduate programs for many years focused on higher education, student affairs, and related fields, and where there are currently approximately 350 such programs across the country at the Masters or Doctoral level (NASPA, 2017), graduate degrees in Canada with an emphasis on student affairs and services have only recently begun to appear. The first such program was launched at Memorial University of Newfoundland in the late 1990s, and several more have appeared since that time, including, for example, the master's program in student development and student services in higher education at the University of Toronto's Ontario Institute for Studies in Education. These graduate education programs are typically designed to support leaders in a variety of higher education roles, with the option to select a specific degree focus such as a specialization in co-curricular learning and administration of post-secondary education. Whereas, in the past, Canadian student affairs and services professionals wishing to gain advanced training in their field were limited to pursuing a graduate program south of the border, the future looks bright for an increasing number of Canadian practitioners to receive graduate training at home in Canada.

Conclusion

This chapter has discussed some of the ways that Canadian higher education institutions use principles of good practice, policy, and programs to support students' learning, growth, and development. While the Canadian higher education landscape is bound to evolve in a variety of ways in the future as it has in the past, we are confident that institutions can continue to effectively support the learning and development of all students by continuing to know and understand their study body, fostering collaboration between administrative and academic staff, and proactively supporting the health and wellness of the entire campus community.

Acknowledgement

This chapter is based upon the presentation by Dr. Donna Hardy Cox at the HER 2014 workshop titled "Student Affairs and Services in Canadian Higher Education."

References

Andrade, M. S. (2006). International students in English-speaking universities: Adjustment factors. *Journal of Research in International Education, 5*(2), 131–154.

Barr, M. J., & Albright, R. L. (1990). Rethinking the organizational role of student affairs. In M. J. Barr & M. L. Upcraft (Eds.), *New futures for student affairs* (pp. 181–200). San Francisco, CA: Jossey Bass.

Baumann, A., Costa, M., Grasselli, M., Kanagaretnam, G., King, J., Mascher, P., ... Zhai, M. (2012, May 4). *Forward with integrity: Internationalization task force position paper*. Retrieved from http://fwi.mcmaster.ca/wp-content/uploads/2013/09/Internationalization-Task-Force-Report.pdf

Bellhouse-King, M. W., Bacon, B. A., Standing, L. G., & Stout, D. (2008). Factors modulating students' attitudes towards homosexuality at a small university located in the eastern townships. *Journal of Eastern Townships Studies, 32–33*, 73.

Bolman, L., & Deal, T. (2003). *Reframing organizations: Artistry, choice, and leadership* (3rd ed.). San Francisco, CA: Jossey-Bass.

DeAndrea, D. C., Ellison, N. B., LaRose, R., Steinfield, C., & Fiore, A. (2012). Serious social media: On the use of social media for improving students' adjustment to college. *The Internet and Higher Education, 15*(1), 15–23.

Dwyer, M. (2013, October 30). *Measuring excellence: Details of how Maclean's ranks 49 universities each year*. Retrieved from http://www.macleans.ca/education/unirankings/measuring-excellence-2-2/

Dwyer, M. (2014, November 6). *University rankings 2015: Methodology-Maclean's 24th rankings evaluate universities across the country*. Retrieved from https://www.macleans.ca/education/unirankings/university-rankings-2015-methodology/

Dwyer, M. (2015, November 5). *Measuring excellence: The methodology behind Maclean's universities rankings – Maclean's 25th rankings evaluate universities across the country*. Retrieved from http://www.macleans.ca/education/measuring-excellence-the-methodology-behind-macleans-universities-rankings/

Dwyer, M. (2016, October 26). *University rankings 2017: How Maclean's selects Canada's top schools: Maclean's 26th rankings evaluate universities across the country*. Retrieved from https://www.macleans.ca/education/university-rankings-2017-how-macleans-selects-canadas-top-schools/

Dwyer, M. (2017, October 19). *Measuring excellence: How we rank Canada's universities: Answers to all of your questions about how Maclean's 27th rankings were determined*. Retrieved from https://www.macleans.ca/education/measuring-excellence-how-we-rank-canadas-universities/

Evans, N. J., & Reason, R. D. (2001). Guiding principles: A review and analysis of student affairs philosophical statements. *Journal of College Student Development, 42*(4), 359.

Fenske, R. H. (1980). Historical foundations. In U. Delworth & G. R. Hanson (Eds.), *Student services: A handbook for the profession* (pp. 3–23). San Francisco, CA: Jossey-Bass.

Fernandez, D., Fitzgerald, C., Hambler, P., & Mason-Innes, T. (2016). *CACUSS student affairs and services competency model*. Retrieved from https://www.cacuss.ca/files/Competency-Docs/CACUSS_Student_Affairs_and_Services_Competency_Model_FINAL.pdf

Hamrick, F. A., Evans, N. J., & Schuh, J. H. (2002). *Foundations of student affairs practice: How philosophy, theory, and research strengthen educational outcomes.* San Francisco, CA: Jossey-Bass.

Hanlon, C. (2012). State of mind: Addressing mental health issues on university campuses. *University Manager,* 1–6. Retrieved from http://www.ucarecdn.com/f7c8e350-7bf9-4bdd-8149-7e45dd12b629/

Hanson, M. D., Moineau, G., Kulasegaram, K. M., & Hammond, R. (2016). Is Canada ready for nationwide collaboration on medical school admissions practices and policies? *Academic Medicine, 91*(11), 1501–1508. doi:10.1097/ACM.0000000000001286

Hardy Cox, D., & Strange, C. C. (Eds.). (2010). *Achieving student success: Effective student services in Canadian higher education.* Montreal: McGill-Queen's University Press.

Hernandez, J., & Hernández, I. (2014). The role of the executive-level student services officer within a community college organizational structure. *New Directions for Community Colleges, 2014*(166), 33–39.

Inkelas, K. K., Daver, Z. E., Vogt, K. E., & Leonard, J. B. (2007). Living–learning programs and first-generation college students' academic and social transition to college. *Research in Higher education, 48*(4), 403–434.

Jones, G. A. (2012). Reflections on the evolution of higher education as a field of study in Canada. *Higher Education Research & Development, 31*(5), 711–722.

Kellogg, K. C., Orlikowski, W. J., & Yates, J. (2006). Life in the trading zone: Structuring coordination across boundaries in postbureaucratic organizations. *Organization Science, 17*(1), 22–44.

Kuk, L. (2009). The dynamics of organizational models within student affairs. In G. McClellan & J. Stringer (Eds.), *The handbook of student affairs administration* (3rd ed., pp. 313–332). San Francisco, CA: Jossey-Bass.

Laliberte, M. R. (2003). *The student affairs profession transformed: Catalytic events of 1968 to 1972.* Retrieved from ProQuest Dissertations & Theses Full Text (No. 305224836)

Lee, K., & Wesche, M. (2000). Korean students' adaptation to post-secondary studies in Canada: A case study. *Canadian Modern Language Review, 56*(4), 637–689.

Lyakhovetska, R. (2004). Welcome to Canada? The experiences of international graduate students at university. In L. Andres & F. Finlay (Eds.), *Student affairs: Experiencing higher education* (pp. 189–215). Vancouver: UBC Press.

Massey, J., Brooks, M., & Burrow, J. (2014). Evaluating the effectiveness of mental health first aid training among student affairs staff at a Canadian university. *Journal of Student Affairs Research and Practice, 51*(3), 323–336.

Massey, J., Field, S., & Chan, Y. (2014). Partnering for economic development: How town-gown relations impact local economic development in small and medium cities. *Canadian Journal of Higher Education, 44*(2), 152–169.

McMaster University. (2012). *Assessment in student affairs.* Retrieved from http://studentaffairs.mcmaster.ca/wp-content/uploads/2014/11/McMaster-Assessment-Full-Document.pdf

McMaster University. (2016). *New changes to internationalization strategy*. Retrieved from http://fwi.mcmaster.ca/story/new-changes-to-internationalization-strategy-at-mac/

NASPA-Student Affairs Administrators in Higher Education. (2017). *Graduate program directory*. Retrieved from http://apps.naspa.org/gradprograms/

Perry, B. (2011). Identity and hate crimes on Canadian campuses. *Race and Justice, 1*(4), 321–340. doi:10.1177/2153368711429304

Rivers, W. P. (1998). Is being there enough? The effects of homestay placements on language gain during study abroad. *Foreign Language Annals, 31*, 492–500.

Robinson, V. W. H. (2011). *Values of Canadian student affairs practitioners*. Retrieved from ProQuest Dissertations & Theses Full Text (No. 920691584)

Saddlemire, G. L. (1980). Professional developments. In U. Delworth, & G. R. Hanson (Eds.), *Student services: A handbook for the profession* (pp. 25–44). San Francisco, CA: Jossey-Bass.

Sandeen, A. (1991). *The chief student affairs officer: Leader, manager, mediator, educator*. San Francisco, CA: Jossey Bass.

Schellenberg, E. G., Hirt, J., & Sears, A. (1999). Attitudes toward homosexuals among students at a Canadian university. *Sex Roles, 40*(1–2), 139–152.

Schuh, J. H., & Gansemer-Topf, A. M. (2010). *The role of student affairs in student learning assessment*. Champaign, IL: National Institute for Learning Outcomes Assessment. Retrieved from http://www.learningoutcomesassessment.org

Seifert, T. A. (2014). Student affairs and services staff in English-speaking Canadian postsecondary institutions and the role of CACUSS in professional education. *Journal of College Student Development, 55*(3), 295–309. doi:10.1353/csd.2014.0031

Seifert, T. A., Arnold, C., Burrow, J., & Brown, A. (2011). *Supporting student success: The role of student services within Ontario's postsecondary institutions*. Toronto: Higher Education Quality Council of Ontario. Retrieved from http://www.heqco.ca/en-ca/Research/ResPub/Pages/default.aspx

Shiri, S. (2015). The homestay in intensive language study abroad: Social networks, language socialization, and developing intercultural competence. *Foreign Language Annals, 48*, 5–25.

Smith, B. (2015, November 27). Canada calls for better focus on international student integration. *The PIE News*. Retrieved from https://thepienews.com/news/canada-calls-for-better-focus-on-international-student-integration/

Stassen, M. L. A. (2003). Student outcomes: The impact of varying living-learning community models. *Research in Higher Education, 44*, 581–613.

Sullivan, B. (2010). Organizing, leading, and managing student services. In D. Hardy Cox & C. C. Strange (Eds.), *Achieving student success: Effective student services in Canadian higher education* (pp. 165–192). Montreal: McGill-Queen's University Press.

STUDENT AFFAIRS AND SERVICES IN CANADIAN HIGHER EDUCATION 97

Tamburri, R. (2011, October 3). Graduate programs for student services professionals grow more common. *University Affairs*. Retrieved from http://www.universityaffairs.ca/news/news-article/graduate-programs-for-student-services-professionals-grow-more-common/

Tanaka, K. (2007). Japanese students' contact with English outside the classroom during study abroad. *New Zealand Studies in Applied Linguistics, 13*, 36–54.

Thompson Rivers University. (2016). *Support services for international students.* Retrieved from http://www.tru.ca/truworld/students/support-services.html

Upcraft, M. L. (2003). Assessment and evaluation. In S. R. Komives (Ed.), *Student services: A handbook for the profession* (4th ed., pp. 555–571). San Francisco, CA: Jossey Bass.

Wilkinson, S. (2002). The omnipresent classroom during summer study abroad: American students in conversation with their French hosts. *Modern Language Journal, 86*, 157–173.

Youth Mental Health. (2016). *The reality of mental health for youth.* Retrieved from https://youthmentalhealth.ca/index.php/advocates-4-change/ymhe/the-reality/

PART 2

The World

∴

CHAPTER 6

Reforms and Myths: University Graduates and the Labor Market in Mexico

Wietse de Vries

Abstract

The future of university graduates in the labor market in Mexico has been surrounded by several myths and speculations. On the one hand, government officials have insisted, since the early 1990s, that access needs to increase in order to catch up with developed countries. At the same time those same officials have stated that graduates face increasing problems in finding jobs, and tend to end up as taxi drivers or salesmen. Unemployment rates among university graduates at times even appear to be higher than among those who have only received primary education. These alarming data have led to several national policies that seek to remedy the situation. However, many assumptions underlying these policies may be erroneous. This chapter will critically review the performance of Mexican graduates as compared to graduates in other countries. The findings show that several assumptions are merely myths. The conclusion is that many policies are based on quicksand, and will clearly not resolve anything.

Keywords

Mexican higher education – unemployed graduates – myths about higher education – policies for higher education – access to higher education

Misinformed and Misdirected Reforms

There are many myths surrounding higher education: There are those who believe that full-time faculty and students produce better learning outcomes, others who believe universities mostly need more funding, while still others judge that private education is better than public. Some of these myths derive from the lack of reliable information. As in other organizations, decision

© KONINKLIJKE BRILL NV, LEIDEN, 2019 | DOI:10.1163/9789004393073_006

makers have limited time and resources, and decisions need to be made under pressure (March, 1994). Not all information is available to everyone and games of power may develop. These limitations imply that decision making takes place under far from ideal circumstances, in situations of "bounded rationality" (Simon, 1991). Over time this situation may become worse. Recent public sector reforms not only have put existing information systems under stress as a result of a call for "evidence-based decision making," they have also led to an increasing need for additional information systems that are capable of evaluating what has changed as a result of reforms (Boston, 2000).

To make matters worse, universities seem to be especially prone to having limited self-knowledge. The doubtful use of data within universities has a time-honored tradition. Already back in 1963, it was observed:

> All over the country these groups of scholars, who would not make a decision about the shape of a leaf or the derivation of a word or the author of a manuscript without painstakingly assembling the evidence, make decisions about admission policy, size of universities, staff-student ratios, content of courses, and similar issues, based on dubious assumptions, scrappy data, and mere hunch. (Ashby, 1963, p. 93)

It does not seem that the situation has improved significantly in 2016 – even if the larger universities have now set up their own planning offices. These offices, however, are more dedicated to complying with government demands than to any form of institutional research (Díaz-Barriga, 2006).

Another cause of myths is adventurous interpretation of the scarce existing data. Mark Twain coined the phrase that there are three types of lies: "lies, damned lies, and statistics," an observation he attributed to Benjamin Disraeli (Twain, 1906). Later, Huff (1954) and Best (2001) observed that lying with statistics is common practice, even in the sciences. Historians tend to be less condemnatory, and talk about "unwarranted speculations" (Schama, 1992). Whatever the qualification, higher education tends to be surrounded by lies, myths or unwarranted speculations.

Changing Perspectives

A fertile soil for myths is the changing idea about what the university is and what it should be. Mexican universities, since their origin in the 16th century, have been surrounded by distinctive debates about their social role. Similar to some of the first European universities, they started as initiatives spurred by well-to-do families in order to educate their children. Teachers were hired directly by those families in an effort to replace home schooling by something more organized and collective (Le Goff, 1992). In the 19th century, other debates arose: Was the university destined to be the centre of research, as Humboldt proposed in Germany, or was its function to prepare educated citizens, as Newman projected in Great Britain? (De Vries & Slowey, 2012). The Mexican answer was: something in between. So the re-foundation of Mexico's national university in 1910 saw the explicit replication of the model of the University of California, Berkeley, and was fully intended to resemble a research university following Humboldt. The national government went as far as handing out PhD titles to the newly hired faculty so they would have the same credentials as their peers abroad (Garciadiego, 1996; Gil, 2000). At the same time, however, the new university had to be at the service of the country and its administration, and provide for educated citizens, whose task it would be to build the state and the nation (Odorika & Pusser, 2007).

Since that time several other issues have sprung up that have renewed the discussion about what the university is and what it should be. On several occasions these discussions have led to policies, generally by the national government, to address these issues and to introduce reform. The important aspect of all these reforms is that when they were introduced, no reliable information existed. On the whole, reliable information was never produced, either, during the actual process of reform. And, of course, the few existing data tended to be manipulated by governments and others in order to further their interests. Even so, for decades, successive governments have set out to devise and implement policies to improve higher education.

Examples are manifold in Mexico. In the 1990s, the Program for the Improvement of the Professorate (PROMEP in Spanish) was launched. It offers professors, after they have already been appointed, scholarships in order to improve their qualifications. The underlying idea was that academics should hold a PhD and be full-time. This, in turn, would increase research and teaching productivity and quality. However, from the beginning (in 1996) there were no reliable data on the number of students or academic staff at Mexican universities (De Vries & Álvarez Mendiola, 1998; Gil, 2000). By the same token, no indicators were developed to measure results, such as increases in research productivity or the number of graduates. The PROMEP continues to this day and a huge amount of money has been spent, but no independent evaluations exist, so the outcomes remain a matter of ongoing debate (Díaz-Barriga, 2013; Gil, 2000).

In the same vein, related to PROMEP, the federal government introduced special funds to public universities to stimulate them to offer new study programs, better geared to the labor market. The benefits for the universities are that the government pays for additional infrastructure and the hiring of additional academic and administrative staff. Not surprisingly, many universities created new programs, and the number of programs offered by most universities jumped from about twenty in the 1990s to around one hundred by 2016. This phenomenon took place with scant information about existing programs, and whether or not the new options are better suited for the labor market remains a mystery.

Much the same has happened with public funding, where after half a century of debate about possible formulas, it remains unclear how much money is spent and what the logic for allocations might be (López-Zárate, 1997). The management of universities is a similar topic: After decades of reforms, reorganizations and shifts in power, it remains far from clear whether or not universities have become more efficient (Acosta Silva, 2009).

The Future of Graduates

The relationship between the university and the labor market is a relatively new topic in this debate. Until the end of the 1990s this relationship was considered unproblematic: Those who entered the university were already part of the national elite, and had their future secured. Overall, the main function of universities seemed to consist of the selection of the "heirs," thus replacing the titles of nobility with university diplomas (Bourdieu & Passeron, 1964).

Contrary to other countries, where the situation started to change after WWII and many systems of higher education made the transition from élite to mass higher education, enrolling more than 15 percent of the relevant age group of 18–24 years old (Trow, 1974), Mexican higher education remained élite until the end of the 1980s (De Vries & Álvarez Mendiola, 2005). Since then, several systems in other countries have become universal, enrolling more than 40 percent of the relevant age group, and traditionally excluded sectors of the population have started to participate in higher education (Unterhalter, 2006). But Mexican higher education remained limited to about 34 percent of the relevant age group by 2015, including only a small proportion of non-traditional groups.

Increasing inclusion in higher education, however, has had various side effects in Mexico. There remains a conviction that "more education is better," based on the persistence of human capital theories (e.g., Becker, 1975; Schultz, 1979), but at the same time a novelty has occurred: Unemployment among university graduates has risen, and at some times turns out to be higher than among those with only primary or secondary education.

In Mexico, the situation turned critical in the 1990s, when recurring crises led to increases in unemployment, especially for those holding a higher education degree. The simultaneous rise of neo-liberal thought introduced new considerations about the role of universities: Their main task should be to prepare students for finding appropriate jobs. The quality of a university began to be measured by indicators such as the absorption of its graduates by the labor market, the salaries received by graduates, the match and link between studies and work, job satisfaction, the opinions of employers or the measurement of skills or competences (Planas, 2014; Rubio, 2006).

This neo-liberal vision does not consider other functions of a university, such as the education of citizens or the training of researchers. Those functions are relegated to a second level: The university has to adjust itself to the demands of the market. Consequently, the backdrop of most recent reforms and policies has been to better adjust the preparation of university graduates to their future jobs.

At first sight, this policy does not seem new. Over the previous three decades, policies had been implemented with the goals of improving the preparation of students, and adjusting this preparation to the demands of the labor market (Comisión Económica para América Latina y el Caribe (CEPAL), 1992). Ever since the expansion of higher education in Mexico started in the 1970s, there have been increasing speculations that something is wrong with the relationship between the university and the labor market. One prevalent conjecture is that the university does not prepare its students adequately, which leads to graduates facing serious problems when searching for jobs. But official discourse on the theme shows evidence of a certain bipolarity (De Vries & Navarro, 2011): On the one hand officials declare that more people should have access to higher education in order to foster socio-economic development, or progress toward the knowledge society (Machin & McNally, 2007; Rodríguez, 2010), while, on the other hand, the same officials with similar data announce that the increase in graduate numbers is leading to a growing number of unemployed (Burgos & López, 2010).

Therefore, the role of higher education has gone through several changes in the second half of the 20th century. A first role was to educate the elites, who were destined to work as government officials or independent professionals. In a second stage, that of mass education, universities prepared students for a wider array of jobs, but still enrolled a limited proportion of the age cohort. In the third stage, with universal education, universities prepare a growing number of students for the knowledge society amid rapid social changes (Brennan, 2004; Castells, 2004; CEPAL, 1992; Trow, 1974). One of these changes seems to be the novelty that a higher education degree leads to unemployment.

However, it is not at all clear in this new context how the relationship between the university and the labor market really operates (Flores-Crespo & Muñoz-Izquierdo, 2009; Márquez, 2008). There is no clear information about unemployment levels, much less about the underlying reasons for unemployment (Vedder, Denhart, & Robe, 2013). Even less clear is what

106   DE VRIES

employers are actually demanding as to competencies, skills or knowledge, and how the university should respond to these demands (Brennan & Little, 2010; Planas, 2014). It is in this context that many myths and speculations flourish, in large part because of a lack of reliable information. We have chosen seven such myths to discuss here.

Data from Comparative Research

The data presented here were obtained in an international comparative study on undergraduate education called PROFLEX ("*El Profesional Flexible en la Sociedad del Conocimiento*" or "The Flexible Professional in the Knowledge Society"), in which 34 countries and nine major Mexican universities participated, three private and six public.

The participating Mexican universities play an important role in the system: Most of them have over 50,000 undergraduate students. In the Mexican case, 4260 questionnaires were completed by graduates who had completed bachelor's degrees (International Standard Classification of Education 5A). For comparative reasons, graduates were interviewed five to six years after leaving the university.[1]

There are some limitations to this study. First of all, the sample did not include some sectors of the Mexican higher education system, such as technological universities, or the large number of (very) small private universities or colleges.

Second, the sample is reliable as to areas of knowledge, but not for individual programs. A growing problem for graduate tracer studies is that most universities have diversified their offerings, to the extent that many Mexican universities now offer over 100 different programs, some with very few students. The areas of knowledge follow the categorization of the European Union (Mora, Carot, & Conchada, 2010).

Myths about Higher Education in Mexico

First Myth: Higher Education Leads to Unemployment

A popular terrain for unwarranted speculations concerns the fortunes of university graduates in the labor market. A common observation is that universities produce a lot of unemployed graduates. As the then undersecretary of higher education, Rodolfo Tuirán, observed in 2010:

> Of the total of university graduates that live in Mexico, 5.6 million are employed or underemployed, 367 thousand are unemployed; 165 thousand are looking for a job. However, 920 thousand more declare

themselves not to be available for a job, they do not look for any and turn down any offer. (Poy, 2010)

The undersecretary went on to confirm that unemployment among university graduates had been on the rise since 2009, and was at the time situated at 15% (Poy, 2010).

At first sight the data from PROFLEX seem to confirm these assertions, as Table 6.1 reflects.

TABLE 6.1   Do you currently hold a paid job (Percentage)?

Country	Unemployed at the time of the interview
Mexico	14.5
France	12.7
Spain	12.5
United Kingdom	10.3
Germany	9.4
Chile	9.0
Japan	10.5
Latin America	11.4
Europe	10.0

SOURCE: DATA FROM PROFLEX

However, these are data about total unemployment. If we follow international directives, as does the Mexican Instituto Nacional de Estadística y Geografía (INEGI), and only consider as unemployed those who are without work but actively searching for a job, Mexican unemployment rates are down to 6.2% for men and 7.5% for women (De Vries & Navarro, 2010). Even so, unemployment rates are slightly higher in Mexico than in the European Union, but the situation does not seem to be alarming. What is alarming, however, is that there are no common guidelines to calculate unemployment. Mexico considers all working in the informal sector as employed, whereas these jobs would be considered as illegal in most of Europe: These jobs are done without contracts, tax declarations, job security, social security provisions or pension plans. Likewise, what is considered as "actively seeking a job" differs by country. Thus, we present these data only for Mexico.

A related myth concerns the different rates of unemployment between those with a university degree and those without one. Here, something seems to

TABLE 6.2   Employment and unemployment (Percentage)

Employment situation	Male	Female	Total
Employed	90.3	82.2	86.0
Unemployed	9.7	17.8	14.0
Unemployed, but actively seeking a job	6.2	7.5	6.9

SOURCE: DATA FROM PROFLEX

happen that defies popular wisdom: Unemployment rates for graduates seem higher than those with only primary education. According to the Mexican press, the Organization for Economic Co-operation and Development (OECD) pointed out in 2014:

> The organization [OECD] confirms that in the Mexican case, unemployment increases when educational level increases. For this reason, the highest levels of unemployment, 20.6%, are found among young adults, while unemployment among older adults is 10.2%. For example, unemployment rates increase when the level of education increases. The unemployment rate is higher in the case of tertiary education than for those who do not have upper-secondary education, according to the OECD. (Educación Futura, 2015, author's translation)

This statement, however, is based on a very doubtful use of data. First, the statement such as it appears above cannot be found in any of the OECD publications on Mexico in 2014 (OECD, 2015). Then, the statement is derived from data by the INEGI, which annually publishes the National Survey on Occupation and

TABLE 6.3   Conditions of employment by educational level, 4th trimester of 2013 (Percentage)

Level of education	Employment status and sector		
	Formal sector	Informal sector	Unemployed
Primary or less	19	78	3.5
Secondary	37	58	5.1
Upper secondary or technical	51	43	5.7
Undergraduate or postgraduate	74	21	4.8

SOURCE: BASED ON DATA OF INEGI, ENOE IV-2013

Employment (Encuesta Nacional de Ocupación y Empleo, ENOE). According to these data, unemployment is effectively lower for those with only primary education, but it should be noted that this group are mostly employed in the informal sector.

Unemployment among people with or without higher education is thus a controversial issue, and depends on how and when it is measured. Official declarations state that overall unemployment for graduates is about 15%. According to other studies (Flores-Crespo & Muñoz-Izquierdo, 2009), unemployment for university graduates was in 2008 around 11%, three times higher than the overall unemployment rate among the Economically Active Population (EAP) of 4%. According to the PROFLEX data, real unemployment is about 6%, based on the data of a sample of graduates who left the universities five years earlier. According to the data from INEGI, based on their ENOE survey, unemployment among those with higher education is 4.8%, slightly higher than for people with only primary education, but lower than for those with secondary or upper-secondary education.

The discrepancy in numbers coming from different sources can be explained by the use of dissimilar criteria and methods. Existing surveys on employment in Mexico do not consider those working in the informal sector as unemployed, or as actively looking for a job. No national database exists that renders reliable information on the total population, on the EAP, or on those who work in the informal sector, so all these data are calculated from a myriad of surveys, each one with its own methodology. This renders international comparisons moot, as working in the informal sector is deemed illegal in all other OECD countries. According to these international criteria, in México, 81.5% of people with primary education should be considered as unemployed, against 25.8% of people with a higher education degree. Therefore, the statement that unemployment for those with higher education is higher than for those with primary education is not only a myth, it is false.

Second Myth: Traditional Programs Are Saturated

Other official declarations state that the labor market for traditional programs – Administration, Law, Accountancy or Medicine – is saturated (Cabrera, De Vries, & Anderson, 2008). According to Undersecretary Tuirán, cited in 2009 by the newspaper *La Jornada*:

> Almost half of graduates, 48 percent, from Administration, do not work in activities related to their field of study. A similar situation applies to 32% who studied Accountancy and Finances and to 29% of those who studied Law. (Poy, 2009)

TABLE 6.4 Do you currently hold a paid job (Percentages)?

Area	Yes	Yes, more than one job	No
Education	71.6	15.7	12.7
Humanities	72.0	12.6	15.4
Social Sciences	78.4	6.6	15.1
Economy & Business	82.3	6.7	10.9
Law	75.2	10.7	14.1
Technical	81.1	8.9	10.0
Health	73.0	10.9	16.1
Sciences[a]	63.7	9.3	27.0

a According to UNESCO, "Sciences" groups together programs such as Mathematics, Physics and Chemistry.

SOURCE: PROFLEX DATA

The data from PROFLEX and other tracer studies paint a very different picture. Problems of unemployment seem to be more acute in areas like Sciences, Health, Social Sciences and the Humanities. In Economy and Business, more than 80% declare themselves to be employed.

At the same time, monthly income appears to be higher for those who studied supposedly saturated programs, which report the highest percentage of graduates earning more than 3,000 US dollars per month. On the other hand, most of those working in the Sciences or in Education earn less than 1,000 US dollars per month.

TABLE 6.5 What is your average monthly income (USD, 2008) (Percentages)?

Area	0–1000	1001–2000	2001–3000	>3000
Education	85.9	12.8	.0	1.3
Humanities	80.0	15.7	2.9	1.4
Social Sciences	69.0	24.2	3.3	3.6
Economy & Business	46.8	35.9	11.7	5.6
Law	62.1	27.0	6.0	4.9
Technical	53.1	29.5	11.8	5.6
Health	81.9	13.5	1.1	3.5
Sciences	83.5	12.6	2.4	1.6
Total	62.3	25.8	7.4	4.5

SOURCE: PROFLEX DATA

REFORMS AND MYTHS   111

Third Myth: Graduates Lack Competencies

A very common myth is that problems in the labor market are due to a lack of competencies of graduates. On this issue, speculations range widely. Some experts state that there are new emerging demands from the labor market (Perrenoud, 1999; Secretaría de Educación Pública [SEP], 2013). Critics consider that basically the term "competencies" has come to replace what was once labeled simply as "skills" (Díaz-Barriga, 2006; Planas, 2014).

These distinctions are important when we review the results of PROFLEX. In the questionnaire graduates were asked about their own level of competencies, about the level of competencies necessary in their current job, and about the role the university had played in their acquiring these competencies. Table 6.6 reveals several interesting data.

First of all, it stands out that the most valued competencies are the following: capacity to make decisions, to work under pressure, to apply knowledge, and to make oneself understood. Therefore, the most important ones seem to refer to social abilities, not to academic ones. Competencies of little importance are the knowledge of a second language and computing skills, both of which figure as priorities in most university curricula (De Vries & Navarro, 2011).

Secondly, there is very little difference between the self reported level and the required level for their current job. Thus, graduates do not seem to lack any required competencies.

TABLE 6.6   Please indicate the level of your competencies

	Own level	Level required at current job	Contribution made by university
Capacity to make decisions	6.0	5.9	5.0
Capacity to work under pressure	5.8	5.8	5.1
Capacity to apply knowledge in practice	5.8	5.8	5.1
Capacity to make oneself understood	5.6	5.8	5.1
Capacity to use time effectively	5.6	5.7	5.0
Capacity to work in a team	5.8	5.7	5.3
Capacity to find new ideas and solutions	5.7	5.7	5.0
Capacity to coordinate activities	5.7	5.7	5.0
Capacity to acquire new knowledge	5.8	5.6	5.2
Capacity to impose authority	5.6	5.6	4.8
Computer skills	5.6	5.6	4.9
Second language	4.1	4.2	3.5

SOURCE: PROFLEX DATA (SCALE 1–7: 1 = UNIMPORTANT, 7 = VERY IMPORTANT)

Fourth Myth: Jobs Held by Graduates Do Not Match Their Studies

Another popular myth is that graduates end up holding jobs that do not match their studies. As an example, in 2009 the then undersecretary for higher education declared to the press that:

> 45 percent of the 7.8 million professionals (people with a higher education degree) are not engaged in activities related to their studies, and have had to conform themselves to occupations such as taxi drivers, vendors or marginal jobs. (Olivares, 2009)

The data from PROFLEX once again contradict this statement. In the case of Mexico, 88.3 percent of those interviewed declared that their current job matches their studies. Mexico, in this aspect, ranks below only Chile and Germany but far above Japan.

TABLE 6.7   To what degree does your current job match your studies (Percentage)?

Chile	95.2
Germany	88.9
Mexico	88.3
Spain	81.5
France	80.1
United Kingdom	74.7
Latin America	90.8
Europe	85.8
Japan	53.2

SOURCE: PROFLEX DATA

Fifth Myth: Graduates Are Forced to Accept Jobs below Their Level of Preparation

A related speculation states that graduates are increasingly occupying jobs that in the past did not require a university degree. According to this speculation, university graduates would be gradually displacing those with only an upper secondary diploma from the labor market. Again, the data from PROFLEX indicate that this is not the case: Only 5 percent of graduates indicate that they hold a job for which no university degree is needed. In fact, more than 40 percent indicate that their current job requires post-graduate studies.

REFORMS AND MYTHS 113

TABLE 6.8   What level of studies is required for your current job (Percentage)?

Required level	Percentage	Number of respondents
Doctorate	3	112
Masters	24	852
Specialization	19	675
Undergraduate	48	1701
No university diploma required	5	184
Total	100	3523

SOURCE: PROFLEX DATA

Sixth Myth: Graduates Are Not Satisfied with Their Jobs

Following the logic of the previous arguments, it seems obvious that Mexican graduates are among those with the least job satisfaction in the world. However, the contrary is true: From a comparative perspective, Mexicans are the most satisfied.

TABLE 6.9   How satisfied are you with your
current job (Mean)?

Mexico	4.10
Chile	4.09
Germany	3.84
France	3.82
United Kingdom	3.78
Spain	3.70
Japan	3.50
Latin America	4.07
Europe	3.83

SOURCE: PROFLEX DATA (SCALE 1 =
NOT SATISFIED – 5 = VERY SATISFIED)

Job satisfaction also varies by areas of knowledge, where Health stands out. The PROFLEX data point to interesting questions regarding the relationship between satisfaction, income, match between studies and work, and gender. In general, satisfaction seems to depend on the match between studies and jobs (Cabrera et al., 2008). Income seems to be a marginal factor: Mexican graduates rank lowest when it comes to income, but highest when it comes to satisfaction. Likewise, women tend to earn less than men, but declare themselves to be more satisfied with their job, although with differences according to areas of knowledge. By the same token, those who work in the worst paid areas of knowledge (Health, Sciences) declare higher levels of satisfaction.

TABLE 6.10   Job satisfaction by areas of knowledge and gender (Mexico)

Area	Gender	Mean
Education	Male	3.74
	Female	4.10
	Total	4.01
Humanities	Male	3.68
	Female	4.08
	Total	3.96
Social Sciences	Male	4.04
	Female	3.98
	Total	4.00
Economy and Business	Male	4.01
	Female	4.01
	Total	4.01
Law	Male	4.08
	Female	4.08
	Total	4.08
Technical	Male	3.98
	Female	4.00
	Total	3.99
Health	Male	4.26
	Female	4.28
	Total	4.27
Sciences	Male	4.10
	Female	4.09
	Total	4.09
Total	Male	4.02
	Female	4.06
	Total	4.04

SOURCE: PROFLEX DATA (SCALE 1 = NOT SATISFIED − 5 = VERY SATISFIED)

Seventh Myth: Public Policies Are Resolving Most of the Above Problems

The myths mentioned above have led to a myriad of public policies enacted by different Mexican federal governments, just as in the case of academic staff or

REFORMS AND MYTHS 115

the creation of new programs. Many official reports boast about the progress being made (Rubio, 2006). However, it is not at all clear if this progress translates into a better positioning of graduates in the labor market. This, however, should not come as a complete surprise. After all, it is common knowledge that policy makers operate in a context of "bounded rationality": They have only partial information on different topics (which compete for attention), the relationship between causes and effects tends to be fuzzy, distinct stakeholders express dissimilar opinions, and time is always pressing.

However, Mexican policies implemented by consequent governments since the early 1990s seem to have been based mostly on quicksand, and the policies regarding the relationship between university graduates and the labor market are no exception to this rule: No serious studies of the match and link between the universities and the labor market were carried out, ideas about causes and effects seem to be very simplistic, and no independent evaluations of the impact or results of these policies exist, although some of them have been in place for two decades. To make matters worse, many of these policies require substantial government funds.

Contradictory signals, mostly coming from research projects, continue to prevail in this area. First, governments and accrediting agencies are eager to point out that the quality of programs has improved, but they base their judgment on the number of full-time academics with a PhD. Research, on the other hand, shows that progress in the qualifications and working conditions of academic staff does not seem to lead consistently to better outcomes in student learning. Several studies have pointed out that full-time professors with a PhD are not better evaluated by their students than part-time academics with only an undergraduate degree (De Vries, González, León, & Hernández, 2008; Estévez-Nenninger, 2009).

At the same time, recently created higher education sectors (such as technological universities offering only short term programs aimed at vocational training), have only been able to attract 5% of students, and their graduates do poorly in the labor market. The reason for this seems to be primarily that both students and employers prefer a 4-year university degree over a 2-year vocational diploma. Subsequent governments have acknowledged this fact by creating polytechnic universities where graduates from the 2-year programs can study an additional 2 years and obtain a university degree (Flores, 2009). But perhaps the biggest mistake in this case has been that government officials travelled abroad to see what worked in France, Germany and Korea, instead of analyzing the Mexican labor market.

The diversification of university programs seems to have resulted in some interesting innovations, but overall the traditional programs continue to do better in the labor market (Cabrera et al., 2008). Finally, it is not at all clear what the contribution of a better infrastructure has been when it comes to learning.

In this context, it is hardly surprising that policies regarding graduates and the labor market have turned out to be simplistic and hold little promise for the future. Many crucial factors in this relationship, such as economic development, family background, or gender, are not taken into account. Other aspects are surrounded by myths and unwarranted speculations.

Conclusions

During recent decades, in spite of several major, well funded policies, no major changes in employment rates among university graduates have occurred. The minor fluctuations that can be observed seem to be due mainly to conditions in the labor market, rather than to the preparation that graduates receive.

However, some differences can be attributed to higher education itself. For example, there is a notable difference between graduates from public and private (elite) universities when it comes to success (measured by income) in the labor market (De Garay, 2002; De Vries, Vázquez-Cabrera, & Treto, 2013): Graduates from private elite institutions tend to earn four or five times the salaries their colleagues from public universities receive. Women graduating from elite private institutions tend to earn much more than men who have graduated from public universities in the same area of knowledge. However, these differences seem to relate more to social and financial background of students than to study plans or to the qualifications of professors, which tend to be lower in the private universities (De Vries & Navarro, 2011).

In general, the analysis of data from the PROFLEX study about the relationship of higher education and the labor market suggests that most policies in Mexico are based on uncertain and inconsistent information and speculations. On occasion, it seems reasonable to assume that some policies were intended to resolve problems that did not exist in the first place, such as high unemployment rates, graduates working as taxi drivers, students insisting on studying traditional programs, or the lack of competencies. Because of this, many policies formulated by the "adjusters" (Planas, 2014) turned out to be incongruous: It does not make much sense to adjust the university to supposedly changing demands in the labor market if many of these demands do not exist.

This, of course, does not imply that universities do not need to reform. However, in order to do so in a sensible way, reliable and relevant data are needed about what is wrong and how to change it. This not only concerns policy makers, but also the universities themselves. After all, it is understandable that policy makers make doubtful decisions, because they lack expertise and information. On the other hand, it should also be said that policy makers hardly ever search and review the information that does exist, and that policies never contemplate any outside evaluation to measure progress. By the same token, it is hard to understand why universities, being places of inquiry, seem to lack even the most basic data on their own functioning and seem very little interested in doing research on what happens internally and in their environment, especially the economy and the labor market. Furthermore, this information should be readily available to the public and various stakeholders, both national and international, in order to facilitate informed discussions about reforms. Up to this moment, much of the existing information is classified as secret or confidential by both policy makers and universities, because it might damage the prestige of some institutions. Moreover, until a constitutional reform in 2007 and the creation of a national institute for access to information (Instituto Federal de Acceso a la Información, IFAI) no one had the right to access (public) information, and nobody had the obligation to provide this information.

Finally, there is an urgency to discuss the type of information and data needed. Traditionally, data are gathered on inputs and some outcomes of university education in order to detect possible problems and make decisions. However, after decades of reform, it is time to introduce indicators that allow for analyses of what has changed and what type of policies contributed to these changes. The lack of this kind of indicators easily leads to situations of unwarranted self-congratulation built upon myths.

Acknowledgements

This chapter was originally presented as a paper at the 11th International Workshop on Higher Education Reform in 2014 in St. John's, Newfoundland, Canada. I would like to thank the audience and most of all Walter Archer and Hans Schuetze for their comments and editorial assistance.

Note

1 Questionnaires were distributed in 2007 and 2008, to those who graduated in 2002 and 2003. The sample was stratified and weighted according to the total number of graduates per university and field of study. The margin of error of the sample is +/- 0.311% for overall data considering $p = q$ and a margin of reliability of 95.5%. The questionnaire consisted of closed questions with multiple options, and was applied by telephone, home visits and via the internet.

References

Acosta Silva, A. (2009). *Príncipes, burócratas y gerentes. El gobierno de las universidades públicas en México* [Princes, bureaucrats and managers. The government of the public universities in Mexico]. Mexico City: Asociación Nacional de Universidades e Instituciones de la Educación Superior (ANUIES).

Ashby, E. (1963). Decision making in the academic world. In P. Halmos (Ed.), *Sociological studies in British university education* (pp. 93–100). Keele: University of Keele.

Becker, G. S. (1975). *Human capital: A theoretical and empirical analysis, with special reference to education* (2nd ed.). New York, NY: National Bureau of Economic Research.

Best, J. (2001). *Damned lies and statistics: Untangling numbers from the media, politicians, and activists*. Berkeley, CA: University of California Press.

Boston, J. (2000). The challenge of systemic change: The case of public management reform. *International Public Management Journal, 3*, 23–46.

Bourdieu, P., & Passeron, J.-C. (1964). *Les héritiers: Les étudiants et la culture* [Heirs: Students and culture]. Paris: Les Éditions de Minuit.

Brennan, J. (2004). Graduate employment: Issues for debate and inquiry. *International Higher Education, 34*, 12–14.

Brennan, J., & Little, B. (2010). Graduate competences and relationships with the labour market: The UK case. In *Development of competencies in the world of work and education*. Ljubljana: University of Ljubljana.

Burgos, B., & López, K. (2010). La situación del mercado laboral de profesionistas [The situation of professionals in the labor market]. *Revista de la Educación Superior, 39*(156), 19–33.

Cabrera, A. F., De Vries, W., & Anderson, S. (2008). Job satisfaction among Mexican alumni: A case of incongruence between hunch-based policies and labor market demands. *Higher Education, 56*, 699–722.

Castells, M. (2000). *The information age: Economy, society, and culture* (Vols. 1–3). Oxford: Blackwell Publishers.

Comisión Económica para América Latina y el Caribe (CEPAL). (1992). *Educación y conocimiento: Eje de transformación productiva con equidad* [Education and knowledge: Axis for a productive transformation with equity]. Santiago de Chile: Comisión Económico para América Latina y el Caribe/Organización de las Naciones Unidas para la Educación, la Ciencia y la Cultura (CEPAL – UNESCO).

De Garay, A. (2002). Un sistema de educación superior, dos realidades distintas: La universidad pública y la universidad privada [One system of higher education, two distinct realities: The public university and the private university]. *Revista de la Educación Superior, XXXI*(122), 69–77.

De Vries, W., & Álvarez Mendiola, G. (1998). El PROMEP:¿ posible, razonable y deseable? [The PROMEP: Possible, reasonable and desirable?]. *Sociológica, 13*(36), 165–185.

De Vries, W., & Álvarez Mendiola, G. (2005). Acerca de las políticas, la política y otras complicaciones en la educación superior mexicana [About policies, politics and other complications in Mexican higher education]. *Revista de la Educación Superior, XXXIV*(134), 81–106.

De Vries, W., González, G., León, P., & Hernández, I. (2008). Políticas públicas y desempeño académico, o cómo el tamaño si importa [Public policies and academic performance, or why size matters]. *CPU-e, Revista de Investigación Educativa, 7.*

De Vries, W., & Navarro, Y. (2011). ¿Profesionistas del futuro o futuros taxistas? Los egresados universitarios y el mercado laboral en México [Professionals of the future or future taxi drivers? University graduates and the labor market in Mexico]. *Revista Iberoamericana de Educación Superior, 2*(4), 3–27. Retrieved from http://ries.universia.net/index.php/ries/article/download/71/109

De Vries, W., & Slowey, M. (2012). Concluding reflections: Between Humboldt and Newman: Marketization and global contributions in contemporary higher education. In H. G. Schuetze & G. Álvarez Mendiola (Eds.), *State and market in higher education reforms: Trends, policies and experiences in comparative perspective* (pp. 215–223). Rotterdam, The Netherlands: Sense Publishers.

De Vries, W., Vázquez-Cabrera, R., & Treto, D. (2013). Millonarios o malparados. ¿De qué depende el éxito de los egresados universitarios? [Millionaires or unfortunates. What does the success of graduates depend on?]. *Revista Iberoamericana de Educación Superior, 4*, 9. Retrieved from http://ries.universia.net/index.php/ries/article/view/273

Díaz-Barriga, A. (2006). El enfoque de competencias en la educación. ¿Una alternativa o un disfraz de cambio? [The focus of competencies in education. An alternative or a disguise for change?]. *Perfiles Educativos, XXVII*(111), 7–36.

Díaz-Barriga, A. (2013). Evaluación de la educación superior. Entre la compulsividad y el conformismo [Evaluation of higher education. Between compulsion and conformity]. In E. Todd & V. Arredondo (Eds.), *La educación que México necesita. Visión de Expertos* [The education that Mexico needs. Vision of experts]. Mexico City: Centro de Altos Estudios e Investigación Pedagógica.

Educación Futura. (2015, January 20). A mayor educación en México, mayor desempleo: OCDE [More education in Mexico means more unemployment: OECD]. *Educación Futura.* Retrieved from http://www.educacionfutura.org/a-mayor-educacion-en-mexico-mayor-desempleo-ocde/

Encuesta Nacional de Ocupación y Empleo (ENOE), IV. (2013). Retrieved from http://www.inegi.org.mx/est/contenidos/Proyectos/encuestas/hogares/regulares/enoe/

Estévez-Nenninger, E. (2009). *El doctorado no quita lo tarado* [The PhD does not resolve foolishness]. Mexico City: Asociación Nacional de Universidades e Instituciones De La Educación Superior (ANUIES).

Flores, P. (2009). *Trayectoria del modelo de universidades tecnológicas en México* [Trajectory of the technological university model in Mexico]. México City: Universidad Nacional Autónoma de México.

Flores-Crespo, P., & Muñoz-Izquierdo, C. (2009, February 19). Crisis y desempleo: ¿podrán hacer algo las universidades? [Crisis and unemployment: Can universities do anything?]. *Campus Milenio*. Retrieved from http://www.campusmilenio.com.mx/309/ensayos/index.php

Garciadiego, J. (1996). *Rudos contra científicos. La Universidad Nacional durante la Revolución Mexicana* [Rude boys against scientists. The National University during the Mexican Revolution]. Mexico City: El Colegio de México/Universidad Nacional Autónoma de México.

Gil, M. (2000). Un siglo buscando doctores [A century of searching for PhDs]. *Revista de la Educación Superior, 29*(113), 23–42.

Huff, D. (1954). *How to lie with statistics*. New York, NY: WW Norton & Company.

Le Goff, J. (1992). *Intellectuals in the middle ages*. Oxford: Blackwell Publishers.

López-Zárate, R. (1997). *El financiamiento a la educación superior 1982–1994* [Financing higher education 1982–1994]. Mexico City: Asociación Nacional de Universidades e Instituciones De La Educación Superior (ANUIES).

Machin, S., & McNally, S. (2007). *Tertiary education systems and the labour market. A paper commissioned by the education and training policy division, OECD, for the thematic review of tertiary education*. Paris: Organization for Economic Cooperation and Development.

March, J. G. (1994). A primer on decision making: How decisions happen. New York, NY: The Free Press.

Márquez, A. (2008). Jóvenes mexicanos: Su horizonte de posibilidades de participación en la educación y el trabajo [Mexican youth: Their horizon of possibilities to participate in education and work]. In M. L. Suárez & J. A. Pérez (Eds.), *Jóvenes universitarios en Latinoamérica, hoy*. Mexico City: Universidad Nacional Autónoma de México/Miguel Ángel Porrúa.

Mora, J. G., Carot, J. M., & Conchada, A. (2010). *Informe resumen del proyecto PROFLEX en América Latina. Comparativa con el proyecto REFLEX en Europa* [Brief report of the PROFLEX Project in Latin America. Comparison with the REFLEX Project in Europe]. Valencia: Universidad Politécnica de Valencia/CEGES.

Odorika, I., & Pusser, B. (2007). La máxima casa de estudios: The Universidad Nacional Autónoma de Mexico as a state-building university. In P. Altbach & J. Balán (Eds.), *World class worldwide: Transforming research universities in Asia and Latin America* (pp. 189–215). Baltimore, MD: Johns Hopkins University Press.

Olivares, E. (2009, February 6). SEP: 45% de profesionistas, en áreas ajenas a su especialidad [Secretary of Public Education: 45% of professionals in areas unrelated to their field of study]. La Jornada. Retrieved from http://www.jornada.unam.mx/2009/02/06/index.php?section=sociedad&article=035n1soc

Organization for Economic Co-operation and Development (OECD). (2015). *Panorama de la educación 2015*. Retrieved from http://www.oecd.org/mexico/Education-at-a-glance-2015-Mexico-in-Spanish.pdf

Perrenoud, P. (1999). *Dix nouvelles compétences pour enseigner. Invitation au voyage* [Ten new competencies to teach. Invitation to the journey]. Paris: ESF.

Planas, J. (2014). *Adecuar la oferta de educación a la demanda de trabajo. ¿Es posible? Una crítica a los análisis "adecuacionistas" de relación entre formación y empleo* [Adjusting the supply of education to the demands of work. Is it possible? A critique of the "adjusters" analyses of the relation between preparation and work]. Mexico City: Asociación Nacional de Universidades e Instituciones de la Educación Superior (ANUIES).

Poy, L. (2010, January 29). Más de 200 mil egresados en el país no buscan ni tienen empleo [More than 200,000 graduates in the country do not have or look for work]. *La Jornada*. Retrieved from http://m.jornada.com.mx/index.php?articulo=043n1soc &seccion=sociedad&amd=20100129

Rodríguez, R. (2010, November 4). Acuse de recibo: Más sobre cobertura [Message received: More about attendance]. *Campus Milenio*. Retrieved from http://www.campusmilenio.com.mx/392/opinion/rrg.html

Rubio, J. (Ed.). (2006). *La política educativa y la educación superior en México. 1995 – 2006: Un balance* [Educational policy and higher education in Mexico. 1995–2006: A balance]. Mexico City: Fondo de Cultura Económica/Secretaría de Educación Pública.

Schama, S. (1992). *Dead certainties and unwarranted speculations*. New York, NY: Vintage Books.

Schultz, T. W. (1979). *The value of higher education in low income countries: An economist's view*. Paris: International Institute for Educational Planning.

Secretaría de Educación Pública (SEP). (2013). *Programa sectorial de educación 2013– 2018* [Sector program for education 2013–2018]. Mexico City: Secretaría de Educación Pública.

Simon, H. (1991). Bounded rationality and organizational learning. Organization Science, 2(1), 125–134.

Trow, M. (1974). Problems in the transition from elite to mass higher education. In *Policies for higher education: General report on the conference on future structures of post-secondary education* (pp. 51–101). Paris: OECD.

Twain, M. (1906). Chapters from my autobiography. *North American Review.*

Unterhalter, M. (2006). Reflections on the transition from elite to mass to universal access: Forms and phases of higher education in modern societies since WWII. In P. Altbach & J. J. F. Forest (Eds.), *International handbook of higher education* (pp. 243–280). Dordrecht: Springer International.

Vedder, R., Denhart, C., & Robe, J. (2013). *Why are recent college graduates underemployed? University enrollments and labor-market realities*. Washington, DC: Center for College Affordability and Productivity.

CHAPTER 7

Policies for Adult Students in Mexican Higher Education and Motives for Returning to Study

Germán Álvarez Mendiola and Brenda Yokebed Pérez Colunga

Abstract

Though the number of adult students in higher education in Mexico has grown over the past 15 years, they have been largely neglected by policy programs, institutions, and, in general, by academic research; consequently, knowledge about them is scarce, as are public policies and institutional programs to serve this group's specific needs and interests. To contribute to filling this gap, we analyze higher education policies related in some way to adult students. Next, we examine the distribution of adult students in Mexico according to sector (public/private) and modality (on-site/open and distance). We also discuss adult students' reasons for starting or resuming higher education. The chapter is based on statistical data provided by the Ministry of Education and on interviews with adult students from private and public institutions in different programs and educational delivery modes.

Keywords

Mexican higher education – adult students – motivations of adult students – public and private higher education institutions – distance education

Introduction

The large group of higher education policies initiated in Mexico during the last ten years has affected the preparation for work and life of a growing number of students. On the one hand, quality assurance policies have encouraged teachers to obtain graduate degrees and promoted the accreditation of academic programs and curricular reforms oriented toward student- and learning-centered models. On the other hand, policies for expanding the higher education system have resulted in the creation of new types of institutions

© KONINKLIJKE BRILL NV, LEIDEN, 2019 | DOI:10.1163/9789004393073_007

and educational offerings and the growth of the student population, as a consequence of which educational opportunities have increased and the student population has become even more heterogeneous, especially due to the growing presence of adult students.

Nonetheless, this important group of policies has not dealt directly with the development of a system based on the paradigms of lifelong learning, which would impact students' education and give more attention to the heterogeneity of the student body. In reality, though the federal government has adopted some ideas similar to the lifelong learning paradigm in adult basic education, job training and (to a lesser extent) in technological secondary education, it has done so based on its economic interest in human capital. Even so, students enter higher education in general with almost no training related to independent learning (Álvarez, 2012).

There has been little progress in terms of policies and programs specific to adult students in higher education in Mexico, despite the fact that these students are becoming an important part of Mexican higher education. In this chapter we will pay special attention to the policies and institutions that have some impact on adults.

The adult undergraduate population has grown significantly in the last 15 years. Yet, while adults currently represent 22% of total enrolled undergraduates, they remain nearly invisible. Few resources have been devoted to study them, public institutions do not typically develop academic programs or specific services for them, and the government lacks explicit public policies to serve this population and stimulate its growth. In fact, the public policy programs used primarily by adult students, such as the Open and Distance University of Mexico (UNADM in Spanish) and other online education programs developed at public institutions, were not originally designed for adult students, but were created instead to help broaden the educational coverage of the 18–23 age group. Only the private sector, with its entrepreneurial bent, includes institutions that have begun to capture the adult demand for higher education.

Thus, in addition to analyzing why adult students receive so little attention within education policy and institutional programs, this chapter examines why these students seek to attend higher education institutions in such an environment.

The chapter begins with a brief discussion of the theoretical and methodological perspective employed. Next, based on the available statistical information, we offer a general overview of higher education in Mexico and the place occupied by adult students in terms of their distribution by sector and type of institution. Third, the chapter presents a brief analysis of policies that, while related in some way to adult students in higher education, have little to do with their needs, interests, and characteristics. Finally, in order to arrive at a greater understanding of the reasons behind the nature of adult student demand, and with the help of interviews, we briefly analyze the motivations and expectations these students have for their studies, taking into account their work and family situations as well as their previous school experiences.

Adult Students and Policies: Theoretical and Methodological Perspective

In this work we define an adult student as someone who is at least 24 years old, who in principle is more mature and possesses greater behavioral complexity and more responsibilities than younger subjects, and who has competing roles (Kasworm, 2003). Students in this population are resuming their studies, whether to finish an undergraduate degree, begin a second career, or formalize knowledge acquired in the workplace. Adult students can be identified as part of the large group of "non-traditional" students

> ... distinct from the "traditional" group with respect to their age and family status (married with dependent children, or single parents) employment and income situation (not supported by their parents but self-supporting with income from full- or part-time work) and patterns of participation (part-time attendance, distance study). Also those without regular school certification ... These attributes are often closely connected and therefore different degrees of "non-traditionality" can be distinguished. (Schuetze, 2014, p. 38)

They give their actions meaning based on certain factors: their interactions with their peers; how they perceive and navigate the tension of juggling yet another role – that of the student; and the value and usefulness of the results of their educational choices.

These subjects' actions are framed by structural contexts that place economic and social conditions on their decisions. An aging population, the job market's increasing demand for credentials, the expansion of upper secondary education, the growth of higher education, and the diversification of educational offerings are a structural scenario with which individuals interact and make certain choices related to their *motivations* for participating in higher education. As Morley (2003, p. 81) reminds us, "choice is frequently structured by gender, social class and ethnicity."

Higher Education in Mexico and Adult Students

Several factors explain the growth of the adult population in Mexican higher education. First, there is a convergence between the demographic phenomenon of an aging population and the job market's increasing demand for greater formal qualifications. Second, an increase in graduation rates for lower levels (i.e., upper secondary), coupled with an improvement in school efficiency and, since 2012, the compulsory status of upper secondary education, has produced an absolute increase in the demand for higher education. Third, the last 15 years have seen a sustained expansion of higher education as well as the increased diversification of institutions and the types of higher education programs offered.

In the first part of this section, we will briefly review these issues in order to provide the context for adult participation at this educational level. In the second part, we will analyze the size of the adult student population as well as its distribution by sector (public/private) and modality (on-site/open and distance).

Adult Population and Job Markets

In Mexico, the adult population (i.e., those aged 18 and over), will reach 90.5 million in 2050, an increase of nearly 18 million from 2015. Nonetheless, age groups will not grow uniformly and, therefore, neither will educational demand. The 50+ age group will experience most growth: In 2030, with 22.6 million people, it will represent 26.5% of adults in the country, reaching 30.7% in 2050. The 40–49 group will remain stable as a percentage of the total population (around 21%) while the relative weight of the 18–23 and 24–29 groups will diminish progressively (Table 7.1).

This population faces pressures from the job market, particularly from those segments that, in demanding greater formal qualifications, diminish the proportion of positions that only require low educational levels. Additionally, as job growth is related to technological development (optimization, continuous innovation, and change management), the demand for high-level competencies in technical areas (such as IT, construction, and engineering) has become more important (STPS & SNE, 2017). Consequently, the supply of credentials generates degree inflation and "credentialism" in the job market and in society in general (Brunner, 2002).

Nonetheless, credential inflation and the decline in the value of degrees have not eliminated the occupational and financial advantages of a professional credential. In 2016, a large percentage of workers in certain sectors had

TABLE 7.1   Mexico: Adult population by age group, 2015–2050 (total numbers and percentage)

Age group	2015	2020	2030	2040	2050
18–23	12,992,295	13,057,474	12,730,709	12,523,352	12,285,712
	17.9	16.8	14.9	14.1	13.6
24–29	11,780,270	12,396,039	12,413,701	12,114,095	11,994,395
	16.2	15.9	14.6	13.6	13.3
30–39	17,741,019	18,355,505	19,903,524	19,782,149	19,398,060
	24.4	23.6	23.4	22.2	21.4
40–49	15,015,273	16,270,763	17,560,744	19,098,921	19,054,426
	20.7	20.9	20.6	21.5	21.1
50 and over	15,050,620	17,720,204	22,589,165	25,398,897	27,739,734
	20.7	22.8	26.5	28.6	30.7
Total	72,579,476	77,799,985	85,197,843	88,917,415	90,472,327
	100.0	100.0	100.0	100.0	100.0

SOURCE: CALCULATED WITH DATA FROM CONAPO, DATA FROM PROJECTIONS,
HTTP://WWW.CONAPO.GOB.MX/ES/CONAPO/PROYECCIONES_DATOS

completed a program of study at an HEI: in the extractive industry (30.8%), government (43.3%), professional services (50.8%), and health and education (67.1%). On the other hand, there is a high but variable correlation between completed studies and job activities (80% on average), depending on the academic major; for instance, health (88.7%), education (91.1%), physics and mathematical sciences (88.6%), and the humanities (86.8%) are very highly correlated (STPS & SNE, 2017).[1]

It should be noted, however, that the programs in HEIs tend to grow less responsive to the changing needs of positions in certain productive sectors and the demand for completed higher education studies follows relatively conventional patterns. For example, the three main professional areas with the highest number of employed individuals (5 million) are Economic & Administrative, Engineering, and Education, representing 64% of all employed professionals. These data are congruent with student demand for certain qualifications. In general, the percentage distribution pattern for areas of knowledge is very similar for both the 24+ and the younger age groups. For example, 42% of students are concentrated in the social sciences, administration, and law, but by taking age into account it becomes clear that a higher percentage of adult students are to be found in these areas (48.6%) compared to their peers who are younger than 24 (40.1%). There are also some variations in adult students' preferences in other areas (Table 7.2).

TABLE 7.2   Mexico: Distribution of student population in higher education by area of knowledge and age (Percentages)

Areas of knowledge	Up to 23 years	24 and older	Total
Agricultural and veterinary sciences	2.4	1.7	2.3
Arts and the humanities	4.0	4.3	4.0
Natural, exact, and computer sciences	5.2	5.6	5.3
Social sciences, administration, and law	40.1	48.6	42.0
Education	6.8	8.8	7.2
Engineering, manufacturing, and construction	28.8	20.3	26.8
Health	11.6	7.7	10.7
Service	1.2	3.0	1.6
Total	100.0	100.0	100.0

SOURCE: ADAPTED WITH DATA FROM ANUIES (2016) (FOR 2015)

Improvement of Graduation Rates and Compulsory Upper Secondary Education

An additional pressure on the higher education system is the improvement of graduation rates from secondary education, part of the expansion of that level. In just four years (2010–2014), enrollment in secondary education went from 4,187,528 to 4,805,981, with an estimated 5,366,491 in 2020. Furthermore, dropout rates have fallen, from 20% in 1996 to 13.1% in 2013. Completion rates have also improved: from 58.3% in 2005 to 64.7% in 2013, with a further projected increase to 68% by 2020. This means that the total number of graduates has increased: 860,327 students graduated in 2005, while 1,159,161 students did so in 2013. According to government projections, there will be 1,419,637 graduates in 2020. Similarly, more of the 15–17 age group will be covered at this level: from 69.4% in 2014 to 81% in 2020 (SEP, 2014).

Though this process of expansion began in the mid-90s, reforms implemented by the Mexican federal government might have accelerated this trend as part of a general revaluation of the importance of secondary education. Riding a wave of reforms, the federal government advanced an ambitious effort in 2008: building a national high school system that would provide greater consistency to a highly-variable curriculum. Furthermore, the educational offering of open and distance secondary education has been promoted more during the past ten years. On the other hand, Congress made upper secondary education compulsory for individuals while guaranteeing access, which has driven an increase in educational requirements in the job market.

There are no specific studies on the influence of these processes on adult demand for higher education, but some partial evidence from certain states indicates that obligatory upper secondary education has increased the demand for higher education, especially open and distance options. The need to update knowledge and abilities will exert pressure on educational demand not only for young people but also for adults. In the case of older adults, an additional incentive to enroll in higher education is their nascent but growing perception of the intrinsic value of learning and broadening one's cultural horizons through lifelong learning.

These factors have driven both the public and private sectors to initiate higher education programs directed at new populations. One example is the roll-out of the Higher Education at a Distance program (ESAD in Spanish) in 2009, which in 2012 became the Open and Distance University of Mexico (UNADM), run by the federal government. On the other hand, the private sector in higher education actively participates in the market of adult education offerings through "executive" or "express" online programs.

Expansion of Higher Education

The public sector has sparked (and, to a large extent, directed) the growth of higher education in Mexico. Setting a goal of expanding the rate of coverage to 40% by 2018, the federal government initiated specific programs to create more public institutions, provide financing to existing institutions so they could serve more students, and provide financial support (grants and scholarships) to low-income students with good performance.

Higher education in Mexico has not ceased its growth, which government projections indicate will continue past 2030. In 2000 there were 1,853,421 students in higher education, including *técnico superior universitario* (ISCED level 5B2), university undergraduate, two-year technical, and *normal* (teacher training), while in 2015 there were 3,718,995, representing a cumulative growth of 100.7%. The federal government estimates that 5,338,499 students will be enrolled in 2030.[2]

Growth rates have varied and will continue to do so. According to the federal government's calculations, a new growth phase will have begun in 2015, finishing by the end of the decade; however, cuts to public funding of higher education in the current economic climate (2016–2017) might halt that growth, with subsequent modifications to these projections, potentially exacerbating the slow rates the government had already predicted would begin in 2020.

Most (70%) of students are concentrated in the public sector, which owes its growth to the government through the creation of public HEIs, the increase in enrollment in existing HEIs, the establishment of new educational programs, and the promotion of open and distance modalities (Mendoza, 2016).

The gross higher education enrollment ratio was 14.6% in 1995, but 19.2% in 2000. It is estimated that in 2015 it rose to 31.4% (SEP, 2014). In addition to the fact that these figures are far removed from the 50% typically used to describe higher education coverage as universal, the system has significant problems with equality in terms of the incorporation of poor and indigenous sectors of the population, as well as unequal coverage from state to state (Mendoza, 2016).

The expansion of the institutional base is notable. In 2000 there were a total of 1,250 institutions of higher education and in 2015 there were 2,960 – an enormous but clearly differentiated and segmented institutional base, the majority of which consists of small, private institutions. The public sector contains 953 institutions of varied types, from several kinds of universities – including federal autonomous, state autonomous, state autonomous with some federal funding, two-year technical, polytechnic, and intercultural – to technological institutes, public research centers, normal schools (teacher training colleges), and a myriad of small and generally specialized institutions. (The difference in classification derives from administrative criteria and the characteristics of their academic offerings, although the academic structure and predominant type of programs are similar.) In the private sector, there are 2,007 institutions of quite divergent sizes, whose educational offering (except in the largest and most prestigious institutions) tends to be small, with no research activities.

The public sector is segmented between autonomous universities and all other institutions. The former tend to attract students with stronger academic performance and, thanks to selection processes, students of greater financial and academic resources than those who attend other types of public institutions. Private institutions are segmented according to the price of programs, brand reputation, and the purchasing power of the socioeconomic sectors they attract. At the top of the pyramid, with the highest educational quality, are consolidated private institutions that cater to the country's economic and political elite. At the base of the pyramid are the low-cost and low-quality establishments that serve students with little purchasing power.

In terms of educational offerings, there are currently 10,375 undergraduate programs (Marúm et al., 2016) and a variety of modalities, from on-site, open and distance, and blended, to short "executive" undergraduate programs that make few demands on students; these modalities are represented across very diverse fields, especially administration.

The growth of higher education was aided by an extensive program of diverse student grants (living expenses, transportation, academic excellence, social service, completion of degree, study abroad, and training in research methods, Science Olympiads, healthcare practices) that provide a modest but important monthly stipend to students. These grants are an effective means to help students defray the cost of transportation, food, and educational materials; at the same time, they are a powerful incentive to remain in school with good grades. Though these grants do not resolve the problems of educational equality, they are a step forward in terms of the creation of opportunities for school access and persistence.

These grants have no age requirements, meaning that adult students have access to them; nonetheless, there are no data available regarding the age of the beneficiaries. We can assume, however, that the large majority of adult students cover their higher education expenses themselves, whether with income from work or with family resources.

Size and Distribution of the Adult Population in Higher Education

The growth and diversification of educational offerings has favored the development of an increasingly heterogeneous student body, a trend that began in the 70s. Low and middle sectors previously excluded from higher education began to make their way into this educational level, while women came to form around 50% of the total student population in a process generally known as the feminization of the student body; moreover, beginning in this century indigenous students entered higher education, though their numbers are still small. The arrival of adults in higher education is part of this general trend of increased student heterogeneity; however, the category "adult student" itself comprises a heterogeneous population of diverse interests due not only to age, but to gender, social roles, and socioeconomic and ethnic origin, a fact that has barely been researched.

Nonetheless, using the typology proposed by Slowey and Schuetze (2012), and based on the qualitative study that informs this chapter's discussion of topics related to student motivations, it is possible to conclude that various types of adult students are present in Mexican higher education. This does not mean *second chance learners*, since Mexico does not have opportunities for access for students without credentials prior to upper secondary. It is possible, however, to find adult students from *equity groups*, i.e., students from minority ethnic groups or those who are working class or migrants, though we lack an estimate of their number. There are also adults who correspond to the *deferrers* type, i.e., who have an upper secondary credential but, for a variety of reasons, postponed their entrance into higher education. The same could be said for the *recurrent learners*: students who already have a degree or ISCED level 5B2-style diploma, and who decide to obtain a degree at a higher level, whether through recognition of

POLICIES FOR ADULT STUDENTS IN MEXICAN HIGHER EDUCATION 131

prior learning programs or simply by starting some higher education program from the beginning. It is also possible to find students who could be classified as *returners*: those who interrupted their studies and resumed them some time later. Of course, one can find *refreshers* among all these types, i.e., students with or without previous higher education degrees who enroll in continuing education programs in order to update their knowledge and skills. Finally, though present in a smaller proportion, there also are *learners in later life*: senior citizens who enroll not only in continuing education programs but even in professional ones in order to obtain a university degree.

The increase in the number of adults demanding higher education is a recent phenomenon that points toward the growing importance of this group. The number of adult students in both on-site and open and distance programs increased by 138.7%, from 343,396 in 2000 to 819,687 in 2015 – a greater increase, incidentally, than that of students generally. In 2000, adult students represented 18.5% of the total student population, but had expanded to 22% in 2015 (Table 7.3).

TABLE 7.3 Mexico: Total enrollment of adult students by age, 2000–2015.[a] On-site and open and distance modalities combined, cumulative growth

Age	2000	2015	% Growth
24–29	254,668	546,061	114.4
30–39	67,288	186,827	177.7
over 39	21,440	86,799	304.9
Total adults	343,396	819,687	138.7
% of total enrollment	18.5	22	
Total enrollment	1,853,421	3,718,995	100.7

a *Técnico superior universitario* (ISCED level 5B2), university undergraduate, two-year technical, and normal (teacher training).
SOURCE: ADAPTED DATA FROM THE SEP'S "911" STATISTICAL DATABASE (FOR 2000 AND 2010) USING ÁLVAREZ AND ORTEGA (2011), AND WITH DATA FROM ANUIES (2016) (FOR 2015)

Considering just the adult population, it becomes clear that older adults have begun to increase their representation within the adult population and will have a greater proportional weight (Table 7.4).

The percentage of women in the total student population is practically the same as for men, but is somewhat lower in the adult population: 45%. That percentage has remained stable since 2000, meaning no relative progress has

TABLE 7.4   Mexico: Total enrollment of adult students by age, 2000–2015.[a] On-site and open and distance modalities combined (Percentages)

Age	2000	2015
24–29	74.2	66.6
30–39	19.6	22.8
over 39	6.2	10.6
Total adults	100	100

a *Técnico superior universitario* (ISCED level 5B2), university undergraduate, two-year technical, and normal (teacher training).
SOURCE: ADAPTED WITH DATA FROM THE SEP'S "911" STATISTICAL DATABASE (FOR 2000 AND 2010) USING ÁLVAREZ AND ORTEGA (2011), AND WITH DATA FOR THE 2014–2015 SCHOOL YEAR FROM ANUIES (2016) (FOR 2015)

been recorded in adult women's participation compared to that of adult men. Nonetheless, some changes can be observed in the composition of each age group according to sex: the growth of the number of young adult women is somewhat more dynamic than that of older adult women, as part of a process of greater female participation in the segments of the job market that demand higher education credentials in order to get better-paid jobs.

But what modalities do adult students prefer, according to available statistics? In 2015, the majority of them (65.4%) preferred on-site options; however, this is lower than in 2000, when the rate was 73.8%. In fact, there has been a significant increase in the preference for open and distance options among the adult student population: from 26.2% in 2000 to 34.6% in 2015.

It is also noteworthy that the majority of adult students are in the public sector, though a slight reduction in their participation (from 67.1% in 2000 to 64.3% in 2015) indicates that the private sector gained some ground in terms of adult offerings. However, this distribution has stabilized, meaning that the percentage of adult student participation in the public and private sectors has remained the same since 2010.

The significant growth in the number of students aged 24 and over, especially in open and distance modalities, has occurred to a greater extent in the public sector thanks to the creation, in 2010, of the Open and Distance University of Mexico (UNADM). In 2015, the UNADM had 59,661 active enrolled students, of which 91.4% were more than 24 years old. The importance of this age group in the UNADM is clear, given a 110.4% increase in only 5 years (2010–2015).

It is also worth noting that 40% of adults enrolled in private institutions participate in open and distance modalities, compared to 31.5% in the public sector. In other words, the private sector has managed to attract a larger portion of adult students to open and distance offerings.

Despite the fact that open options appear to be better adapted to adult students and enrollment in them tends to grow in absolute and relative terms, adults nonetheless prefer programs in on-site modalities at public universities. This paradox is worthy of further research, as adults in on-site modalities face institutional barriers to achieving their goals, in academic spaces designed for the ideal student (young, full-time, fully dedicated to studying). In Mexico and elsewhere, "[f]or too many adults who want to earn postsecondary credentials, the traditional structure and organization of higher education pose significant barriers to access and, particularly, to persistence and success" (Kazis et al., 2007, p. 3).

For many adult students, some course content is irrelevant. These students have acquired practical knowledge through their occupational experience and, consequently, already have a general idea of what they need to learn and are able to identify content that is meaningful for them. According to Cross and Zusman (1977, p. 22) the barriers these students encounter are primarily related to "practices and procedures which exclude or discourage working adults from participating in educational activities – inconvenient schedules or locations, full-time fees for part-time study, inappropriate courses of study, etc."

In an analogous sense, Fairchild (2003) notes that schools are often not structured to accommodate adult students, and colleges and universities are poorly equipped to handle career orientation for adults. According to Fairchild:

> ... class work may do little to meld life experiences into academic subject matter. Office and class hours may not meet the needs of students who work and care for families, and the institution may ignore or discredit the civic and school involvement important to adult students. (p. 13)

Policies Related to Adult Students in Higher Education

Various higher education policies and programs coincide with some aspects of lifelong learning paradigms: the broadening of educational coverage, the creation of new public institutions, reforms to student-centered educational models, the establishment of tutoring sessions as a formal space for accompanying students, some programs regarding student mobility, degree equivalence and recognition of prior learning, as well as the expansion of the open and distance educational offerings and programs with lateral or intermediate degrees that permit students to combine study and work.

However, there is no unified approach orienting these reforms and resources toward the construction of a coordinated system of institutions and programs, nor are there comprehensive initiatives for adult students. This expansion of coverage is a far cry from the universalization of higher education, and the reforms to educational models were not even designed to incorporate adult students (though they still may not have produced the desired results in terms of a solid development of students' autodidactic abilities) (Álvarez, 2012). The situation in developed countries is completely different, given their greater experience in programs related to adult education, such as recurrent, continuing, permanent, or lifelong education; lifelong learning; open programs; virtual universities; and prior learning assessment.

There are some efforts in Mexico related to adults in higher education: the prior learning assessment program (launched in 2004 by the federal government), which to date includes nearly 50 programs that individuals can complete with a proficiency examination; the promotion of open and distance higher education through the creation of the Open and Distance National University (UNADM) as well as financial support for public institutions to develop programs of this type; and, finally, the growth of continuing education at universities and other HEIs through a varied offering of *diplomados* – courses (generally of short duration) that do not lead to certifications but are meant to serve training and professional "refresher" needs. None of these initiatives, however, have been conceived and launched as part of an overarching policy (strictly speaking) regarding adult students – even less so regarding lifelong learning.

The capacity of distance learning is quite different from that of continuing education. In the public sector, the National Autonomous University of Mexico (UNAM) stands out due to its facilities and equipment, and for the enormous gamut of courses it offers. In the private sector, this position is occupied by the Monterrey Institute of Technology and Higher Education (ITESM or *Tec de Monterrey*). Since the beginning of the past decade the variety of models has expanded, but they lack coordination and duplicate work; moreover, given the uneven quality of programs, there is a need for specific standards that define and regulate the field, as well as for frameworks and mechanisms to evaluate programs and their results.

The creation of the UNADM is the most important government policy related to adult students, which also contributed to the expansion of the student population in higher education and to the development of open and distance modalities. This university caters to different segments of the working-age population: high school graduates, and people who wish to resume their studies or seek academic recognition for their knowledge and skills (Álvarez & Pérez, 2013).

The Nature of Adult Student Demand for Higher Education[3]

In this section we will delve into the motivations of adult students at the moment they decide to resume university studies, which will provide some valuable explanations regarding the nature of the adult demand for higher education. In general, we can identify three motivations that drove the adult students interviewed to participate in higher education:

a. a willingness to continue with their education;
b. the perception that a university degree confers prestige or value on the person who possesses it;
c. concrete experience that suggests a need for certification, specialization, or professionalization of acquired knowledge.

When their interest in obtaining an undergraduate degree stems from the workplace, students base their choices on rational or financial considerations, meaning they focus on the practical utility of their education. Here we observe motivations such as finding a better job or becoming self-employed. The interviewees (especially those who interrupted their academic path) mentioned a constant need to study. In the school sphere of interaction, we can observe motivational factors such as developing or improving abilities or an enjoyment of learning.

The interviewees brought up additional factors such as educational expectations. In general, those who chose on-site modalities touched upon the need to be in a classroom and interact with their teachers in order to learn. These students prefer conventional classes because they are uncomfortable with open options, mediated by technology.

The interviewees from public universities (the National Autonomous University of Mexico [UNAM in Spanish] and the Autonomous University of Mexico City [UACM in Spanish]) cited the direct admissions process and the low cost as the main reasons for their choice. The UNAM offers graduates of its associated high school complete access to undergraduate programs as long as they have finished on time with a satisfactory GPA. At first, the UACM allowed graduates of its evening high schools in Mexico City who had achieved a minimum GPA of 8/10 to enter the university. The expectations of these students were tied to a desire for self-improvement (not associated with specific occupational or financial goals) and a general enjoyment of learning.

This situation differs for adult students who decided to study in a private institution, which is located in Ciudad Nezahualcóyotl, a part of the Mexico City metropolitan area characterized by poverty and high crime rates. They were motivated by the proximity of the institution, the low fees and the prestige they attributed to it. It is interesting to observe that their idea of prestige is not the concept of professional or scientific prestige employed in the academic world, but instead centers on fame or social reputation, a function of various real or fictitious attributes disseminated by publicity and word-of-mouth. Students' choices can also be explained by related factors outside their control, such as schedule constraints resulting from work commitments and the availability of financial resources needed to pay fees. These students expect to improve their quality of life by acquiring better jobs that allow them to move elsewhere.

A lack of time and flexibility in the workplace leads other students to opt for open and distance modalities. They have a clear expectation of acquiring the tools to develop new abilities (strongly linked to the workplace) and to learn, as they put it, the "theory" behind their occupationally-derived knowledge. As such, their expectations are concrete, practical, and work-related. Those who chose a public university considered the flexibility of schedules offered by the open and distance modality, which enables them to perform school-related tasks in their free time. Students in this modality at private institutions considered the same factors as their peers in on-site modalities: the proximity of the institution and, in some cases, the cost as well as prestige they attribute to the institution. On top of this, private HEIs provide open and distance modalities that include mixed offerings with unusual class schedules that allow students to fit school activities into the constraints of their jobs.

General Conclusions

Adult students in higher education are a growing population with specific characteristics and educational needs; consequently, the lack of attention paid them by researchers, higher education institutions, and the government must be remedied. In Mexico, some policies are related to this population, but not explicitly targeted at it. For example, the recognition of prior learning and the existence of open and distance options attract adult students, but this is an unintended consequence of these policies. Similarly, short courses (*diplomados*) draw adult students, but this is due to the market, and not due to policies designed for them. In the case of Mexico, it is noteworthy that adult students prefer on-site educational programs, which are aimed at traditional students. There is, consequently, a convergence between the lack of specific options for adults and their preference for traditional options. The growing incorporation of adults into open and distance programs presents serious challenges for education policy in terms of developing models and strategies appropriate for adults' needs and interests, not only considering training requirements, but also the conditions resulting from different stages of life.

The growth of the adult population in higher education can be explained by the general aging of the population, the inflation of the value of educational degrees, compulsory upper secondary education and the improvement in graduation rates from this level of the education system, and the expansion of higher education. Possessing a university degree continues to confer advantages in terms of obtaining better jobs and increased earnings; moreover, there is a high (though variable) correlation between completed studies and occupational activities, depending on the specific program, thereby reinforcing the creation of demand for higher education. Nonetheless, the higher education system is diverse and segmented by type of institution, quality, and the socioeconomic sector(s) targeted by institutions. Consequently, in addition to their specific problems, adult students face the same issues as students in general, especially regarding the quality of educational programs.

Students are a heterogeneous social cohort that includes various subgroups such as adults, but adults are themselves a diverse group that must be studied in detail to account for differences according to age group, socioeconomic status and geographic origin, gender, ethnicity, and disadvantaged and special needs populations. Similarly, there is a need for specific studies on the influence of external factors in the creation of adult demand for higher education, especially regarding how higher education is perceived by students.

A matter of the greatest importance, which future research must address, concerns the factors and conditions that permit students to complete their studies, which relates to how adult students navigate obstacles to completing their studies, not only in the school sphere but also at home and at work. Studies of school "success" would have to shed light on the impact on employment and changes to family life resulting from adult students' completion of an undergraduate program.

The results of our research lead us to conclude that, for adult students who continue their university studies, their initial motivations for pursuing an undergraduate degree remain almost the same, but their roles and identities undergo changes (generally positive), both in the family and at work.

Notes

1 This phenomenon calls into question the adaptationist perspective of education and employment and highlights the existence of two related but different markets: the education market and the job market, as discussed by Planas (2014).

2 Unless stated otherwise, data from 2000 to 2010 are drawn from Álvarez and Ortega (2011), with ANUIES (2016) providing data for 2015.

3 This part of the chapter is based on doctoral research by Brenda Pérez (in progress), which will be presented at the Department of Education Research of the Center for Research and Advanced Studies (CINVESTAV in Spanish). Here we present a summary of the main findings related to the reasons adult students have for returning to university. Twenty-four individual interviews were conducted: nine with women and 15 with men. The interviews were conducted at six different universities (three public and three private), in on-site as well as and open and distance modalities, and in nine undergraduate programs. Though this is hardly a representative sample, the stories from these interviews give us a glimpse into the range of experiences, choices, and motivations of adults in undergraduate programs.

References

Álvarez, G. (2012). Mexico: Great expectations, scattered approaches, disjointed results: The rocky road to lifelong learning in Mexican higher education. In H. G. Schuetze & M. Slowey (Eds.), *Global perspectives on higher education and life-long learners* (pp. 157–172). Abingdon: Routledge.

Álvarez, G., & Ortega, J. C. (Eds.). (2011). *Sistema de Consulta de la Base 911 de la SEP* [System for Consulting the SEP's "911" Statistical Database]. Retrieved from https://consulta911.wikispaces.com/

Álvarez, G., & Pérez, B. (2013). Open and distance university of Mexico. In E. Gruber et al. (Eds.), *Opening higher education to adults. Appendix G – Case studies*. European Union, European Commission.

ANUIES – Asociación Nacional de Universidades e Instituciones de Educación Superior [National Association of Universities and Higher Education Institutions]. (2016). *Anuarios Estadísticos de Educación Superior* [Statistical Yearbooks for Higher Education]. *Ciclo Escolar 2014–2015* [2014–2015 School Year]. Mexico City: ANUIES.

Brunner, J. J. (2002). Nuevas demandas y sus consecuencias para la educación superior en América Latina [New demands and their consequences for higher education in Latin America]. In J. J. Brunner (Ed.), *Información, análisis y discusión sobre educación y políticas educacionales* [Information, analysis and discussion about education and educational policies]. Retrieved from http://www.brunner.cl/?p=345

POLICIES FOR ADULT STUDENTS IN MEXICAN HIGHER EDUCATION   139

Cross, K. P., & Zusman, A. (1977). *The needs of non-traditional learners and the responses of non-traditional programs*. Berkeley, CA: Center for Research and Development in Higher Education. Retrieved from http://files.eric.ed.gov/fulltext/ED150900.pdf

Fairchild, E. (2003). Multiple roles of adult learners. *New Directions for Student Services, 102*, 11–16.

Kasworm, C. E. (2003). Setting the stage: Adults in higher education. *New Directions for Student Services, 102*, 3–10. Retrieved from http://citeseerx.ist.psu.edu/viewdoc/download?doi=10.1.1.546.1980&rep=rep1&type=pdf

Kazis, R., Callahan, A., Davidson, C., McLeod, A., Bosworth, B., Choitz, V., & Hoops, J. (2007). *Adult learners in higher education: Barriers to success and strategies to improve results*. Washington, DC: US Department of Labor, Office of Policy Development and Research, ETA Occasional Papers. Retrieved from http://www.jff.org/sites/default/files/publications/adultlearners.dol_.pdf

Marúm, E., Moreno, C. I., Rodríguez, C., Curiel, F., Becerra, J. A., Partida, I., ... Aguilar Peña, V. (2016). Informe Nacional: México [National Report: Mexico]. In J. J. Brunner (Ed.), *Educación Superior en Iberoamérica, Informe 2016* [Higher Education in Iberoamerica, Report 2016]. Retrieved from http://www.cinda.cl/wp-content/uploads/2016/11/MEXICO-Informe-Final.pdf

Mendoza, R. J. (2016). *Retos de la Cobertura de Educación Superior* [Challenges of Coverage for Higher Education]: *1er Foro Regional Metropolitano sobre Educación Superior* [First Regional Metropolitan Forum on Higher Education]. Mexico City: Consejo Regional Área Metropolitana de la ANUIES [ANUIES' Regional Council for the Metropolitan Area]. Retrieved from http://cram.ibero.mx/wp-content/uploads/2016/04/zppd_4COBERTURAJMendoza140420162.pdf

Morley, L. (2003). Reconstructing students as consumers: Power and assimilation. In M. Slowey & D. Watson (Eds.), *Higher education and the lifecourse* (pp. 79–92). Maidenhead: Society for Research into Higher Education.

Planas, J. (2014). *Adecuar la oferta de educación a la demanda de trabajo. ¿Es posible? Una crítica a los análisis "adecuacionistas" de relación entre formación y empleo* [Adapting the Educational Offering to Labor Demand. Is It Possible? A Critique of the "Adaptationist" Analysis of the Relationship Between Training and Employment]. Mexico City: ANUIES.

Schuetze, H. (2014). From adults to non-traditional students to lifelong learners in higher education: Changing contexts and perspectives. *Journal of Adult and Continuing Education, 20*(2), 37–55.

SEP – Secretaría de Educación Pública [Ministry of Public Education]. (2014). *Reporte de Indicadores Educativos* [Report on Educational Indicators]. Mexico: SEP. Retrieved from http://www.snie.sep.gob.mx/descargas/indicadores/reporte_indicadores_educativos_sep.xls

Slowey, M., & Schuetze, H. G. (2012). All change – no change? Lifelong learners and higher education revisited. In M. Slowey & H. G. Schuetze (Eds.), *Global perspectives on higher education and lifelong learners* (pp. 4–21). New York, NY: Routledge.

STPS & SNE – Secretaría del Trabajo y Previsión Social & Servicio Nacional de Empleo [Ministry of Labor and Social Services & National Employment Service].

(2017). Ocupación por sectores económicos [Occupation by economic sector]. In *Observatorio laboral*. Mexico City: STPS & SNE. Retrieved from http://www.observatoriolaboral.gob.mx/swb/es/ola/ocupacion_por_sectores_economicos?page=3

CHAPTER 8

The Value of Degrees and Diplomas in Japan

Shinichi Yamamoto

Abstract

This chapter describes a unique feature of the Japanese university system: the age structure of its students, the great majority of whom are between 18 and 23 years of age whereas just two percent are older than 25 years. The author points to the "Japanese way of employment," and hence the unique job-seeking system for Japanese students, which is at the origin of this phenomenon. Larger firms, in particular, prefer to hire young graduates rather than older candidates, and rely for their hiring decisions more on their own examinations, including achievement tests and interviews, rather than on university degrees. Employees thus hired into "regular" employment with good salaries, fringe benefits and high job security (tenure) will then undergo firm-specific training to fit the skill profiles required. Large firms also prefer graduates from highly rated universities, which explains why university *entrance* examinations are so important. The author concludes that a reform of the existing job seeking system is necessary since the current process negatively affects the quality of education, as well as the value of university degrees.

Keywords

higher education in Japan – student age, hiring process of large firms – graduate employment – university entrance examination

Composition of the Student Body in Japan

Massification of higher education is a common phenomenon affecting both advanced and emerging countries around the world. Japan is no exception. Nearly 3 million students are now studying at universities and colleges. Japan's Ministry of Education says 56.5% of young people advanced to universities and colleges in 2015.[1] In other words, more than a half of high school graduates continue on to college or university. However, this huge enrollment is mostly

© KONINKLIJKE BRILL NV, LEIDEN, 2019 | DOI:10.1163/9789004393073_008

comprised of young students aged 18–23. A recent survey by the OECD and Japan's Ministry of Education indicates that only 2% of first year students in universities and colleges in Japan are over 25 years old, while 20% is the average among other OECD member countries.[2] There are still very few adult students in Japan, according to the most recent survey by the Ministry of Education as shown in Table 8.1. This may sound strange to people outside Japan because, with the advent of the knowledge-based economy, earning a university degree or diploma should be a major advantage, not only for young students but also for older students.

TABLE 8.1 Number of entrants by age and program levels (2015)

Age	Junior colleges	Undergraduate	Master's	Doctoral	Total
18 or below	52,138	484,042	–	–	536,180
19	5,523	101,320	–	–	106,843
20	750	17,074	–	–	17,824
21	419	5,558	264	–	6,241
22	348	2,609	37,250	–	40,207
23	267	1,699	16,775	91	18,832
24	195	1,206	5,188	2,701	9,290
25	164	878	2,388	2,053	5,483
26	128	694	1,406	1,318	3,546
27	97	482	1,026	1,003	2,608
28	94	348	731	930	2,103
29	62	262	567	865	1,756
30 or over	813	1,335	6,370	6,322	14,840
Total	60,998	617,507	71,965	15,283	765,753

SOURCE: MINISTRY OF EDUCATION, SCHOOL BASIC SURVEY (2015)

Why does this big gap between the numbers of older students in Japan, as compared to the numbers in other OECD countries, exist? It is mostly explained by the unique job-seeking system for Japanese students. It implies that the value of university degrees and diplomas in Japan is not high if students are too old. In Japan, leading companies (Dai-Kigyo in Japanese) maintain the so-called "Japanese way of employment," in which they hire new graduates, under the age of about 25, only once a year as permanent employees. Therefore, students tend to begin serious job-seeking while they are in only their third year of university. Students in Japan who major in humanities and social sciences

THE VALUE OF DEGREES AND DIPLOMAS IN JAPAN

TABLE 8.2 Distribution of enrolment per 1,000 students in 2010

		Humanities	Social sci.	Science	Engineering	Medical	Education	Others
Undergraduate	public	18	35	12	51	27	24	27
	private	113	265	16	83	58	33	99
Master's	public	1	2	4	17	3	3	7
	private	3	4	1	8	2	1	4
Doctoral	public	1	1	2	4	6	0	4
	private	1	1	0	1	2	0	1
Professional	public	0	2	–	0	0	0	0
	private	0	5	–	0	0	0	0
Junior college	public	1	1	–	–	0	0	1
	private	5	5	–	1	4	15	16

SOURCE: THE MINISTRY OF EDUCATION, SCHOOL BASIC SURVEY (2011)

do not study very hard because they know that companies do not require them to achieve good academic grades. But they do require more basic competencies such as communication skills, common sense, positive attitudes toward work, etc. Such students think that the value of a university degree is very limited; a degree is of value only because it helps them to get a job at a very early stage of their life. After being employed, they usually work for the companies as generalists, not specialists based on the disciplines that they learned, and are later promoted from lower ranked positions toward top ranked positions, such as senior managers or even CEOs.

Public institutions include both national and local public universities. As indicated by the figures in Table 8.2, humanities and social sciences are the major fields of study at the undergraduate level. *Graduate enrolment* is relatively small, especially in doctoral programs.

This causes another problem. Graduate education in Japan is small in scale compared with the huge undergraduate enrolment, especially in the humanities and social sciences. The reason for the very small enrollment in graduate programs is because taking the time required to engage in graduate study may make it more difficult for students to find a good job, as compared to ending their studies at the bachelor's level. By the time they have completed a graduate degree they are too old (over 25) and too narrowly trained. An exception is engineering, where getting a master's degree is regarded as the best way for the students to work as engineers, not technicians, after their graduation. This virtuous cycle, better job opportunities for engineers with graduate degrees, and, therefore, more students entering graduate programs in engineering, began in the 1960s, when engineers of high quality were needed because of the rapid industrial and economic growth at that time. Since then, this trend has continued. However, even in engineering, enrollment in doctoral programs is not large. Thus, enrollment in graduate programs generally indicates an intention to work for universities or laboratories as teaching stuff or researchers, not for business companies.

Because of these factors related to employment, the value of graduate degrees in Japan, including the Ph.D., is not high except in academia.[3] With the advance of the knowledge-based economy and globalization, however, the Japanese way of employment and the meaning of study at universities are being greatly challenged. The so called "collapse of the bubble economy" in the early 1990s damaged the Japanese economy seriously and changed the management systems of Japanese companies in various ways. It is now more expected that universities in Japan take on a more significant role as the engine for revitalizing the Japanese economy, both through research and teaching. The Japanese government has implemented university reform policies, including the introduction of a national accreditation system, to improve the quality of university

THE VALUE OF DEGREES AND DIPLOMAS IN JAPAN   145

education so that students can adapt to global changes. The intention is that the value of the degrees and diplomas earned by the students should be increased. This change will entail deeper consideration and intense discussion of the relationship between university education and the job market in Japan.

The Japanese Way of Job-Seeking

Every year, in spring and summer, one often sees many young men and women walking around the streets of Marunouchi, Otemachi, and other business districts in Tokyo.[4] Almost all wear business suits, mostly black but some in dark gray if they are women, carrying their cell-phones and briefcases. They seem to be nervous. Are they working for companies nearby? No, they are not working there; they are university students who are visiting companies where they want to be employed after their graduation next year. The purpose of their visit is to get information about the companies and also to find out the possibility of employment by talking with the people who are in charge of recruitment. They have sent papers called "entry sheets" to the companies, and the companies have informed them whether or not they will accept the students' visits to the companies. Then, if the students pass through some form of pre-selection, they will take examinations, including achievement tests and interviews that may lead to employment.

The process of recruitment takes several months or even longer. Students usually visit more than a few companies that may accept them. This kind of job seeking takes a lot of the students' time. Thus, in their third and fourth years of university, much of their time must be used for job seeking rather than for their academic study. Both universities and companies have recognized that this job-seeking system detracts from the students' academic progress and they have tried to make a kind of guideline so that students may not take too much time for their job seeking. According to the guideline, companies hold information sessions about themselves in the period of March through May, and during the same period students send their entry sheets to the companies where they want to be employed. Then the companies start their selection from among the students who have applied; students who pass the selection will be employed in April of the following year.[5]

Although the job-seeking activities might detract from their studies, universities have a reason for sending as many students to as possible be employed in industry. The number of students who succeed in gaining employment in big companies is a valuable indicator that enhances the reputation of the universities. Therefore, most universities have an office of employment where several or more professional staff are working. Such offices are commonly called "career centers" or "employment centers." Their mission is to give consultation and advice to the students who are seeking jobs after graduation, and also to bring to the students' attention all the available jobs at companies.

It was not so several decades ago. At that time, only a limited number of students, those studying at leading universities such as the Universities of Tokyo, Keio, or Waseda, were allowed to be involved in this kind of job seeking with big companies. The leading companies had a strong preference for accepting students from such famous universities only. This system of privileged institutions was referred to as the "Designated School System" (*Shitei-ko* in Japanese). When the author (Yamamoto) was a student at the Faculty of Law of the University of Tokyo in the early 1970s, one day he received a thick volume of companies' catalogues from a corporation called "Japan Recruit Center" in which various kinds of information, such as job descriptions, salary, and expected career path, as well as office addresses and phone numbers were written. Such catalogues were not sent to all students but only a limited number of them, including the students of the University of Tokyo. Students of the privileged universities might make phone calls to and visit offices of the companies that they were interested in. Then the way to employment was relatively easy, if the students would, in this way, show their willingness to be employed by those companies.

This system, however, was very much hated because so many students, those who were not at the leading schools, tended to be excluded in the competitive job seeking race to the big companies. In 1987, the National Council of Educational Reform pointed out, in its recommendations to the Prime Minister, that the Designated School System was unfair and that all students must be given an equal opportunity to compete in the job seeking race (Ministry of Education, 1987, p. 21).

With this notion of equality and also with the development of information technology, including e-mail and the Web, now very many university students are given an opportunity to join the job seeking race. Why do they join such a difficult or even stupid race? Because they believe that the big companies give them opportunities of employment only once in their lifetime, which means that they can get full-time and "tenured" employee positions only upon their graduation. In addition, the big companies have a strong preference for employing young students without any specific job skills because companies think the job skills can be acquired after employment through their own on-the-job training systems. Like drawing a picture on a blank paper, companies want to train employees as they like, without interference from any academic influences that students may have picked up at universities.

If they fail to get regular employment (full-time and tenured) at the big companies upon their graduation, students' futures will be quite uncertain.

THE VALUE OF DEGREES AND DIPLOMAS IN JAPAN   147

TABLE 8.3   Top 50 universities which sent many graduates to 400 leading companies in 2015

	Graduates total	Employed by 400 leading companies	Continue to study
National			
Tokyo	7,905	1,540	2,527
Osaka	6,215	1,506	1,974
Kyoto	6,277	1,288	2,226
Kyushu	5,273	911	1,619
Kobe	4,504	870	1,157
Tohoku	4,855	861	1,659
Tokyo Institute of Technology	2,795	832	1,252
Nagoya	3,939	820	1,373
Hokkaido	4,719	691	1,555
Hitotsubashi	1,081	573	91
Other 10 Universities	10,783	2,058	3,764
Local Public			
Osaka Prefectural	2,197	375	486
Other 2 Universities	1,589	293	417
Private			
Waseda	13,160	3,997	2,088
Keio	8,082	3,151	1,287
Doshisha	7,009	1,759	959
Meiji	7,726	1,706	657
Ritsumeikan	8,111	1,614	1,068
Kwansei	5,571	1,402	314
Hosei	6,961	1,351	470
Kansai	6,977	1,246	630
Other 19 Universities	36,917	8,684	4,625
Top 50 Total	1,62,646	37,528	32,198

SOURCE: *SUNDAY MAINICHI WEEKLY NEWS MAGAZINE* (15 NOVEMBER 2015)

Today, according to the Ministry of General Affairs, more than one-third of employees in Japan are non-regular employees. Their salary is far less than that of regular employees and their continuity of employment is always uncertain. Companies have had a great incentive to reduce the cost of labor to survive in the difficult economic situation after the "bubble collapse" of the economy since the early 1990s. Once the students get non-regular employment, it is very difficult for them to move to regular employment on a tenured basis. Thus the first job just after their graduation of from university is extremely important.

Table 8.3 shows an example of the relationship between prestigious universities and leading companies. According to this source, in 2015 the top 50 out of nearly 800 universities in Japan sent 37,528 students to 400 leading companies. The University of Tokyo, Hitotsubasi, Waseda and Keio are included in the 50 top universities. In Table 8.3, graduates include students who finish undergraduate and graduate programs.

The Ministry of Economy, Trade and Industry states that there are about 40 million employees working for companies in Japan, of whom about 12.3 million are working for big companies. This number is about 30% of all employees in Japan. If employees work about 40 years for these big companies, we can estimate that the companies hire about 300,000 new employees every year, both on a regular (tenured) and non-regular basis. Since, in recent years, universities and colleges produce about 400–450,000 bachelor's degree holders who manage to find jobs every year, the way to the big companies is no longer so easy.[6]

This is especially true for the students who majored in humanities and social sciences. Science and engineering majors, however, are somewhat different. It is generally recognized that students in these fields must have the knowledge and skills which are necessary for them to work as scientists or engineers in industry. The medical and allied health fields are also different. In these fields students must pass national examinations for certification by the government, not by the universities where they study, if they want to work as professionals such as medical doctors, pharmacists and nurses. Thus they must study very hard. But enrollment in the medical and related fields comprises only 10% of all enrollments. Therefore, the discussion focuses on the humanities and social sciences, which comprise nearly half of the total enrollment.

The Importance of the University/College Entrance Examination System

In the previous section, the Japanese way of job-seeking for the students in humanities and social sciences was discussed. Big companies do not so much care about students' academic scores but more about generic skills, such as ability to communicate with others. In this regard, these companies, as well as the general public in Japan, have tended to think that the *potential* ability of the students is much more important than knowledge and skills that are acquired through academic work at universities and colleges. Given this belief, how do they find such students with potential ability? This potential is discovered through the entrance examinations that the students must pass in order to *enter* the higher education system. The examinations at prestigious universities are very difficult to pass, and thus, passing those examinations has been regarded as the best indicator for the companies to judge whether the students have potential for good performance after their employment.[7]

This attitude held by companies has had a great impact on study patterns, especially among high school students. They have been taught that passing the entrance examinations of prestigious universities will promise them a good future. A "good future" means to be employed by a big company with a sizable salary and to continue to work there until their retirement at about age 60. If they become managers of the company, their opportunity to work will continue until they are 70 or older. The difference of life-time income is apparent, between people who are winners and who are losers. The university entrance examination has, therefore, been regarded as a very important event for the students. It is an event which all the students who wish to study at universities must go through, and must prepare for diligently. But after surviving the ordeal of the university entrance examination, they tend to forget another important matter, i.e., studying at their university itself. But both the students and their potential employers have not been worried about studying because they believe the students have already shown their potential by passing the university entrance examinations.

Observers, both inside and outside Japan, sometimes criticize this attitude of Japanese students who major in humanities and social sciences because they do not study hard. But their lack of interest in academic study fits very well with the system that results in employment after graduation, although this fitness applies only in humanities and social sciences. As noted above, in science and engineering students must study hard so that they can gain the level of knowledge and skills required to work as scientists and engineers.

Also as noted above, in the medical, pharmaceutical and nursing science fields students must study even harder than in other fields of science because they must pass national qualification exams if they wish to work as professionals in those fields. It is quite reasonable that high school students with good achievement tend to choose medical studies which may result in their becoming medical doctors. The social status and economic rewards of medical doctors in Japan have been very high, and will be even higher because medical doctors are protected by the exclusive credential of "medical doctor," and there are many kinds of medical treatment that only medical doctors are allowed to decide upon and practice. In addition, medical doctors are paid more than non-medical staff if they work for hospitals and medical clinics. If they work as independent medical practitioners, they may become even richer. A study shows that the typical rich person in Japan is a medical doctor or company manager (Tachibanaki & Mori, 2015). Indeed, the entrance exams of medical schools have become extremely difficult, in spite of the general trend that entrance exams have become much easier in other fields such as humanities and social sciences due to the decline of the 18-year-old population.

Because of the situation described above, the university entrance examination system has been of the deepest interest to Japanese people. The examination system has become an end in itself, instead of a means to select talented individuals for study at universities. The so called "examination hell" has been a key to understanding the Japanese system of education, not only in higher education but also in primary and secondary education until recently. Children have been forced to study hard even in primary and secondary education if they wish to go to prestigious universities. Unlike the American and European systems of admission, the Japanese system has put its emphasis on achievement as measured by the entrance examinations set by universities. As an OECD review of Japanese education system stated, Japanese higher education has greatly relied on its entrance examination system, and people have their future decided on the basis of the examination which they undergo at about the age of 18 (OECD, 1971).

Recently, however, the entrance examinations have become very important not only for the high school students *but also for university managers and administrators*. Because of the sharp decline of the 18-year-old population, admission into higher education institutions has become much easier than it was in the 1970s and 1980s. The 18-year-old population has been declining since the early 1990s. In 1992, there were about two million 18-year-olds in Japan, but now this segment of the population is only 1.2 million – a 40% decline. It is estimated to be about one million in 2030 and 0.8 million in 2040, according to the calculation by the Ministry of Welfare and Labor. The "examination hells" are now limited to a few institutions which are highly competitive, such as the Universities of Tokyo, Keio, and Waseda. The majority of Japanese universities are now competing with each other for students. The Japan Agency for the Promotion of Private Schools (*Shigaku-Jigyodan* in Japanese) says more than 40% of universities and nearly 70% of junior colleges cannot attract as many students as they are allowed to accept. Fewer students means less income for the universities because private universities depend heavily on revenue from tuition and fees.[8]

Therefore, the universities have tried to attract as many students as they can by introducing an easier and more attractive examination system. Some universities admit students without any academic achievement test but only on the basis of documents and recommendation letters from high schools and interviews by the institutions. Thus the important function performed by the university entrance examinations of gauging the potential abilities of students has become weaker. The universities must now find another role, instead of only discovering the potential abilities of the students. An important function of universities and colleges, of course, must be found in their teaching, which may give the students useful knowledge and skills that should be relevant for their future vocations. Indeed, many universities and colleges, especially in humanities and social sciences, put an emphasis on career and vocational education in their curriculum.

But it is not easy for them to achieve the intended recruitment because vocational qualifications in humanities and social sciences, unlike medical sciences, are only remotely related to many vocations which the students may be fitted for. Although the Ministry of Education has tried to encourage universities to improve or reform their curriculum so that they may teach more practical and vocational subjects for the students, teaching staff with academic backgrounds are not good at teaching practical subjects and companies still do not care very much about the knowledge and skills which the students acquire at universities. Therefore, recently, the creation of another kind of university has been discussed. In May, 2016, the National Council on Education issued a recommendation regarding a new type of university called "Special Vocational University" (provisional name) which may resemble the former polytechnics in the UK or *Fachhochschulen* in Germany. Some universities may move to this new structure, but more attention to this new development is now being paid by the current special training colleges which may want to get university status. Ironically, big companies still require basic knowledge and skills, which used to be tested by the difficult university entrance examinations, not practical skills.

Another important strategy for the universities that are trying to recruit more students is to attract adult students and international students. Both of these groups are expected to replace the lack of enrollment by young Japanese. However, universities and colleges are not ready to increase the number of international students by providing lectures in English or other non-Japanese languages. Instead, universities have mainly accepted international students who have studied Japanese as a working language and, therefore, accept students mainly from China and Korea. Although the Ministry of Education encourages universities to increase the number of non-Japanese speaking students by introducing competitive grants such as the SGU (Super Global Universities) program, the situation seems not to change rapidly. Adult students are also difficult to attract in greater numbers. This is because the value of a degree is not high for the adult students who must pay tuition and fees.

The Value of a Degree

The value of a university education should be expressed by the degrees which students receive on their graduation. In this sense, various kinds of university degrees should show the ability of the graduates to perform well both in academia and business (Senoh, 2011, pp. 259–260). Thus, university degree holders are expected to earn more than non-degree holders. According to the OECD survey, the economic benefit of a university education is apparent in all countries. Table 8.4 shows, by comparing the internal rate of return in each country, the percentage by which the average salary of a degree holder exceeds that of a person who does not have a degree.

Japan is no exception to the general rule that a degree confers some economic benefit, but the benefit seems to be less than among other major countries and OECD member countries as the whole.

Why is the economic benefit of a degree so much less in Japan? One of the reasons is that Japanese companies and other organizations usually do not much care about whether an employee holds a university degree or not. Instead, the basic structure of the salary scale is based on age, years of job experience, and the positions that employees are in. The difference of salary between university graduates and high school graduates, for example, can be explained by the difference in positions that those workers have. Generally speaking, a higher position earns higher salary, and people who have university degrees are expected to have more chances for promotion because of their ability. This is an indirect benefit of having a degree; a university degree does not have much of a direct effect. In addition, there is a big difference in salary among different industries. In finance and security, people earn more than in manufacturing industries. And those who have university degrees tend to go to

TABLE 8.4   Economic benefit of higher education

	Men (%)	Women (%)
Japan	7.4	7.8
Canada	10.8	11.0
U.S.A.	11.5	8.8
Germany	9.6	8.2
OECD average	12.4	11.4
EU21 average	13.9	10.8

SOURCE: OECD (2012)

THE VALUE OF DEGREES AND DIPLOMAS IN JAPAN 153

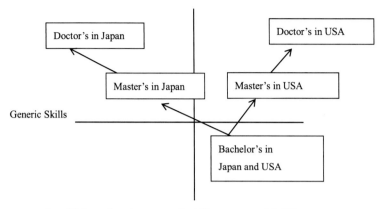

FIGURE 8.1   Higher education – generic skills versus special skills

finance and other non-manufacturing industries. The difference of economic benefit is much narrower among bachelor's, master's and doctoral degrees in Japan as compared to other countries. Some companies even have no difference in salary scales between holders of bachelor's degrees and those who finish graduate studies. The salary is almost the same, if the difference in age at graduation is taken into account. Except in the field of engineering, students graduating with master's degrees find difficulty in finding appropriate jobs outside of academia. Doctoral degrees are even more difficult to connect to jobs in business. This situation can be explained by Figure 8.1.

In Japan, people generally regard university education as the place for getting generic knowledge and skills that will be applicable to various kinds of jobs after their graduation. Companies also welcome students with strong generic skills such as communication skills and problem solving skills. Special or professional skills, they believe, should be added by the companies through on-the-job training. Thus, students with many special skills are not welcomed because companies think their skills do not always fit the requirements of the companies. Therefore, holders of Bachelors of Arts are most welcomed, master's degree holders come second (with a few exceptions in science and engineering, fields in which specialized knowledge and skills are desirable in a new employee) and holders of doctor's degrees are least welcome in business.

It is completely different from the situations in other countries like the U.S.A., where doctorate degrees are highly regarded both in academia and business because those who have doctorate degrees have been trained to have both generic skills and special skills which are useful for practical problem solving as well as academic research. In Europe, and even in developing countries, doctorate degrees show professional capacity to work for government, business and academia. Indeed, graduate degrees are effective tickets to the globalized society.

Japanese higher education is a very large system in terms of total enrollment, but graduate schools still attract very few students, especially in social sciences (see Table 8.1). That is largely explained by the fact that people do not highly regard graduate degrees, both master's degrees and doctorates. Instead, people still put much reliance on the name and, of course, reputation of the university where a student has completed their undergraduate program. The idea that bachelor's degrees are the most desirable still influences people's way of thinking. For graduate degrees to be more valued, some strong measures for university reform are required (Yamamoto, 2007, p. 197).

Conclusion: Toward a Future System of Higher Education in Japan

Japanese higher education has several unique features, compared with other advanced countries. First, the private sector accounts for the majority of enrollments. About three-fourths of all enrollment is in private universities and colleges. This is completely different from most European systems, which consist mainly of public institutions. And it is largely different from the U.S. system also, where private universities play a big role both in education and research but only about 40% of students are in the private sector. Thus, private universities in Japan must adapt to the practical needs of students in mass higher education. This means that private institutions do not, or cannot, care much about graduate education, which is not popular among students in humanities and social sciences. But these institutions should care about bachelor's degree programs.

Second, most students start studying at the age of 18 or 19. There are very few adult students in Japan. This is the result of the Japanese way of job seeking; students have a very narrow window of time for getting jobs after graduation. If the value of graduate degrees, including master's and doctoral degrees, were much higher, students might have more choice regarding their future, even after they are 30 years old. Due to the decline of the 18-year-old population in Japan, higher education institutions, especially private universities, must review their admission policies in order to attract more adult students. In addition to the review of higher education admission policies, corporations should value university degrees earned by such adult students much more than they have to date.

Third, most undergraduate students currently start to seek jobs in big companies even when they are still in the third year of their four year bachelor's programs. In 2016, the job seeking race officially started on March 1, which allows students to visit companies to get information and to discover the employment possibilities. Actually, the race had already started the previous year. This situation is very bad for the study activities of the students. Seeking a job is the official excuse for absence from classes that the students must normally attend. The Ministry of Education, on the other hand, recently stated a requirement that universities should offer classes at least 30 weeks a year so that students have enough time to study. Under the current system of university education in Japan, students must get 120 academic credits or more for graduation. One academic credit requires students to study 45 hours, both in class and at home, and universities must offer their classes for more than 30 weeks in each year. How do those students manage to find adequate time for study during their period of job seeking? While the quality of learning is not always correlated with the amount of study time, university officials are concerned that too much absence from class may detract from the quality of learning in university courses.

To reform the existing job seeking system in Japan will not be easy, but it must be done. The job seeking system clearly affects the quality of education, and thus the value of university degrees.

Notes

1   School Basic Survey conducted annually by the Ministry of Education. In this survey, the ratio of advancement to universities and colleges is calculated by dividing the number of entrants into universities and colleges in a year by the 18-year-old population in the same year.
2   http://www.mext.go.jp/component/b_menu/shingi/toushin/__icsFiles/afieldfile/2012/10/04/1325048_6.pdf
3   In academia, even in Japan recently, the Ph.D. is almost a mandatory requirement for those who seek academic positions in universities and colleges. Therefore, students hoping for an academic career face a quite risky choice near the end of their bachelor's program. Preparing for an academic career requires years of graduate school, but devoting those years to graduate level study will tend to disqualify them for other forms of desirable employment.
4   *Marunouchi* and *Otemachi* are the names of the most famous and prosperous business districts in Japan. Many big companies locate their headquarters there and from there control their offices around the world as well as in Japan. This area is very near the government agencies, called *Kasumi-ga-seki*, which makes it convenient for them to maintain good relations with the government.

5 https://job.rikunabi.com/2017/contents/article/edit~schedule~index/u/

6 http://www.chusho.meti.go.jp/koukai/chousa/chushoKigyouZentai9wari.pdf

7 U.S. Department of Education (1987) states that "Many secondary school graduates who fail to gain admission try again the following year and commonly devote full time to the preparation process."

8 In Japan, universities and colleges are informed by the Ministry of Education as to the number of students that they may accept each year. The aim of this system is to maintain the quality of teaching. This comes from Article 4 of the School Education Law and related Orders by the Minister of Education.

References

Ministry of Education. (1987). The recommendations of the national council on educational reform, MESC 61. *The Monthly Journal of the Ministry of Education* (Monbu-Jiho), 1327. Tokyo: Gyosei Publishing. (In Japanese)

OECD. (1971). *Reviews of national policies for education: Japan.* Paris: OECD.

OECD. (2006). *Thematic review of tertiary education: Country background report of Japan.* Paris: OECD.

OECD. (2012). *Education at a glance 2012: OECD indicators.* Paris: OECD. Retrieved from http://dx.doi.org/10.1787/eag-2012-en

Senoh, W., & Higeta, T. (2011). Some characteristics of, and issues in higher education in Japan implied by the "rate of return to education." *Journal of National Institute for Educational Policy*, 249–263.

Tachibanaki, T., & Mori, T. (2015). *Nihon no Okanemochi Kenkyu* [A Study of Japanese Rich People]. Tokyo: NIKKEI Newspaper Publishing.

US Department of Education. (1987). *Japanese education today.* Washington, DC: Government Printing Office.

Yamamoto, S. (2007). Doctoral education in Japan. In S. Powel & H. Green (Eds.), *The doctorate worldwide* (pp. 181–193). Maidenhead: Open University Press.

Yamamoto, S. (2012). Lifelong learning and higher education in Japan. In M. Slowey & H. G. Schuetze (Eds.), *Global perspectives on higher education and lifelong learners* (pp. 217–229). Abingdon: Routledge.

Yamamoto, S. (2019). Higher education reform: Why did it start and has it ended? An analysis of the Japanese case. In P. Zgaga, U. Teichler, H. G. Schuetze, & A. Wolter (Eds.), *Higher education reform: Looking back – looking forward* (2nd ed., pp. 129–142). Frankfurt: Peter Lang.

CHAPTER 9

MOOCs, Students, Higher Education and Their Paradoxes

Maureen W. McClure

Abstract

Massive Open Online Courses (MOOCS) have attracted a great deal of attention in the media. Some of this coverage has promoted myths to the effect that MOOCS are completely new (not a continuation of previous practices in education), monolithic, and inevitable. They are not. The author provides an extensive discussion of how MOOCS have developed from previous practices of distance education, lifelong learning, and open educational resources. She then explains why MOOCS are "fragile," mainly because they are in clear danger of not living up to the hype that has surrounded them. And they are not monolithic: various types have emerged, and more continue to emerge. The author concludes with the observation that the MOOC movement is one of many "wicked paradoxes" that will be very challenging for higher educational institutions to address.

Keywords

MOOCS – distance education – lifelong learning – open educational resources – accreditation of MOOCS

Introduction

Massive Open Online Courses (MOOCS) have often been reported in the media as: (a) *ab nihilo* new; (b) monolithic; and (c) inevitable (McClure, 2015). They are none of these. They are not "out of nothing" new because they are descended from three longer-term traditions of: (a) distance education technologies; (b) lifelong learning; and (c) scholars' traditions of open access to their research. MOOCS were never monolithic and are currently morphing at very rapid rates into multiple, often contradictory forms. MOOCS' currently high production costs, however, prevent them from being inevitable.

© KONINKLIJKE BRILL NV, LEIDEN, 2019 | DOI:10.1163/9789004393073_009

Today's average MOOCers differ significantly from on-campus students, as they are likely to live off campus, have degrees and work full-time. Their needs tend to focus on career building and educational enrichment (Coursera, University of Pennsylvania, & University of Washington, 2015). Higher Education Institutions (HEIs) should consider how they can balance MOOCs' access, accreditation and cost paradoxes with their own sustainability needs. This is critical because entering the fray are a new global generation of social media savvy students pursued by new: (a) competitors; (b) technologies; (c) pedagogies; and (d) credentials (McClure, 2016).

There is much good news. MOOCs and their derivatives have generated educational access for millions of students both young and old. In 2015, about 35 million students signed up for at least one course, roughly double the number in 2014 (ICEF Monitor, 2016).

TABLE 9.1   Basic MOOC trends

	2012	2013	2014	2015
Signed up for at least one MOOC course	~2,000,000	~10,000,000	16–18,000,000	~35,000,000
Number of participating Universities	~33	~200	400+	500+
Number of courses offered	~100	~900	2400+	4200

SOURCE: ED SURGE NEWS, (2013); ICEF MONITOR, (2016); PAPPANO, (2012)

The benefits for students are many, from global access to radical convenience to elite quality. Professors can teach and students can learn from almost anywhere (Anderson, 2012). MOOCs also offer greater diversity in classroom peers across place and age. Managed well, this can create many opportunities for rich, complicated discussions.

MOOCs Are Not New, Monolithic or Inevitable

MOOCs have deep roots. They evolved internationally from the longstanding traditions of correspondence education dating back to the late 1800s (Karsenti, 2013). In Juliana Marques' "A short history of MOOCs and distance learning," she writes that distance learning continuously morphed during the 20th century, first from correspondence courses to multi-media instruction using radio, television, tapes, CDs, etc., and then to today's online learning (2013).

Distance Learning

In the second half of the 20th Century, the United Nations Educational, Scientific and Cultural Organization (UNESCO) built multi-media radio and television education programs by working with governments in developing countries for large-scale outreach into isolated regions globally. The origins of these programs can be found in the work of Canadian educators who, in the early 1940s, developed the "Farm Radio Forum," an early mass radio education program. The success of these forums led to their later adaptation by UNESCO in many developing countries. Globally, "By 1968, a total of about 15,000 [forums] was reported" (Nwaerondu & Thompson, 1987).

By the late 1960s, the UK's Open University had taken a global lead in supporting education massification movements by providing international access to both higher education and lifelong learning. Other countries followed suit, establishing their own open universities. For example, Indonesia established the Universitas Terbuka (UT) as a way of reaching students and teachers across its large number of isolated islands. MOOCs, therefore, have been firmly rooted within traditions of mass, open and lifelong learning across multiple countries.

The Open Educational Resources (OER) Movement

With the advent of the Internet and computer-assisted learning, the William and Flora Hewlett Foundation funded the Open CourseWare project at the Massachusetts Institute of Technology (MIT) in 2002 (McClure, 2014a). It encouraged professors to provide open access to their syllabi, and where possible, other course materials on the Internet. edX, a major provider of MOOCs, is a descendent of this project. The OER movement facilitated two important strategic shifts. Not only did it provide mass, global access to faculty-vetted materials, it also extended a global *research* culture to shared *teaching*.

It did not, however, provide direct access to online courses. MOOCs did that. And, more importantly to some, the OER movement helped create new rules for intellectual property rights related to Internet use. The now ubiquitous Creative Commons created multiple levels of agreements for intellectual property rights, an important issue for scholars (McClure, 2014a). The OER movement allowed for both author attribution and the widespread sharing of materials.

Despite their many global public benefits, most HEIs' incentive systems still weigh heavily against the OER movement's efforts to help all students. Corporate publishers publish most top journals. Their business models are not compatible with OER access. Publication in corporately published journals most often counts decisively more than OERs for fundamental decisions on tenure, promotion and annual raises, despite their cost and increasingly limited global reach. It is a chronically overlooked problem that needs to be addressed at the highest levels.

Fragile, Not Inevitable

When the press wasn't comparing MOOCs to university degree programs, it often framed them in terms of the technology industry. Gartner's Hype Cycle™, for example, has been cited frequently (Tapson, 2013). According to the Gartner model, MOOCs, like most technology rollouts, were first over-promised, then pilloried for not living up to the unrealistic hype. Finally, reality and pragmatics settles in and moves the field forward.

Right from their introduction, the hype around MOOCs was almost limitless. They have been touted as (McClure, 2015):

- low cost access for some HEIs to extend their international reach strategy for recruitment, placement, networking for teaching and research, etc. (McClure, 2013b);
- sources of domestic and international media visibility for HEIs (McClure, 2013b);
- cooperative outreach to the remote and isolated (McClure, 2013a);
- access to global, cosmopolitan discussions (Dolan, 2014);
- global access to Open Educational Resources (OER) and concomitant intellectual property rights issues (Peralta, 2012);
- sources of remedial education for college entrants (Kolowich, 2013);
- new methods for building alumni relations through professional development and cultural enrichment (McClure, 2013b);
- new opportunities for cross-university teaching (Jaschik, 2013);
- low cost access to elite education for students in developing countries (especially with mobile use) (McClure, 2014b).

In sum, there is great promise for students who have realistic understandings of what MOOCs can do. The future of MOOCs, however, remains fragile due to the cost-related risks for HEIs as well as their relatively weak marketing efforts.

The Grand Intentions: Democratizing Content, Platforms and Accreditation

Looking beyond frames of new, monolithic and inevitable, it may be useful to reframe thinking about MOOCs in terms of their democratizing intent. This intent was made visible in three strands: (a) content; (b) platforms; and (c) accreditation. MOOCs provided free or low cost access to: (a) elite university teaching (Anderson, 2012); (b) global peer networks for professionals, faculty and students; (c) technology that included social networking; and (d) lifelong learning beyond the campus (McClure, 2013a). Together, these democratizing efforts led to: (a) access to open source platforms and resources; (b) more agile forms of online learning; (c) access to employers embedded in courses as teaching faculty; and (d) new forms of mobile use with cloud storage (Mitra & Dangwal, 2010; Vivian, Falkner, & Falkner, 2014).

As MOOC designers realized the need for student incentives both to complete courses and to pay small fees, accreditation democratized through the development of: (a) certificates, badges, nanodegrees, etc. through university and non-university providers; (b) more flexible time requirements for completion; (c) new entrants from cultural institutions as well as both the private and non-profit sector; and (d) shifts toward self-paced courses. While media interest in MOOCs has waxed and waned, public interest as indicated by online searches for them has shown both erratic and steady growth (see Figure 9.1).

FIGURE 9.1   Google searches for "Massive open online course" or "MOOC" 2012–2016

Democratizing through Self-Organizing Approaches

MOOCs were first named and designed in Canada in the late 2000's to generate self-organizing, low cost, Internet-based networks for cooperative learning. Later, MOOCs of this type were called cMOOCs. George Siemens at the University of Manitoba, Stephen Downes at the Canadian Research Council, and others at Athabasca University worked with the Canadian government, UNESCO and other countries to support education not only in rural and remote areas of Canada, but also in developing countries, especially remote villages and islands (Cormier, 2010; Downes, 2008; UNESCO, n.d.).

These "CMOOCs" were the most organic in terms of providing simultaneous access to content, process and accreditation. They built networks of peers and mentors using software platforms already in common use (Cormier, 2010). These required some technological literacy and a great deal of patience. Their designers relied on patchworks of applications (email, word processing, databases, analytics, presentations etc.). For example, a CMOOC today might create a course using MS Word to generate documents, Box to share and comment on them, LinkedIn to share links and discussions related to course readings, and Zoom for videoconferences. (Downes, 2010; Siemens, 2010a, 2010b). CMOOC networks were often intentionally temporary, as they were often designed and managed by faculty members, rather than by large HEIs with degree programs.

Democratizing through Expert Approaches

Unlike the self-organizing CMOOCs, others were designed by experts willing to share their knowledge and experience. Called "XMOOCs," they focused on the democratization of access to elite teaching through externally and centrally controlled platforms. XMOOCs have come to dominate the popular discourse.

In the fall of 2011, Stanford professors Sebastian Thrun and Peter Norvig put their course CS221: Introduction to Artificial Intelligence online for free, thinking they might attract a few thousand students. Instead, 160,000 showed up, globally launching the XMOOC movement. It was built on traditional university classroom lectures by professors with substantial expertise. Soon after, several innovative XMOOC platform providers were launched. Out of Stanford emerged Thrun's Udacity and Andrew Ng's and Daphne Koller's Coursera. Harvard and MIT generated Anat Agarwal's edX (McClure, 2014a).

All three startups had breakthrough centralized platform designs and startup company entrepreneurship. They were both radically convenient and provided free global access to high quality content and production. Soon they attracted other elite HEIs willing to teach online through external and centralized platforms that included course design teams. These platform providers built networks, domestically at first, and soon after went global (McClure, 2014a).

Democratizing Platforms

CMOOC platforms were highly decentralized by definition. XMOOC platform designers at edX and Google soon began democratizing their centralized platforms. They created access to their Open edX platform codes. This openness encouraged a whole new industry based on democratizing access to platform design globally (McClure, 2016). National governments soon became interested in supporting national platform providers. These new providers designed MOOCS in local languages and other world languages other than English (Despujol, Turro, Orts, & Busquets, 2015). These were located in various countries including China (XuetangX), France (France Université Numérique), Jordan (Edraak), and Spain (Miríada X) (Gibney, 2013; Walters, 2014b). For example, the UK's British Broadcasting Corporation (BBC)-based platform, FutureLearn, helped recruit international students by designing study skills improvement MOOCS (Gibney, 2013).

Democratizing Pedagogy

XMOOCS provided access not only to syllabi and reading materials, but also to online pedagogy using multiple short lecture videos. These short videos were often broken into modules containing only one or two critical points. Students benefited from using this new pedagogy by: (a) slowly building conceptual frameworks through brief modules; (b) watching them on their own time; (c) replaying them as needed; and (d) changing the speed of the video, fast for familiar areas (1.5x), normal (1.0), or slow (.5) for more complicated topics or learning in a different language (Walters, 2014a). In addition, they generated valuable new sources of "big data" on learning for both researchers and evaluators.

The founder of edX, Anat Agarwal referred to this online pedagogy as "Pause, rewind, and speed up" (Agarwal, 2014), and keep trying until mastery (Walters, 2014a). In addition, small quizzes were often embedded in the videos so students could self-check their comprehension. As research on online teaching and learning becomes more sophisticated, there is a growing interest in shifting from lecture-based monologues to engagement (Chi, Kang, & Yaghmourian, 2016) through "active" or "hands-on" learning and "gamification" (Andone, Mihaescu, Ternauciuc, & Vasiu, 2015).

An overlooked pedagogical gift of the XMOOCS has been the high tech industry's culture of failure tolerance. Students were given greater opportunities to fail often and still succeed. This modular and repetitive approach shadowed the ways social media savvy students already learned while online.

High quality content, platforms and pedagogy, however, are expensive to produce. Many MOOCS appeared to have more significant investments in content quality than in production. One problem with this approach was that it overlooked the social media experiences of many students. Another problem was that it overlooked whole new classes of competition. For example, new content and platform providers like the Smithsonian, the BBC and Udacity began offering expensively produced courses designed with high quality content and production values. MOOC pioneer Sebastian Thrun puckishly mused that if the entertainment industry could produce movies that cost $100 million, why not the same for MOOCS (Walters, 2014b).

MOOCs have been transformative because of their rapid innovation and globalization, but their future has never been inevitable. Whatever their growing pains, MOOCs have opened up online career building and educational enrichment to millions. The problem has been paying for them.

MOOCs Morph

MOOCs were an idea that threw accelerants on the already rapidly developing online learning movement using the Internet (Keohane, 2013; McClure, 2015; Pappano, 2012). MOOCs morphed early, translating rapidly into new forms as follows (see McClure, 2015). MOOCs quickly became BOOCs (big but not massive open online courses) aimed for enrollments of about 500. DOCCs (distributed open collaborative courses) were blended learning courses taught for degree-related credit, simultaneously by multiple faculty members from multiple institutions. These have great promise, but few takers so far ("State of the MOOC 2016"). Henry Mintzberg at McGill University in Montreal designed GROOCs (GRoup open online courses) using work teams across networks rather than having students studying individually. They have remained popular. HOOCs (hybrid open online courses) are conducted online, both synchronously and asynchronously. LAPs (local access points) restructured MOOCs from totally online courses to hybrids, based on students' "meetups" that were organized informally in cities; faculty then held online office hours, city by city, globally. These meetups have gone on to a significant life of their own.

LOOCs (little open online courses) were kept small because they were intended for some level of credit or certification. MOODs were either massive open online discussions or massive open online data-big data use. An example of big data use would be analyses of the many thousands of individual student paths through course materials, quiz scores and discussions generated during a single course. In China, MOOE (massive open online experiments) and MOORs (massive open online research) began to adapt MOOCs' teaching aims for other academic uses. POOCs (personalized open online courses) used big data for adaptive learning. ROOCs had a couple of meanings (re-mixable open online course or regional open online course). Remixable materials means open educational resources (OER) that are not only free, but are also available for re-use elsewhere by students anywhere. ROOCs also meant regional interests with regional designs. SMOCs (synchronous massive online course) were taught online to those willing to pay tuition costs. SPOCs (small private online courses) were designed for on-campus use in hybrid or blended learning courses for free or fee (McClure, 2015).

Once the reality of cost and upkeep settled in, MOOCs morphed in directions so complex they fell into the category of "wicked problems" (Connery & Hasan, 2015; McClure, 2014a, 2014c). First, students shifted interest away from democratizing access to elite education toward career building in the areas of science, technology, engineering and mathematics (STEM) (Alcorn et al., 2015; Coursera et al., 2015). Second, there was a gradual shift from free to fee.

MOOCs as Paradox

MOOCs present paradoxes that can't be solved. For example, elite HEIs democratized online education. Sebastian's Thrun's xMOOC course created a paradox of design. Stanford and edX's Harvard and MIT provided democratic access to elite education by investing their discretionary resources into high quality production. Few HEIs could have done that. Elite HEIs created an entire market by making MOOCs with their brands available to millions of others who otherwise could not enroll. Sometimes paradoxes are not necessarily problematic.

In addition to edX's self-funding model, Coursera used venture capital for their platform and organized other top universities globally. Each partner HEI provided course content and often production value through self-funding teams of specialists with expertise and experience in discipline, pedagogy and instructional design. Despite uneven quality, millions of students of all ages had radically convenient access to thoughtful content. An early and iconic example was a young student in Mongolia who snagged both an MIT scholarship with top performance on a sophomore level MOOC, and a lot of press for MIT (Pappano, 2013) Mentioned less often was a reference to his mentor, an MIT graduate.

The Paradox of Access
Access remains a persistent dilemma both domestically and globally. The good news is that Internet access has grown wildly in the last few years. Today, about 46 percent of the world's population, or about 3.4 billion people, have an Internet connection. The bad news is about 4 billion people still do not have Internet access (Internet live stats, 2016).

In addition, Internet quality is a problem for the poor and isolated in some countries with large youth populations. Internet quality as it is used here means access to bandwidth sufficient to easily run MOOC courses on a laptop or mobile. In more developed countries, both the public and private sectors help create a working technology infrastructure for the Internet and MOOC development. HEIs in communities with fewer resources, however, may lack the bandwidth needed for a quality Internet infrastructure and/or the expertise needed for MOOC development of courses in local languages (McClure, 2014b).

For those with access to mobile technology and the Internet, the possibilities for education are exploding (UNESCO, n.d.). For those without it, they remain, for better or worse, outside these communities of knowledge. The gaps grow. Sir John Daniel argues that openness trumps scale in developing countries (Vander Ark, 2012). Given the high costs of access to the publishers of scholarly work, this is understandable. Some corporate publishers, however, have responded to the OER movement by charging authors and/or their institutions for open access publications (Elsevier, 2016). Few HEIS have been thrilled by these prospects.

Dan Wagner, UNESCO Chair at the University of Pennsylvania, as well as Francophone colleagues globally have been working on sustainable MOOCS in areas of Africa where mobile phones provide the only Internet access (MOOCs4D, 2014). This can open access to millions of people in regions where many, if not most people have access to mobile phones. Interestingly, mobile use for MOOCs also benefits commuters stuck in traffic in modern urban areas.

In addition, access to MOOCs designed in different countries could benefit students not only by encouraging them to expand their intellectual boundaries, but also by expanding their awareness of study abroad. Paradoxically, HEIS could find their boundaries nibbled by corporate interests (Noble, 1998) acting as new entrants into online education. These new entrants not only include other HEIS, but also well-resourced, global publishing corporations like Pearson, media giants like the BBC, or assessment corporations such as the Educational Testing Service (ETS).

On one hand, democratizing global access to high-status university teaching may also help raise student expectations for local HEIS in a practical and realistic virtuous cycle. On the other hand, global access to elite university teaching may also help raise students' expectations for local HEIS that cannot be met. Elite interests in globalization and standardization should not crowd out students' local/national languages and cultures. The futures are many and uncertain. Who will take responsibility for simultaneously supporting both the domestic and international views needed to provide millions of students with educational opportunities?

The Paradox of Costs

Younger students in many countries have grown up with and benefited from expensively produced social media with a high degree of engagement. These students' online expectations for production values may be higher than many

MOOCS, STUDENTS, HIGHER EDUCATION AND THEIR PARADOXES

HEIS currently acknowledge. Consequently, many MOOCs have been grossly undercapitalized in terms of instructional design, online pedagogy and production. As competitive markets expand, the problem grows.

HEIS in the US have reported a wide range of costs. In 2013 the US National Association of College and University Business Officers (NACUBO) reported average costs for MOOC development to be between $50k and $100k (Jackson, 2013). Later, Hollands and Tirthali reported a wider cost range (2014).

> We find costs ranging from $38,980 to $325,330 per MOOC, and costs per completer of $74-$272, substantially lower than costs per completer of regular online courses ... key variables in determining costs do not appear to include course length. (p. 125)

Some framed MOOCs as expenditure investments, others as revenue streams. Expenditure investments included: (a) a relatively small investment in otherwise expensive global brand building; (b) providing relatively low-cost global recruitment; (c) supporting alumni's lifelong learning; and (d) helping to suppress competition. Revenue streams included expanding professional development and educational enrichment opportunities.

MOOCs have distributed cost risk unevenly: low costs for students and high upfront costs for HEIS (Anderson, 2013; Brady, 2013; Carr, 2013; Hollands & Tirthali, 2014; Straumsheim, 2016). Soon, HEIS designed the new business models needed to access more substantial levels of capitalization. For example, a Georgia Tech, Udacity and AT&T partnership designed an expensive online computer science degree using twenty MOOCs.

> Course development has been a major expense – Peterson said the institute spends about $350,000 to create each course ... AT&T subsidized the program's launch with a $2 million investment, then later made an additional $1.9 million commitment. ... AT&T offers a tuition assistance program, and its employees made up more than 20 percent of the 2,359 applicants to join the first cohort. About five employees are among the program's first 20 or so graduates, who finished the program in December [2015]. (Straumsheim, 2016)

Georgia Tech's $7 million ($350,000 per course x 20 courses) investment in a single online degree program focused on immediate career placement. In addition to the degree's high initial production costs, their courses also needed chronic maintenance and upgrades. This was not inexpensive. Few HEIS could afford this model alone.

In light of these cost challenges, more MOOCs designers are turning from free to fee through certificates, badges and nanodegrees (Friedman, 2016; Whitthaus et al., 2016). Some HEIS are also broadening their appeal along the Open University model with its long-term, sustainable commitments to low cost lifelong learning.

The Paradox of Accreditation

Accreditation is no longer the almost sole province of universities; new institutional entrants are expanding and challenging this traditional role of HEIS. These new entrants include: (a) corporate trainers; (b) publishers; (c) cultural institutions (museums, libraries, etc.); and (d) individual content providers using centralized platforms such as Udemy or P2PU (Oremus, 2013; P2PU, 2016).

MOOCs appeal to students outside of the degree-oriented enrollment pool (Baker, 2013; Kolowich, 2013). By expanding the enrollment pool, however, MOOCs may also threaten the value of HEIS' degrees. The growth of certificates, digital badges and Udacity's nanodegrees have refocused MOOCs around shorter and far less expensive forms of accreditation keenly focused on job placement and educational enrichment. As some MOOCs deliver on job placement, especially in STEM, HEIS risk being reframed as expensive middlemen (Oremus, 2013; Porter, 2014; Whitthaus et al., 2016).

Students' career placement focus has generated a significant shift away from early intentions of free, democratic access to elite degree-oriented education. MOOCs taught by faculty who are also employed in the tech industry have also gained credible traction. Short-term certificates have helped tech workers stay current in the rapidly changing industry (McClure, 2016).

These certificates won't count as much as a degree from Stanford, but employers may value the timely knowledge and skills that generate tangible benefits for students. These include career change, promotion and entrepreneurship (Coursera et al., 2015). The paradox created by expanding markets offset by expanding competition could end splendidly for all – or not. Exploring new paths, students could benefit if HEIS, both domestically and internationally, began more systematic sharing of accreditation.

MOOCs: Broadening the Student Base for Lifelong Learning

According to Evans and Myrick (2015), MOOCs have been designed for different purposes. The top three purposes, according to the results of their study were to:

MOOCS, STUDENTS, HIGHER EDUCATION AND THEIR PARADOXES 169

a democratize higher education so that underprivileged students may take courses from top universities;
b allow professionals (primarily in sciences, technology, engineering and mathematics – STEM) to improve the skills that are important to their profession; and
c give intellectually curious adults an easy way to learn new skills or explore new ideas (p. 8).

Together these three help frame networks of lifelong learning paths for today's students. Access to lifelong learning has drawn in a MOOC student base that tends to be older, educated and interested in careers and enrichment. This profile is reasonable and should be expected, not problematized. MOOCs give students viable complements to academic degrees. While current users may not be the originally intended audience, these students are good news. With the revenues generated by low cost fee models, HEIs may be able to expand access to poorer students.

Quality content, convenient platforms and low costs for continuing professional development are both useful and scarce for working students. US platform providers (edX, Coursera, Udacity, etc.) offer certificates that are shorter, cheaper and more closely targeted to employers than traditional degrees. Also, recent work in the UK suggests that shorter (two week) courses led to both larger enrollments and higher completion rates (McIntyre, 2016). For students in the US, many of them mired in debt, improved low cost access to employment is good news.

MOOC Critiques

Critiques of MOOCs are generally well known. They are framed as degree-light. They are security risks. HEIs are existentially threatened both internally and externally (Anderson, 2013; Brady, 2013; Carr, 2013; Coursera, 2013; Noble, 1998). These critiques cannot be easily ignored. MOOCs should not, however, be tightly compared with face-to-face on-campus courses. For most students, MOOCs' low cost, certificated futures do not correspond well with HEIs' expensive, degreed pasts.

MOOC critiques, however, point to some problems that could be reframed as expectations. The three most posited problems are: (a) low completion rates; (b) high levels of students with degrees; and (c) many HEIs' reluctance to translate MOOCs into degree credits. While all three points are descriptive, they are also in part outdated. New research is discovering that some of these problems are rational outcomes.

Low Completion Rates

Low completion rates are in part less of a problem and more of an expectation for social media savvy students. MOOCers may have low completion rates in part because they are successful Internet "tourists."

> Students who are enrolled in MOOCs tend to have different motivational patterns than fee-paying college students. A majority of MOOC students demonstrate characteristics akin more to "tourists" than formal learners. As a consequence, MOOC students' completion rates are usually very low. (Xiong, Li, Kornhaber, Suen, Pursel, & Goins, 2015, p. 23)

Their study suggested that in some cases low completion rates should be expected for MOOCs. Many of today's users are already deeply immersed in social media so they know how to benefit from being an Internet "toe dabbler" or "tourist." These tourists often work efficiently through online "just-in-time" learning strategies (Vivian, Falkner, & Falkner, 2014), and do-it-yourself (DIY) learning with cloud support (Mitra & Dangwal, 2010). Students can manage both asynchronous and synchronous connections, swooping in to learn just what they need at the time. Then they move on. They can be highly committed to the quality of their own education and careers, but may not be at all motivated to complete a course (Xiong et al., 2015). This is not necessarily problematic. Indeed, it is understandable because: (a) it is an efficient Internet learning strategy; (b) until more recently HEIs offered few incentives for MOOC completions; and (c) most MOOC users are not full-time students (Xiong et al., 2015).

The MOOC movement, however, has been improving student completion rates through better alignment with student needs. First, some content providers are promoting more technical career development courses targeted to students' growing demand for them (Alcorn et al., 2015; Coursera et al., 2015). Second, some providers have developed more concrete incentives for completion by creating courses in resume-building sequences through certificates at substantially lower fees than course credits. MOOCs are now also earning degree credits. For example, the pioneering MOOC provider MIT now allows successful MOOCers to opt out of required courses (Bradt, 2015).

Perhaps more importantly, MIT has divided a popular one-year master's program in order to lower costs. The first semester can be spent online from anywhere in the world. Only the second semester must be on campus (Bradt, 2015). The boldest move belongs to Arizona State's Global Freshman Academy and its corporate partner. Students spend their first year online using McGraw-Hill Education's adaptive software to personalize student learning. They claim to have the first MOOCs with this feature (Howard, 2012; Marsh, 2016).

MOOCS, STUDENTS, HIGHER EDUCATION AND THEIR PARADOXES 171

Building on another important niche, the UK's FutureLearn offers MOOCs to help students prepare for study abroad. These MOOCs are intended to increase academic motivation, which a recent study shows can in turn improve engagement; and that in turn can improve retention (Xiong et al., 2015).

Older Users, Higher Levels of Education

In addition to being tourists, MOOC students globally tend to be older, to have a bachelor's degree and to use MOOCs for career promotion (Alcorn et al., 2015; Coursera et al., 2015; Ho et al., 2014). This was not the intention, but it was an inevitable consequence. Of course MOOC users are well educated and computer immersed. Who else would know about them? How would those outside of HEI networks learn about them?

The MOOC "industry" appears to grow primarily by word of mouth through social media. Personal *ad hoc* inquiries made of colleagues in the K-20 education community, both domestically and internationally, suggested that many, if not most, had limited notions of either MOOCs or of their benefits for students. There are only a few national MOOC advertising campaigns to promote their use. "For example, every citizen of Singapore over the age of 25 gets a $500 credit from the Singapore government to take a MOOC" (iSpring Solutions, 2016). International agencies such as UNESCO and their partners were pioneers in distance education and with more resources to invest, could reach more disadvantaged audiences.

Today's educated MOOCers are in the information network streams (Internet access, social media, word-of-mouth, conferences, etc.) needed to find and use them. These students already have the knowledge and skills to become early adopters as attainment costs are relatively low. In contrast, the information costs required to successfully reach the poor globally with democratizing technology are high. So too, access costs are much lower for those who are already technology literate and who speak passable English or other world languages.

Studies of both Coursera and edX students generally agree. The Coursera survey respondents were older than on-campus students; 69% held either a bachelor's or a master's degree, and 58% said they were employed full time. Most students were engaged in career building. Most were, for the most part, taking courses in STEM subjects (Alcorn et al., 2015; Ho et al., 2014).

Respondents claimed substantial tangible and intangible benefits from their experiences (2015). The Coursera study separated students into career builders (52%) and education seekers (28%). Of the career builders, 87% reported career benefits and 33% reported tangible career benefits. Of the education seekers, 88% reported educational benefits and 18% reported tangible educational benefits. These tangible benefits included successfully: (a) entering or re-entering the job market; (b) advancing their current position; and (c) starting new businesses (Coursera et al., 2015). These results held across developed and developing countries, low and high education levels and low and high socio-economic status.

Conclusion

Education is first a generational investment. HEIs should consider how MOOCs align with generations of students' life trajectories. This alignment should not simply reinforce current career-focused trends, but also reach out both domestically and globally to those who can benefit from the democratic access that low cost MOOC education can provide. For example, more HEIs could lower their costs by creating and sharing introductory courses on how to learn using MOOCs. This could encourage a broader audience to learn how to learn from them.

We can't solve the wicked paradoxes MOOC create. Elite HEIs have designed MOOCs' democratizing technology. They have the most discretionary resources to invest, and free/low fee courses can be expensive to design and maintain. The cautious good news is there is a lot of room to grow the enrollment pool. We do need, however, to pay close attention to what is emerging.

Students who are considering investing in MOOCs should assess three types of benefits. First are transactional benefits. MOOCs can provide radically convenient, low cost access to the knowledge and skills needed for both career development and educational enrichment. Student risks are low because they can usually withdraw at any time without significant penalties. Second are transformational benefits. Education can help students think more carefully about their personal identities and how they see the world. For example, MOOCs can help students learn how to think with greater discipline and cultural complexity about their generational roles and responsibilities for the civil discourse essential for self-governance. Third are life trajectory benefits. MOOCs have tangibly helped many students: (a) change jobs; (b) be promoted; and (c) become entrepreneurs (Coursera et al., 2015).

Despite their low costs, as the markets for MOOCs expand, students may need consumer protection. Not all MOOCs are created equal. Most HEIs rely on the reputation of their platform providers; most platform providers rely on the credibility of the HEIs in their networks. As the MOOC field continues to grow, the need for consumer protection will also grow, especially as revenue stream planning drifts toward advertisements.

Students needs should inform HEIS' sustainability planning. From a transactional perspective this means right-priced student fees, internal and/or external public/private support, or some combination. From a transformational perspective, HEIS need to help students design their identities in areas such as STEM, critical thinking, civic engagement and/or personal enrichment in an increasingly complex world.

Finally, MOOCs threaten HEIS' traditional strategic thinking about students. In the past, institutional planning focused on students on campus. What students did before they arrived on campus, what they did after they graduated, or when and where they were online, were important but relatively minor considerations. MOOCs, however, offer students opportunities to re-center their educational needs across their life trajectories. HEIS' strategic relationships are increasingly generational, beginning in basic education and lasting into old age. These lifelong learning trajectories are both personal for students and, given their scale, fundamentally generational. The future of MOOCs may be a bit uncertain, but the century's needs for open access to educational resources, online learning and improved life trajectories are not. If HEIS can't adequately address them, perhaps someone else will.

References

Agarwal, A. (2014, April 6). Anant Agarwal describes six advantages of online education. *Online Education in Canada* [blog]. Retrieved from http://www.onlineeducationincanada.com/online-study-tips/anant-agarwal-describes-six-advantages-online-education/

Alcorn, B., Christensen, G., Eriksson, N., Ezekiel, E., & Zhenghao, C. (2015, September 22). Who's benefiting from MOOCs, and why. *Harvard Business Review*. Retrieved from https://hbr.org/2015/09/whos-benefiting-from-moocs-and-why

Anderson, N. (2012, November 3). Elite education for the masses. *The Washington Post*. Retrieved from http://www.washingtonpost.com/local/education/elite-education-for-the-masses/2012/11/03/c2ac8144-121b-11e2-ba83-a7a396e6b2a7_story.html

Anderson, N. (2013, May 01). As Amherst rejects online lecture model, educators ponder what's to gain from trend. *The Washington Post*. Retrieved from http://articles.washingtonpost.com/2013-05-01/local/38945447_1_moocs-edx-coursera

Andone, D., Mihaescu, V., Ternauciuc, A., & Vasiu, R. (2015, May). *Integrating MOOCs in traditional higher education*. Proceedings Papers, European MOOCs Stakeholders Summit, Université catholique de Louvain, Mons, Belgium. Retrieved from http://www.emoocs2015.eu/sites/default/files/Papers.pdf

Baker, D. (2013, March 14). *The MOOC debates on the future of the university. Group panel discussion.* New Orleans, LA: Comparative and International Education Society (CIES).

Bradt, S. (2015, October 7). *Online courses + time on campus = a new path to an MIT master's degree: Pilot program reimagines admissions process, introduces "Micro-Master's."* Cambridge, MA: Massachusetts Institute of Technology. Retrieved from http://news.mit.edu/2015/online-supply-chain-management-masters-mitx-micromasters-1007

Brady, H. E. (2013). Let's not railroad American higher education! *PS: Political Science & Politics, 46*(1), 94–101. doi:10.1017/S104909651200159X

Carr, D. (2013, July 18). San Jose state university suspends udacity MOOC project. *Information Week.* Retrieved from http://www.informationweek.com/software/san-jose-state-u--suspends-udacity-mooc-project/d/d-id/1110807

Chi, T. H., Kang, S., & Yaghmourian, D. L. (2016, June 23). Why students learn more from dialogue- than monologue-videos: Analyses of peer interactions. *Journal of Learning Sciences.* doi:10.1080/10508406.2016.1204546

Class Central. (2014, December 27). *Online courses raise their game: A review of MOOC stats and trends in 2014.* Retrieved from https://www.class-central.com/report/moocs-stats-and-trends-2014/

Connery, A. M., & Hasan, H. (2014). *Towards a modified framework for informer emancipation in complex contexts* (pp. 91–102). Proceedings of Informing Science & IT Education Conference (InSITE). Retrieved from http://proceedings.informingscience.org/InSITE2014/InSITE14p091-102Connery0646.pdf

Cormier, D. (2010). *MOOC definition* [video]. Retrieved from http://www.youtube.com/watch?feature=player_embedded&v=eW3gMGqcZQc#

Coursera. (2013, January 9). Introducing signature track. *Coursera* [blog]. Retrieved from http://blog.coursera.org/post/40080531667/signaturetrack

Coursera, University of Pennsylvania, & University of Washington. (2015, September). *Impact revealed: Learner outcomes in open online courses.* Retrieved from https://d396qusza40orc.cloudfront.net/learninghubs/LOS_final%209-21.pdf

Despujol, I., Turro, C., Orts, J., & Busquets, J. (2015, May). *Sizing an on-premises MOOC platform: Experiences and tests using open edX* (pp. 71–75). Proceedings papers, European MOOCs Stakeholders Summit, Université catholique de Louvain, Mons, Belgium. Retrieved from http://www.emoocs2015.eu/sites/default/files/Papers.pdf

Dolan, V. L. (2014). Massive online obsessive compulsion: What are they saying out there about the latest phenomenon in higher education? *The International Review of Research in Open and Distance Learning, 15*(2). Retrieved from http://www.irrodl.org/index.php/irrodl/article/view/1553/2849

Downes, S. (2008). *MOOC and Mookies: The connectivism and connective knowledge online course.* Seminar Presentation Delivered to eFest, Auckland, New Zealand by

Elluminate. Stephen's Web Presentations. Retrieved from http://www.downes.ca/presentation/197

Downes, S. (2010, June 15). *The role of open educational resources in personal learning* [video file]. Retrieved from http://www.youtube.com/watch?v=AQCvj6m4obM&feature=relmfu

EdSurge News. (2013, December 22). *MOOCs in 2013: Breaking down the numbers.* Retrieved from https://www.edsurge.com/news/2013-12-22-moocs-in-2013-breaking-down-the-numbers

Elsevier. (2016). *Open access.* Retrieved from https://www.elsevier.com/about/open-science/open-access

Evans, S., & Myrick, J. G. (2015). How MOOC instructors view the pedagogy and purposes of massive open online courses. *Distance Education, 36*(3), 295–311. doi:10.1080/01587919.2015.1081736

Friedman, J. (Ed.). (2016, January 22). What employers think of badges, nanodegrees from online programs. *U.S. News & World Report.* Retrieved from http://www.usnews.com/education/online-education/articles/2016-01-22/what-employers-think-of-badges-nanodegrees-from-online-programs

Gibney, E. (2013, September 19). FutureLearn plans to stand out from MOOC crowd. *Times Higher Education.* Retrieved from http://www.timeshighereducation.co.uk/news/futurelearn-plans-to-stand-out-from-mooc-crowd/2007482.article

Ho, A. D., Reich, J., Nesterko, S., Seaton, D. T., Mullaney, T., Waldo, J., & Chuang, I. (2014). *HarvardX and MITx: The first year of open online courses* (HarvardX and MITx working paper No. 1). Retrieved from http://papers.ssrn.com/sol3/papers.cfm?abstract_id=2381263

Hollands, F., & Tirthali, D. (2014). Resource requirements and costs of developing and delivering MOOCs. *The International Review of Research in Open and Distributed Learning, 15*(5). Retrieved from http://www.irrodl.org/index.php/irrodl/article/view/1901

Howard, J. (2012, September 17). Publishers see online mega-courses as opportunity to sell textbooks. *The Chronicle of Higher Education.* Retrieved from http://chronicle.com/article/Can-MOOCs-Help-Sell/134446/

ICEF Monitor. (2016, January 5). *MOOC enrolment surpassed 35 million in 2015.* Retrieved from http://monitor.icef.com/2016/01/mooc-enrolment-surpassed-35-million-in-2015/

Internet live stats. (2016). *Internet users in the world.* Retrieved from http://www.internetlivestats.com/Internet-users/

iSpring Solutions. (2016, July 7). *Why are MOOCs a trend: Facts and figures.* Retrieved from http://www.ispringsolutions.com/blog/why-are-moocs-a-trend-facts-and-figures/

Jackson, N. M. (2013, July/August). Mind the MOOCs: Business officer. *NACUBO*. Retrieved from http://www.nacubo.org/Business_Officer_Magazine/Magazine_ Archives/JulyAugust_2013/Stretching_Campus_Boundaries/Mind_the_ MOOCs.html

Jaschik, S. (2013, August 19). Feminist anti-MOOC. *Inside Higher Education*. Retrieved from http://www.insidehighered.com/news/2013/08/19/feminist-professors-create-alternative-moocs#ixzz38WAhMtoF

Karsenti, T. (2013). The MOOC: What the research says. *International Journal of Technologies in Higher Education, 10*(2), 23–37. Retrieved from https://www.researchgate.net/publication/266374293_MOOC_What_the_ research_says

Keohane, N. O. (2013). Higher education in the twenty-first century: Innovation, adaptation, preservation. *PS: Political Science & Politics, 46*(1), 102–105. doi:10.1017/ S1049096512001734

Kolowich, S. (2013, February 7). American council on education recommends 5 MOOCs for credit. *The Chronicle of Higher Education*. Retrieved from http://chronicle.com/ article/American-Council-on-Education/137155/?cid=at&utm_source=at&utm_ medium=en

Marques, J. (2013, April 17). A short history of MOOCs and distance learning. *MOOC News and Reviews*. Retrieved from http://moocnewsandreviews.com/a-short-history-of-moocs-and-distance-learning/#ixzz3zJjRmAUz

Marsh, N. (2016, May 3). McGraw-Hill education establishes its software status with GFA deal. *The PIE (Professionals in International Education) News*. Retrieved from http://thepienews.com/news/mcgraw-hill-education-establishes-its-software-status-with-gfa-deal/

McClure, M. W. (2013a). MOOCs: Hope and hype in viral technologies and policies. *Excellence in Higher Education, 4*(1), 7–24. doi:10.5195/ehe.2013.83. Retrieved from https://ehe.pitt.edu/ojs/index.php/ehe/article/view/83/71

McClure, M. W. (2013b, October 2–4). *MOOCs: Hype or hope: Conflicting narratives in higher education policy* (pp. 159–171). In Higher Education Reforms: Looking Back – Looking Forward: Proceedings from the 10th International Workshop on Higher Education Reform, University of Ljubljana, Slovenia. Retrieved from http://www.pef.uni-lj.si/uploads/media/HER_proceedings_2013.pdf

McClure, M. W. (2014a). MOOCs, wicked problems and the spirit of the liberal arts. *Journal of General Education, 63*(4), 269–286. doi:10.1353/jge.2014.0024

McClure, M. W. (2014b, April). *Who owns development? MOOCs in a "wicked" world.* Presentation at the MOOCs4d: MOOCs for Development Conference, University of Pennsylvania, Philadelphia, PA. doi:10.13140/RG.2.1.3414.2968

McClure, M. W. (2015). MOOCs: Hype or hope: Conflicting narratives in higher education policy. In P. Zgaga, U. Teichler, H. G. Schuetze, & A. Wolter (Eds.), *Higher education reform: Looking back – looking forward* (pp. 385–400). Frankfurt: Peter Lang.

MOOCS, STUDENTS, HIGHER EDUCATION AND THEIR PARADOXES 177

McClure, M. W. (2016). Investing in MOOCs: "Frenemy" risk and information quality. In D. Zajda & V. Rust (Eds.), *Globalisation and higher education reforms* (pp. 77–94). Dordrecht: Springer.

McIntyre, C. (2016). *UK MOOC report 2016: An insight into MOOCs provided by UK institutions*. Retrieved from http://www.mooclab.club/Reports/UK%20MOOC%20Report%202016.pdf

Mitra, S., & Dangwal, R. (2010). Limits to self-organising systems of learning—The Kalikuppam experiment. *British Journal of Educational Technology, 41*(5), 672–688. doi:10.1111/j.1467-8535.2010.01077.x. Retrieved from https://www.youtube.com/watch?v=y3jYVe1RGaU

MOOCs4D. (2014, April). *MOOCs for development: Conference report*. Retrieved from http://www.gse.upenn.edu/pdf/moocs4d/conference_report.pdf

Noble, D. F. (1998). The automation of higher education. *First Monday, 3*, 1–8. doi:10.5210/fm.v3i1.569

Nwaerondu, N. G, & Thompson, G. (1987). The use of educational radio in developing countries: Lessons from the past. *Journal of Distance Education, 2*(2), 43–54. Retrieved from http://web.worldbank.org/archive/website00236B/WEB/RAD_01.HTM

Oremus, W. (2013, June 24). Get rich quick: Become a teacher. *Slate*. Retrieved from http://www.slate.com/articles/technology/technology/2013/06/online_learning_startup_udemy_rookie_teachers_make_big_money_teaching_online.html

P2PU (Peer-2-Peer University) website. (2016). Retrieved from https://www.p2pu.org/en/about/

Pappano, L. (2012, November 2). The year of the MOOC. *The New York Times*. Retrieved from http://www.nytimes.com/2012/11/04/education/edlife/massive-open-online-courses-are-multiplying-at-a-rapid-pace.html?pagewanted=all

Pappano, L. (2013, September 15). The boy genius of Ulan Baatar. *The New York Times*. Retrieved from http://www.nytimes.com/2013/09/15/magazine/the-boy-genius-of-ulan-bator.html

Peralta, C. (2012, November 1). Online courses raise intellectual property concerns. *Stanford Daily*. Retrieved from http://www.stanforddaily.com/2012/11/01/intellectual-property-concerns-for-moocs-persist/

Porter, E. (2014, June 17). A smart way to skip college in pursuit of a job: Udacity-AT&T 'nanodegree' offers an entry-level approach to college. *The New York Times*. Retrieved from http://www.nytimes.com/2014/06/18/business/economy/udacity-att-nanodegree-offers-an-entry-level-approach-to-college.html

Siemens, G. (2010a, March 6). *TedX/NY* [video file]. Retrieved from http://www.youtube.com/watch?v=4BH-uLO6ovI&feature=related

Siemens, G. (2010b, June 15). *Connectivism: Socializing open learning* [video file]. Retrieved from http://www.youtube.com/watch?v=rqL_lsogeNU&feature=youtu.be

State of the MOOC 2016: A year of massive landscape change for massive open online courses. (n.d.). *Online course report*. Retrieved from http://www.onlinecoursereport.com/state-of-the-mooc-2016-a-year-of-massive-landscape-change-for-massive-open-online-courses/

Straumsheim, C. (2016, April 27). Georgia tech's next steps. *Inside Higher Ed*. Retrieved from https://www.insidehighered.com/news/2016/04/27/georgia-tech-plans-next-steps-online-masters-degree-computer-science

Tapson, J. (2013, September 13). MOOCs and the Gartner Hype cycle: A very slow tsunami. *PandoDaily* [blog]. Retrieved from http://pando.com/2013/09/13/moocs-and-the-gartner-hype-cycle-a-very-slow-tsunami/

UNESCO. (n.d.). MobiMOOC: Using a mobile MOOC to increase educational quality for a diversity of learners through dialogue and ubiquity. *UNESCO: ICT in Education*. Retrieved from http://www.unesco.org/new/en/unesco/themes/icts/m4ed/unesco-mobile-learning-week/speakers/inge-ignatia-de-waard/

Vander Ark, T. (2012, September 25). Sir John Daniel: Openness rather than scale is MOOC contribution. *Education Week* [blog]. Retrieved from http://blogs.edweek.org/edweek/on_innovation/2012/12/sir_john_daniel_openness_rather_than_scale_is_mooc_contribution.html

Vivian, R., Falkner, K., & Falkner, N. (2014). Addressing the challenges of a new digital technologies curriculum: MOOCs as a scalable solution for teacher professional development. *Research in Learning Technology*. Retrieved from http://dx.doi.org/10.3402/rlt.v22.24691

Walters, H. (2014a, January 27). We need to change everything on campus. *Ideas.Ted.Com* [blog]. Retrieved from http://ideas.ted.com/2014/01/27/we-need-to-change-everything-on-campus-anant-agarwal-of-edx-on-moocs-mit-and-new-models-of-higher-education/

Walters, H. (2014b, January 28). Two giants of online learning discuss the future of education. *Ideas.Ted.Com* [blog]. Retrieved from http://ides.ted.com/in-conversation-salman-khan-sebastian-thrun-talk-online-education/

Witthaus, G., Inamorato dos Santos, A., Childs, M., Tannhäuser, A., Conole, G., Nkuyubwatsi, B., & Punie, Y. (2016). *Validation of non-formal MOOC-based learning: An analysis of assessment and recognition practices in Europe (OpenCred)*. Retrieved from https://ideas.repec.org/p/ipt/iptwpa/jrc96968.html

Xiong, Y., Li, H., Kornhaber, M. L., Suen, H. K., Pursel, B., & Goins, D. D. (2015). Examining the relations among student motivation, engagement, and retention in a MOOC: A structural equation modeling approach. *Global Education Review, 2*(3), 23–33. Retrieved from http://ger.mercy.edu/index.php/ger/article/view/124/138

CHAPTER 10

The Expansion of Higher Education and First Generation Students in Germany: Increasing Participation or Continuing Exclusion?

Andrä Wolter

Abstract

Massification of higher education in Germany has occurred since the middle of the 20th century. This has been aided by the absence of tuition fees except for a short period between 2006 and 2013, when fees were charged in seven of the 16 German states, as well as the establishment of a non-university sector of higher education (*Fachhochschulen*). The author discusses the question of whether or to what extent this expansion of participation in higher education has fostered equality of opportunity within Germany. After examination of this question, including through comparisons with other OECD countries, the author reaches the rather surprising conclusion that the expansion of the higher education system has, in fact, not corrected social inequality but rather has reinforced the role of higher education as an institution of social reproduction. He discusses a number of factors that may have led to this result.

Keywords

massification of higher education – German higher education – widening participation in higher education – education for labor market – social class reproduction

Introduction

From its beginning, the expansion of higher education in Germany has been embedded in several partly political, partly academic discourses about its causes and impacts (Friedeburg, 1989). In the context of the labor market discourse, expansion was considered to be a response to the increasing qualification needs, both in quantitative terms (the quantitative scale of the requirement for a quali-

© KONINKLIJKE BRILL NV, LEIDEN, 2019 | DOI:10.1163/9789004393073_010

fied workforce) and in qualitative ones (the type of qualification required), of the post-industrial, or even knowledge-based society. In the equality or equity discourse – recently the diversity discourse – massification was regarded as a vehicle to widen participation in terms of different criteria, e.g., social origin, gender, migration background or even age, including also adult students. The issue of widening participation is primarily relevant because of the close linkage between level of education, the distribution of social positions and status, and later life opportunities in a highly stratified society (Hillmert, 2009a, 2009b).

In particular, in Germany the growth of the higher education sector, especially the growth of participation in higher education, has been accompanied since the 1960s by the expectation that socially disadvantaged groups should profit from the expansion to a disproportionately large extent and that this development would balance out the social distribution of opportunities to study (Mayer, Müller, & Pollak, 2007). Furthermore, the expansion as well as the widening of participation had been considered to be the prerequisite for meeting the changing demands of the labor market as a consequence of an increasingly human capital intensive economy. In particular, the recommendations and the "philosophy" of the OECD education policy have played a significant role in this development (Papadopoulos, 1990).

For these reasons several reform strategies, initiatives and activities were implemented during the 1960s and 1970s to achieve the vision of more equality of opportunities in the German higher education system. The spectrum of these reforms extended from compensatory measures in pre-school education, strategies to reform the school system – e.g., to open the transition from primary to secondary schools, to promote permeability within the German tracking system at secondary level or to establish comprehensive schools – to various measures in the area of higher education. The latter included, e.g., the introduction of a state funded system of financial support for needy students, the establishment of a non-university sector of higher education (*Fachhochschulen*) and – as a temporary model until the 1980s – comprehensive institutions offering university courses as well as non-university courses. Furthermore, since 1970 there have been no tuition fees in Germany except for a short time span between 2006 and 2013 limited to seven of the 16 German states (see chapter by Timmermann in this volume). Without a doubt, these actions reinforced the expansion of participation in higher education, but the question is whether they also fostered equality of opportunities in the social participation patterns.

The topic of this chapter addresses the question of whether, or, more precisely, to what extent this expectation and objective have been realized. It will start with a short comparative consideration concerning the relationship between social origin and access to higher education in a European perspective

THE EXPANSION OF HE IN GERMANY 181

and then follow on with the special case of Germany. Furthermore, some theoretical approaches and terminology issues will be discussed to explain the results of this empirical stocktaking, including the separation between primary and secondary effects of social origin and the concept of maximally maintained inequality. In particular, some reasons will be given for the shift from the concept of working-class children to the concept of first-generation students as the main social category for socially disadvantaged students.

The Social Dimension of the European Higher Education Area

In the European context one of the main topics of higher education policy debates over recent decades has been the social make-up of national student populations. The social dimension of the European Higher Education Area (EHEA) is one of the central action fields of the Bologna Process on which the presently 47 participating countries concur. The original Bologna declaration (1999) did not mention the social dimension. The focus was on "the objective of increasing the international competitiveness of the European system of higher education." A series of conferences of ministers that have normally taken place every two years since Bologna has pushed ahead the progress and further development of the agenda of this process, introducing the social dimension along the way. The social dimension was put on the agenda of the Bologna process for the first time in the Prague communiqué (2001) – even though rather *en passant*, meriting only one sentence without any further explanation: "Ministers reaffirmed the need, recalled by students, to take account of the social dimension of the Bologna process." In another sentence the declaration referred to "the idea that higher education should be considered a public good and is and will remain a public responsibility."[1] Generally, compared with these previous manifests, the follow-up conferences assigned a considerably larger importance to the social dimension of the European higher education area.

Recapitulating the development from Bologna (1999) to the last conference in Yerevan (2015), it might be possible to state that at the least a more precise and operational understanding of the term "social dimension" has emerged. Overall it is noticeable that the concept of the social dimension has become an established element in the European discourse on future higher education. It has often been reinforced that higher education in the Bologna context is considered to be a public good and a public responsibility. However, sometimes it seems a bit as if this concept is becoming more and more an all-embracing catchphrase (Banscherus, Himpele, & Staack, 2011). The intended objective is not only general growth ("increasing participation") but also a more balanced relationship in the social structure of participation in higher education ("widening participation"), based on the arguments of equality of opportunities and social cohesion. The understanding of this concept has been differentiated so that is now possible to consider the "social dimension" to be a multi-dimensional concept and to identify its most important elements as follows:

- Equality of opportunities at the stage of access/admission based only on achievements (and capacity)
- Enlarging participation of underrepresented, socially disadvantaged groups
- Lifelong learning: recognition of prior learning, widening access for non-traditional students
- Improving the allocation function of access, co-ordination between school and university
- Guaranteeing an adequate student social infrastructure during studying
- Successful completion of studies within an appropriate period of time without social and economic obstacles
- Measures to promote and to support student mobility, in particular of disadvantaged groups
- Reducing existing gaps between the European countries, in particular supporting mobility from poorer countries.

The focus of the debate about the social dimension of the EHEA is partly on the relationships between the vision of social cohesion and social equity and partly on the mainstream issues of the international higher education policy debates such as competitiveness or excellence. On the one hand, the social concern of Bologna and the excellence aspiration have often been regarded as a contradiction. On the other hand, among many higher education stakeholders there is broad consensus that a well-balanced relationship between excellence and social equity or cohesion must be reached. But it is important to note that there are also some serious issues and arguments provoking a controversial debate on what is meant by the social dimension. These include:

- Are the social dimension and the related values only a topic of secondary priority on the European agenda, compared with the main concerns of higher education policy linked with a market- and competition-based understanding and efficiency orientation of higher education?
- Are there any indications or signals for trends and developments which contradict the idea of the social dimension, e.g., the establishment of tuition fees in some European countries?
- Is there also a contradiction between the common striving of higher education institutions for excellence and a high rank status on the one hand, and their involvement in social issues or objectives like social inclusion or widening access on the other hand?

The Social Structure of the Student Body in Selected European Countries

The following section is based on a few selected, specific indicators for the social structure of students[2] for which some data from European surveys are available – the most important of which is the Eurostudent project. This Europe wide monitoring system has been implemented as a part of the Bologna process to provide some empirical information about the state of realization of the idea of a social dimension. Thirty countries participated in the most recent sequence of this project from 2012 to 2015, which means that the study is one of the broadest internationally comparative studies in higher education or student research (Hauschildt, Gwosc, Netz, & Mishra, 2015).[3] The project has a decentralized structure which considers the country participants as members of a monitoring network. All information and data are a by-product of national surveys or national administrative data based on several conventions and agreements about the standards, the form and processing of data provision.

In the Eurostudent study different educational levels are distinguished with respect to students' parents based on the International Standard Classification of Education (ISCED) according partly to the 1997, partly to the 2011 version (Hauschildt et al., 2015, p. 47). For Germany it is important to take into account that level 6 includes some non-university post-secondary programs and institutions such as *Fachschulen* or *Berufsakademien*. This classification causes some statistical differences between the Eurostudent study and some national surveys that do not include non-higher education institutions in level 6.

A relatively simple measure of social inequality is based on the highest level of education achieved by at least one parent – comparing students from families who have a tertiary education background with those who do not. Social mobility exists in a higher education system when a student, whose parents have not achieved tertiary education themselves, enters a tertiary education institution. There is strong evidence that the key determinant factor for the long arm of the family is not the socio-economic status but the socio-cultural family background of students (Wolter, 2011). The main difference in participation can be seen between students from families with a tertiary and those with a non-tertiary background.

As shown in Figure 10.1, in each of the Eurostudent countries the share of students from each of these groups differs (Hauschildt et al., 2015, p. 50 ff.). This indicates large variation between the participating countries with respect to the social openness of tertiary or higher education institutions. In 12 countries more than half of the students have parents without a tertiary education background, including Italy, Austria, Norway and many of the former socialist eastern or southeastern European countries. These are countries with a high degree of

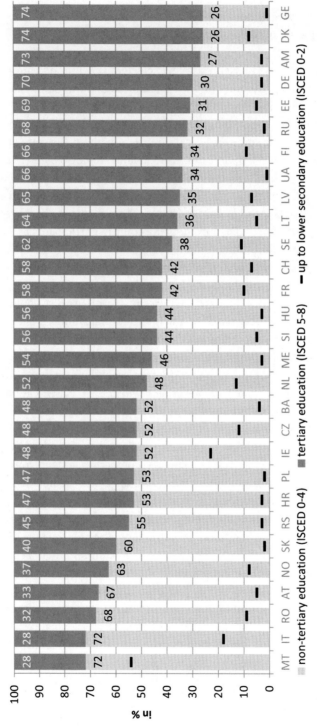

FIGURE 10.1   Level of education of students' parents in European countries, 2014. (The country abbreviations are listed before the references.)
SOURCE: EUROSTUDENT 2015, HIGHEST EDUCATIONAL ATTAINMENT OF EITHER FATHER OR MOTHER

THE EXPANSION OF HE IN GERMANY
185

upward social mobility via higher education. At the opposite end of the spectrum, in some countries more than two thirds of the students come from families with a tertiary background; that means that access to higher education or other tertiary institutions fulfills a social self-reproduction function. This is obvious in Germany and Denmark but also in some eastern European countries.

The methodological limitation of this indicator is the "absolute" measurement of the social composition of the student body, not referring to any reference point or group to determine the extent of over- or underrepresentation. Therefore, a more complex measure – even though this is also a proxy – is based on the statistical relationship between both student groups – those with and without a tertiary education family background – and the share of the group with this status in the general population in a country (Figure 10.2). Inequality in favor of the social or educational elite means that the share of students whose parents achieved tertiary education is overrepresented compared to the general population of a country in the corresponding age group of students' parents (index higher than 1). Relative exclusion of the other social groups (index lower than 1) means that their share in the student body is lower than their proportion of the general population.

The results (Figure 10.2) show large differences in the social structure of the student body related to the population. Three country clusters can be identified (Hauschildt et al., 2015, p. 52 ff.).

The first cluster contains those few countries in which students from low educational background are more or less largely overrepresented. This is true for some eastern European countries and for Ireland, very slightly for Finland, and even more slightly still for Malta. But all these countries also show an overrepresentation of students from families with a high educational status and, furthermore, an underrepresentation of medium level students.

A relative balance between the social structure of students and the population can be observed in another small group of countries. This cluster includes Austria, the Netherlands, Norway and Switzerland, which can be identified as socially more inclusive: they display a minimal under-representation of students with low education background and a minimal over-representation of the high education group.

In all other countries, students with highly qualified parents are overrepresented and those from families with a low – and mostly also with a medium – level of education are underrepresented. Besides Germany, some eastern European countries can be found in this cluster that can be classified as socially exclusive according to these measures.

With regard to this indicator it can be stated that the social composition of the student body varies considerably between European countries, and

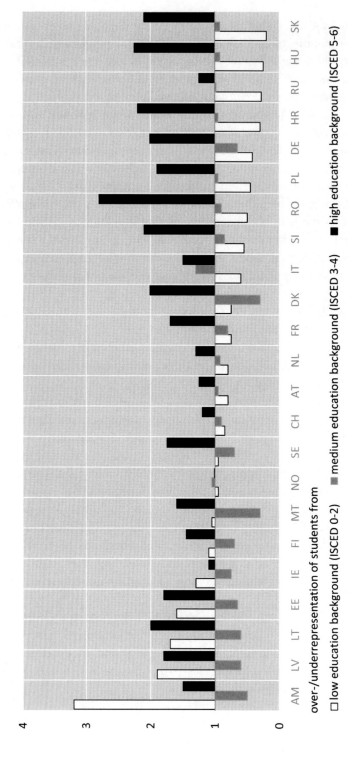

FIGURE 10.2 Representation of students from families with high, medium or low educational background in European countries, 2014
SOURCE: EUROSTUDENT 2015, INDEX BASED ON THE SHARE OF STUDENTS' FATHERS WITH A CERTAIN LEVEL OF EDUCATION WITH THE CORRESPONDING SHARE OF 40–59 YEAR-OLD MEN IN THE NATIONAL POPULATION

that in the majority of the countries included in the Eurostudent study the social mix is far away from diversity (in the meaning of proportional diversity). Unfortunately, these findings are only cross-sectional so it is not possible to say anything about the development over time. The data verify that in the large majority of countries belonging to the EHEA area the social structure of participation in higher education does not meet the political objectives of the Bologna process as manifested in the concept of the social dimension. Students from families without a higher education background are underrepresented in most countries, and vice versa students from an academically qualified family are strongly overrepresented in almost all countries. However, this pattern of social preference or discrimination is not primarily generated at the level of access to higher education but continuously throughout the pre-university school career and the selective mechanism in this process.

The international comparison of patterns of more exclusive or inclusive participation in higher education in these 30 countries directly calls for a macro-theoretical explanation such as Peter Hall's and David Soskice's concept of varieties of capitalism (Hall & Soskice, 2001) or Gösta Esping-Andersen's concept of different welfare state regimes (1990). Whereas Hall and Soskice distinguish between liberal and coordinated market economies, Esping-Andersen differentiates between three types of welfare states: conservative, liberal and social-democratic. However, such attempts at theoretically based interpretation encounter some difficulties. The first one is the fact that the type of a liberal market economy (according to Hall and Soskice) and the type of a liberal welfare regime (according to Esping-Andersen) are not frequent among the European countries participating in the Eurostudent study (and England could not be taken into account or only partly because of a lack of data).

The second reason is that it seems that the variety within the same type of economy or welfare state is considerably larger than it should be. There is no common pattern for the Scandinavian countries nor for the eastern European ones or for any other cluster. The only deviating pattern exists for the four countries with a relatively balanced representation pattern that all belong to the type of highly developed welfare states. But other welfare states show a different pattern. Obviously, the landscape is more colorful than the theoretical models (Hölscher, 2016).

Higher Education and Social Inequality in Germany[5]

Germany has often been considered, in particular in the OECD context, as an example of a country in which expansion has been carried out in a rather

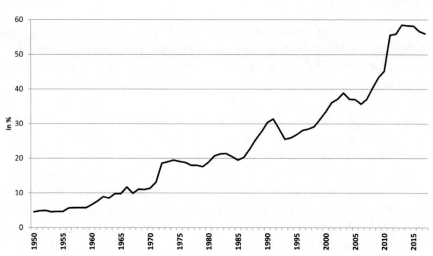

FIGURE 10.3 Percentage of new entrants in higher education related to the age cohort, 1950–2017, Germany
SOURCE: DESTATIS, GERMAN OFFICIAL STATISTICS

delayed and tentative manner albeit in a constant direction (Powell & Solga, 2011; Wolter, 2009, 2014). It is important to consider that Germany has a very well established sector of vocational training outside tertiary education that has been very attractive for young people, including those with a study entitlement (i.e., they have passed the examination at the end of upper secondary school – primarily the *Abitur* – that allows them entry into higher education). And many programs, which in other countries are part of higher education, are part of upper secondary or post-secondary education in Germany – e.g., the training for non-physician health care professions.

Nevertheless, particularly in the last ten years there has been massive growth in the proportion of first-year students, as compared to the age cohort. This proportion has increased since the beginning of the 1950s, interrupted only periodically and, in the case of interruption, followed by an even larger rise in the following years. The decrease in the first half of the 1990s was caused by German reunification (until 1991 the data refer only to West Germany) because the share of students leaving the school system in East Germany with a study entitlement was much lower than in West Germany. After 1993 a rapid process of adaptation took place. An extremely steep rise can be observed since 2006, so that the proportion of new students is now more than half of the age cohort, including international students. Without international students it is roughly half of the age cohort. This enormous rise has also been due to certain conditions, such as the reduction of the length of schooling up to the *Abitur* from

13 to 12 years during recent years. Because this conversion came to an end in 2014, the subsequent development was slightly declining. However, the main reason for the strong increase is the sustainable rise in educational participation, generated through the changing educational aspirations and decisions in families, and transmitted through the school system (Wolter & Kerst, 2015). Special factors such as the shortening of school time have only reinforced this sustainable growth.

Obviously, as a result of this strong increase the gap between Germany and the OECD average has become narrower, and there has been a clear process of alignment. The obviously continuous expansion of participation in higher education has revitalized the general question – or the hope – whether or to what extent the process of expansion has been accompanied by a social opening up of access to the university, as expected in the past. In an internationally comparative perspective it might be possible to distinguish two pre-dominant models of access to higher education (Teichler, 1984, 2003):

> Those countries in which access to higher education is the central stage of allocation and selection. These countries are mostly characterized by a horizontal structure of the school system and a large share of graduates from upper secondary school who basically are entitled to apply for enrollment, and the higher education institutions practice their own selection procedures.
>
> Then there are those countries in which the burden of allocation is assigned primarily within the school system, and the stage of access to the university normally is only an additional but weak instance of selection. This is often the case in countries with a tracking school system, with a vertical organization of the secondary school into different types of programs of which only one type is the main route to university, often linked with a formal study entitlement, and only parts of the young generation are awarded the study entitlement. There is no doubt that Germany, with its characteristic tracking school system and with the grammar school as the main feeder for higher education, belongs to this type.

Access to higher education in Germany is based in principal on the precondition of having a formal study entitlement that is normally acquired with the *Abitur*, the successful completion of the final exam of the grammar school, or other school degrees. Therefore, the social distribution of opportunities to get access to higher education comprises two processes. The main selection and allocation on the way to university takes place during the school career from primary school to upper secondary school, along the route to the

Abitur. Those who finish their school career successfully with a study entitlement turn out to be a strongly pre-filtered population. Therefore, allocation and selection for higher education are built up as a biographically cumulative or gradual process. However, there is some evidence that the social disparities on the way to the *Abitur* have become slightly smaller with the massive expansion of participation in the grammar school track even though these discrepancies are still pronounced (Mayer et al., 2007). The second hurdle is the allocation and selection mechanisms at the stage of transition from upper secondary school to higher education among those who finished school with a study entitlement.

Based on a multivariate analysis it can be shown that – in Germany – the relative opportunity of a child with an academic family background to attend a grammar school is approximately twice as great as for a child with a working class background – even in the case of the same proven literacy or general cognitive competence (Baumert & Schümer, 2001, p. 357). The series of PISA studies since 2001 has produced much evidence to verify this disparity (Reiss, Sälzer, Schiepe-Tiska, Klieme, & Köller, 2016). That means that there is a certain potential of students who reach a level of competence sufficient to attend grammar school but who do not get the opportunity to do that. The main explanation for this distinction between cognitive competence and school career is the fact that decisions about the further school career and the allocation between alternative school types are only partly based on educational diagnostic results about competencies and achievements. Rather, they are influenced by many other motives, reflections and prognoses from parents as well as from teachers.[6] The long educational pathways leading to a study entitlement are full of screening mechanisms, ensuring that this discrepancy is maintained (Maaz, 2006).

Despite the fact that only a highly pre-selected, socially homogenized population reaches the stage of *Abitur* and is faced with the decision to study or not (and in this case to choose a non-academic path of vocational training), the transition point between upper secondary school and university comprises some further social selection mechanisms (Autorengruppe Bildungsberichterstattung, 2016, p. 126). During the last two decades, an average of 70–75% of a cohort of school-leavers with study entitlement have transferred to the academic sector and taken up studies. About 25–30% have not taken that opportunity. The most important factor determining the likelihood to study is previous school achievement, usually measured by the average *Abitur* grade.

However, based on multivariate analysis (binary logistic regression), it can be shown that there is a very strong secondary origin effect on the decision to study when other variables such as gender, type of school, school achievement

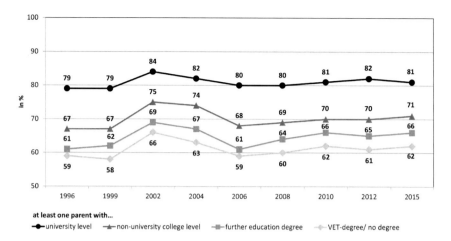

FIGURE 10.4   Study probability of school leavers with a study entitlement in Germany, differentiated according to the highest qualification of their parents, 1996–2015
SOURCE: DZHW, STUDIENBERECHTIGTENPANEL

(the Abitur grade) or regional origin are controlled. The probability of studying varies considerably with the educational background of the family (Autorengruppe Bildungsberichterstattung, 2016, p. 126 ff.). The difference in the study likelihood between the highest and the lowest educational level of parents is about 20 percentage points – despite the fact that every school-leaver in this population has acquired a formal study entitlement (Figure 10.4). That means that descendants of families with an academic status take up studies even in the case of lower achievement and marks below average. On the other hand, descendants with a working class background or low educational family status do not take up studies to the same extent even in the case of good performance and marks above average. The complete time series reveals that the difference between the different parents' qualification levels is nearly constant over 16 years except for a very small short-term interruption in 2002.

Over time there is no convergence in the study decision behavior between the different status groups. Despite the massive increase in the number of first-year students the distribution patterns have not changed – and the social distinctions have not become smaller, even if the absolute number of first-year students with a working class background may have increased to a certain extent. The main reasons not to study, despite having the entitlement to do so, include financial concerns or, conversely, the expectation of earning money as quickly as possible by transferring to vocational training. Another important reason is the fear of failure at university (Watermann, Daniel, & Maaz, 2014).

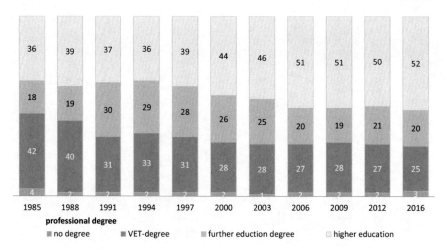

FIGURE 10.5   Social composition of students in Germany according to the highest qualification of parents, 1991–2016
SOURCE: SOZIALERHEBUNG 2016

The socially selective study decisions in favor of young adults who can already rely on an academic tradition in their family result in a corresponding composition of the student body. The share of students with at least one parent with an academic degree has increased steadily from 1991 to 2006 and stagnated at this high level afterwards (Figure 10.5) (Middendorff et al., 2017). At the current time, half of all students have a father or mother with an academic degree. In other words, about half of the students are first-generation students. But their proportion has continuously decreased from nearly two-thirds. Therefore, it can be stated that the university has become socially more exclusive with the expansion of participation, not more inclusive or open – at least relatively. That means that the absolute number of first-generation students may have grown but, in a structural perspective, their share has declined.

Germany has a binary system of higher education embracing the university and a non-university college sector (*Fachhochschulen*). Despite a clear process of convergence, the two segments are distinctive with respect to several academic characteristics – and they vary in their social composition (Middendorff et al., 2013). In the university sector the share of students with an academic family status has already reached approximately 60%. In contrast, the sector of non-university colleges has proved to be a little bit more open; here the proportion is about 40%, with first-generation students making up the rest. This type of college seems most likely to be an institution of social upward mobility. One of the reasons for this is that about half of the student body in the college sector is enrolled in engineering – a cluster of subjects that is more attractive for educational climbers. Within that sector there are also differences between the different subjects in the spectrum from more exclusive (like medicine or arts) to more inclusive (like engineering), but not very pronounced. The observation that the non-university college sector is socially more open than the traditional university sector is compatible with the notion that the internal differentiation of higher education systems fosters social permeability, especially in the lower ranked sector.

There are two explanations for this more or less surprising result that the expansion of higher education has been accompanied by a process of reinforcement of the traditional educational elite among students. A first explanation refers to the changing composition of the population, reflecting a social and educational upgrading. Generated by former waves of expansion, the share of the academically qualified part of the population has tripled in the last four decades. But all in all, it only makes up less than half of the student population. Therefore, this argument is not sufficient to explain the link between the expansion and the increasing proportion of students with an academic family background. A second explanation refers to Raftery and Hout's theory (1993) of maximally maintained inequality. This will be explained in more detail in the last section.

The enormous disparities in the distribution of social opportunities to study become even more evident when comparing the relative chances of different population groups in getting access to higher education. To show this, the social composition of the student body (based on student survey data) is related to the corresponding composition of the population in the typical age cohort of their parents (based on micro census data). The advantage of this procedure is that there is a reference point for the evaluation of the composition of the student body as being over- or underrepresented. That is exactly the reason why this procedure is more meaningful for the issue of equality or equity of opportunities than merely the composition of the student body. The data show the probability of students whose parents have a certain education background in gaining access to higher education.

Therefore, being a descendant of a family with a higher education tradition is the most important factor influencing the relative chance to enroll (Figure 10.6). The social differentiation of study opportunities corresponds exactly to the distinction between academic and non-academic families. Children from families in which one parent has already earned a degree show a probability of more than 75% for access – with a maximum of 90% in civil servant families. On the other hand, the chance for children from non-academic families is lower than 50% – with a minimum of 12% in families with the lowest educational background. As a result, the participation quota of young people with an academic family background is more than six times greater than that of those with the lowest educational status. Unfortunately, we currently do not have any comparable competence data for the complete age cohort, so that we cannot say anything about the interrelation between participation and competence development at this stage. However, it is obvious that the differences would become a little bit smaller but still continue when such variables such as cognitive competencies or school achievements are controlled.

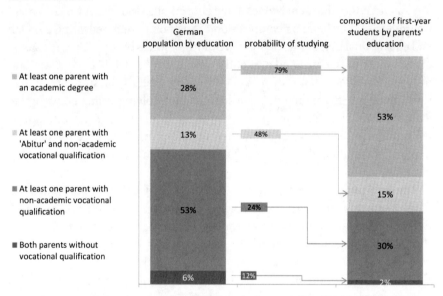

FIGURE 10.6   Probability of studying in correlation with the highest educational background of students' parents in Germany, 2016
SOURCE: KRACKE, BUCK, AND MIDDENDORFF (2018)

Some Theoretical Explanations

Overall, the reported empirical evidence provides reasons for not overestimating the results of the massification of higher education with respect to the correction of social inequality in the distribution of participation opportunities. Rather, it seems that one of the great hopes linked to educational expansion since the 1960s – the spirit of optimism – has been frustrated. There are different theoretical approaches to explain this amazing structural consistency in the distribution of participation chances, in particular in access to higher education, even though disparities related to educational or social background may have slightly decreased, especially in the school system. The focus is on the continuity of selection and allocation mechanisms throughout the educational life-course from early childhood to adult age, including higher education, as a biographically cumulative process (Hillmert, 2014; Neugebauer & Schindler, 2012; Reimer & Pollak, 2010).

Class-Theory Based Approach

The question is whether these mechanisms of social reproduction will partly change along with massive expansion of participation. In the context of class-based theoretical approaches the educational participation patterns are understood as the result of the collective competition and struggle between social groups for the distribution of educational capital in a society (Bourdieu & Passeron, 1971; Bourdieu et al., 1981). Because the allocation of social rank and status depends more and more on educational capital in terms of titles, degrees or certificates, the distribution of educational capital becomes more important. The continuity of disparities can be explained as mutual reinforcement between two conditions: on the one hand, the strategies of social classes to maintain their cultural capital and advance under the conditions of stronger educational competition, and on the other hand, the specific requirements through which educational institutions execute their social reproduction function. Both factors interact with each other and promote in this way the preservation of the predominant position of the educational elite even under the conditions of massification. Smaller distinctions within the same educational status become crucial.

Different Origin Effects

Based on Boudon's differentiation between the primary and secondary effects of social origin (Boudon, 1974), there is much evidence that proves the major importance of the educational status of the family of origin. The main reasons for the under-representation of students with a non-academic background in upper secondary education or in the grammar school are not primarily cognitive or achievement deficits but a lack of support and encouragement in family and school. Primary origin effects refer to the influence of the cultural capital of the family on the development of individual competences – e.g., cognitive abilities or literacy (language skills) – and also on school performance. Secondary origin effects embrace those distinctions in educational decisions in institutional settings like families or schools that are caused by social origin. Whereas during the school career a complex entanglement of primary and secondary effects determines the probability of finishing school with a study entitlement, evidence shows that at the stage of study decisions and transition to higher education the relevance of secondary effects becomes larger.

According to rational choice theories this might be a result of origin-caused varying evaluation of costs and benefits associated with the often non-rational balancing of chances, risks and success probabilities (Neugebauer & Schindler, 2012). Because of this, school-leavers with a study entitlement often turn away from studying in favor of an alternative option such as non-academic vocational training.

Saturation Hypothesis

A third approach refers to the result of an increasing proportion of students with an academic family background. As argued before, this is partly due to the changing demographic composition of the population due to a growing proportion of highly qualified people resulting from previous sequences of educational expansion. In a more general perspective, according to Raftery and Hout's concept of maximally maintained inequality (Lucas, 2001; Raftery & Hout, 1993) based on data for developments in Ireland (1921–1975), education inequality will not decrease until the participation of the upper classes reaches something like a saturation point. If the educational reserves of the upper classes are almost exhausted there is a realistic chance of opening up access and reducing the social inequality in participation. Students with an upper class or academic family background strive to maximally maintain inequality in the educational outcomes between them and their peers from lower classes until their potential is completely realized. Raftery and Hout argue that this point of saturation is reached if "the transition rates approach or reach 100 percent" (1993, p. 57). However, because of the intersectionality between social origin and other factors it is reasonable to suppose that this point is reached far below this value. But Figure 10.6 shows that there are hidden reserves for further expansion even among families with an academic status.

First-Generation Students

There are several terms used to conceptualize socially disadvantaged students. In Germany, the traditional concept in educational research or sociology of education was that of working-class children. Currently, this notion has been more and more replaced by the concept of first-generation students (London, 1989; Miethe, Boysen, Grabowsky, & Kludt, 2014; NCES, 1998; Pascarella, Pierson, Wolniak, & Terenzini, 2004; Terenzini, Springer, Yaeger, Pascarella, & Nora, 1996). But neither in German nor in international research is there a common understanding of these terms or a comparable or even standardized method of measurement. Sometimes these groups are subsumed under the term "non-traditional students," but this term has often been even more widely defined than the other ones. There are numerous reasons for rejecting the concept of working-class children. Firstly, the class structures of the traditional industrial society have been widely dissolved and have merged with the new social entities of post-industrial, service-oriented societies or the knowledge-based economy. Secondly, especially in Germany, the social law differentiation between workers and employees was abolished several years ago, and now all these groups are legally equal. And thirdly, evidence shows that the main line of social differentiation in educational behavior and decisions is not along the socio-economic conditions of families but primarily along their socio-cultural distinctions, in particular their educational status. With respect to higher education the most important distinction runs between students with an academic or non-academic family background (as shown in Figure 10.6). That is the reason for the introduction of and preference for the term "first-generation students." However, this concept still remains a bit fuzzy because it refers only to the parents' background and not the longer family education tradition in former generations (Gofen, 2009).

Conclusions

The social composition of the student body has changed in Germany considerably as a result of the previous expansion of participation in higher education – but in a probably unexpected direction. It has not led to more social inclusiveness and social equity, making institutions accessible for new social groups. Rather, the contrary has happened. It is fair to say that the German university was still an institution of social upward mobility in the first part of the last century, but it has become more and more an institution of social reproduction for those who want to pass on their academic tradition to the next generation – in other words, the university as an institution of social and cultural inheritance. Most of this social selectivity takes place during the school career, not at the stage of access to university. What is called secondary inequality – the social differentiation of educational decisions in the family context and the reinforcing influence of institutions (or vice versa) – seems to be the most important factor responsible for the existing social disparities. Given equal average marks of students at the end of upper secondary school, the relative study chance of young people with an academic family background is considerably higher than that of young people with the same achievements but a lower social origin.

But many studies show that there is an additional process of screening at the level of access, showing the same dynamic: The educational status of the family is more important than the individual achievement of the student. Nevertheless, about half of the student population is now made up of first-generation students; but 30 years ago their share was still two-thirds. At a more general level, it can be stated that obviously the ongoing expansion of partici-pation has been driven primarily by its own momentum, by competition based forces of self-reinforcement. In the light of increasing competition on the edu-cational and labor market, a higher level of education and qualification seems to be the best precondition for a professional career, or sometimes only the best prevention against social decline. The dynamic observed is a confirma-tion of Raftery and Hout's theory (1993) of maximally maintained inequality, at least for Germany. Because of these mechanisms of self-reinforcement, the upper classes tend to maximize their potentials to a critical limit before the social hurdles become lower. However, the European comparison shows that there is great variety in the balance between social exclusion and social inclu-sion among the European countries.

The key issue involves the strategies or measures to intervene in the obvi-ously stable primary and secondary origin effects. Of course, the first instance (except pre-school education) is the school system. One approach would be the diversification of routes, awarding a study entitlement beyond the gram-mar school and the promotion of vocationally oriented paths in the school system to gain a study entitlement. The improvement of the diagnostic com-petencies of teachers is also very important because there is a high volume of false diagnoses during the school career. At the transition point between school and university the connection between origin and access can be circumvented by more and better information and counselling of parents, especially those with a lower class or educational status, about the available sources of finan-cial support and the future life and labor market opportunities. A very recent study reveals that more and better information about the benefits of studying can raise the study probability considerably (Peter, Rusconi, Solga, Spieß, & Zambre, 2016). Opening up access to higher education for vocationally quali-fied people would be another approach (Wolter, 2015b). Lastly, the further development of public financial support for students that is not contingent on the burden of debt is an important prerequisite to increase the participation of first-generation students.

Country Abbreviations

In all figures, the following abbreviations are used to refer to the participating countries.

AM	Armenia	LT	Lithuania
AT	Austria	LV	Latvia
BA	Bosnia and Herzegovina	ME	Montenegro
CH	Switzerland	MT	Malta
CZ	Czech Republic	NL	The Netherlands
DE	Germany	NO	Norway
DK	Denmark	PL	Poland
EE	Estonia	RO	Romania
FI	Finland	RS	Serbia
FR	France	RU	Russia
HR	Croatia	SE	Sweden
HU	Hungary	SI	Slovenia
GE	Georgia	SK	Slovakia
IE	Ireland	UA	Ukraine
IT	Italy		

Notes

1 All documents of the Bologna process can be found under:
http://www.bildungsserver.de/Die-Bologna-Konferenzen.-Hintergrunddokumente-3401.html
2 In the following explanations the term "student" refers only to people attending higher education institutions (and "studies" only to higher education programs – i.e., programs leading to degrees).
3 Compared with Wolter (2015a) based on data from 2008, the results presented here report data from the 2014 Eurostudent study. Shortly before the manuscript went to print the new Eurostudent study (DZHW, 2018) was published, but could not be taken into account. The study presented new data now for 28 countries. The basic social structures of participation in higher education do not differ even if there is a relatively high degree of inconsistency in the national data.
4 Different from the statistics in the former section, the data in this section refer to the national classification of higher education institutions, including only institutions with programs leading to academic BA or MA degrees (and doctorates).
5 Boudon's conceptual differentiation between primary and secondary effects of social origin takes up this discrepancy and will be explained in more detail in a later section.

References

Autorengruppe Bildungsberichterstattung. (2012). *Bildung in Deutschland 2012* [Education in Germany 2012]. Bielefeld: wbv.

Autorengruppe Bildungsberichterstattung. (2016). *Bildung in Deutschland 2016* [Education in Germany 2016]. Bielefeld: wbv.

Banscherus, U., Himpele, C., & Staack, S. (2011). Die soziale Dimension: Der blinde Fleck im Bologna-Prozess [The social dimension: The blind spot in the Bologna process]. *Die Hochschule, 1,* 142–154.

Baumert, J., & Schümer, G. (2001). Familiäre Lebensverhältnisse, Bildungsbeteiligung und Kompetenzerwerb [Family life conditions, participation in education and competence acquisition]. In Deutsches PISA-Konsortium (Ed.), *PISA 2000* (pp. 323–410). Opladen: Leske & Budrich.

Boudon, R. (1974). *Education, opportunity, and social inequality: Changing prospects in western society.* New York, NY: Wiley.

Bourdieu, P., Boltanski, L., de Saint Martin, M., Maldidier, P. (1981). *Titel und Stelle: Über die Reproduktion sozialer Macht* [Title and position: About the social reproduction of power]. Frankfurt: Campus.

Bourdieu, P., & Passeron, J. C. (1971). *Die Illusion der Chancengleichheit* [The illusion of equal opportunities]. Stuttgart: Klett.

DZHW, German Centre for Higher Education Research and Science Studies. (Ed.). (2018). *Social and economic conditions of student life in Europe. Synopsis of indicators. EUROSTUDENT VI 2016–2018.* Bielefeld: wbv.

Esping-Andersen, G. (1990). *The three worlds of welfare capitalism.* Cambridge: Polity Press.

Friedeburg, L. v. (1989). *Bildungsreform in Deutschland* [Educational reform in Germany]. Frankfurt: Suhrkamp.

Gofen, A. (2009). How first generation higher education students break the intergenerational cycle. *Family Relations, 58*(1), 104–120.

Hall, P. A., & Soskice, D. (Eds.). (2001). *Varieties of capitalism.* Oxford: Oxford University Press.

Hauschildt, K., Gwosc, C., Netz, N., & Mishra, S. (2015). *Social and economic conditions of student life in Europe: Synopsis of indicators. EUROSTUDENT V 2012–2015.* Bielefeld: wbv.

Hillmert, S. (2009a). Bildung und Lebensverlauf – Bildung im Lebensverlauf [Education and life course – education across the life course]. In R. Becker (Ed.), *Lehrbuch der Bildungssoziologie* [Textbook of sociology of education] (pp. 215–238). Wiesbaden: Verlag für Sozialwissenschaften.

Hillmert, S. (2009b). Soziale Inklusion und Exklusion: Die Rolle von Bildung [Social inclusion and exclusion: The function of education]. In R. Stichweh & P. Windolf

(Eds.), *Inklusion – Exklusion: Analysen zur Sozialstruktur und sozialen Ungleich-heit* [Inclusion – exclusion: Analyses of social structure and social inequality] (pp. 85–100). Wiesbaden: Verlag für Sozialwissenschaften.

Hillmert, S. (2014). Bildung, Ausbildung und soziale Ungleichheit im Lebenslauf [Education, qualification and social inequality in the life course]. In K. Maaz, M. Neumann, & J. Baumert (Eds.), *Herkunft und Bildungserfolg von der frühen Kindheit ins Erwachsenenalter* [Origin and educational success from early childhood to adulthood] (Special edition). *Zeitschrift für Erziehungswissenschaft, 24,* 73–94.

Hölscher, M. (2016). *Spielarten des akademischen Kapitalismus* [Varieties of academic capitalism]. Wiesbaden: Springer.

Kracke, N., Buck, D., & Middendorff, E. (2018). *Beteiligung an Hochschulbildung. Chancen(un)gleichheit in Deutschland* [Participation in higher education in Germany]. Hannover: DZHW-Brief 032018.

London, H. B. (1989). Breaking away: A study of first-generation college students and their families. *American Journal of Education, 97*(2), 144–170.

Lucas, S. R. (2001). Effectively maintained inequality: Education transitions, track mobility, and social background effects. *American Journal of Sociology, 106*(6), 1642–1690.

Maaz, K. (2006). *Soziale Herkunft und Hochschulzugang* [Social origin and access to higher education]. Wiesbaden: Verlag für Sozialwissenschaften.

Mayer, K. U., Müller, W., & Pollak, R. (2007). Germany: Institutional change and inequalities of access in higher edusssscation. In Y. Shavit, R. Arum, & A. Gamoran (Eds.), *Stratification in higher education* (pp. 240–265). Stanford: Stanford University Press.

Middendorff, E., Apolinarski, B., Becker, K., Bornkessel, P., Brandt, T., Heißenberg, S., & Poskowsky, J. (2017). *Die wirtschaftliche und soziale Lage der Studierenden in Deutschland 2016* [The economic and social situation of students in Germany 2016]. Berlin: BMBF.

Miethe, I., Boysen, W., Grabowsky, S., & Kludt, R. (2014). *First generation students an deutschen Hochschulen* [First-generation students in German higher education]. Berlin: edition sigma.

NCES, National Center for Education Statistics. (1998). *First generation students: Undergraduates whose parents never enrolled in postsecondary education.* Washington, DC: U.S. Department of Education.

Neugebauer, M., & Schindler, S. (2012). Early transitions and tertiary enrolment: The cumulative impact of primary and secondary effects on entering university in Germany. *Acta Sociologica, 55*(1), 19–36.

Papadopoulos, G. (1990). *Education 1960–1990: The OECD perspective.* Paris: OECD.

Pascarella, E. T., Pierson, C. T., Wolniak, G. C., & Terenzini, P. T. (2004). First generation college students: Additional evidence on college experiences and outcomes. *The Journal of Higher Education, 75*(3), 249–284.

Peter, F., Rusconi, A., Solga, H., Spieß, K., & Zambre, V. (2016). Informationen zum Studium verringern soziale Unterschiede bei der Studienabsicht von AbiturientInnen [Information about studying reduces social distinctions in study intentions]. *DIW Wochenbericht, 26,* 555–565.

Powell, J. W., & Solga, H. (2011). Why are higher education participation rates in Germany so low? Institutional barriers to higher education expansion. *Journal of Education and Work, 24,* 49–68.

Raftery, A. E., & Hout, M. (1993). Maximally maintained inequality: Expansion, reform, and opportunity in Irish education, 1921–1975. *Sociology of Education, 66,* 41–66.

Reimer, D., Pollak, R. (2010). Educational expansion and its consequences for vertical and horizontal inequalities in access to higher education in West Germany. *European Sociological Review, 26*(4), 415–430.

Reiss, K., Sälzer, C., Schiepe-Tiska, A., Klieme, E., & Köller, O. (Eds.). (2016). *PISA 2015 – Eine Studie zwischen Kontinuität und Innovation* [PISA 2015 – A study between continuity and innovation]. Münster: Waxmann.

Teichler, U. (1984). Hochschulzugang und Hochschulzulassung im internationalen Vergleich [Access and admission to higher education in an international comparison]. In P. Kellermann (Ed.), *Studienaufnahme und Studienzulassung* [Transition and admission to higher education] (pp. 9–24). Klagenfurt: Kärntner Verlagsgesellschaft.

Teichler, U. (2003). Hochschulzulassung und Struktur des Hochschulwesens [Admission to and structure of higher education]. In G. Schned & S. Ulrich (Eds.), *Hochschulrecht, Hochschulmanagement, Hochschulpolitik* [Higher education law, management, policy] (pp. 143–158). Wien: Böhlau.

Terenzini, P. T., Springer, L., Yaeger, P. M., Pascarella, E. T., & Nora, A. (1996). First generation college students: Characteristics, experiences, and cognitive development. *Research in Higher Education, 37*(1), 1–22.

Watermann, R., Daniel, A., & Maaz, K. (2014). Primäre und sekundäre Disparitäten des Hochschulzugangs [Primary and secondary disparities of access to higher education]. In K. Maaz, M. Neumann, & J. Baumert (Eds.), *Herkunft und Bildungserfolg von der frühen Kindheit ins Erwachsenenalter* [Origin and educational success from early childhood to adulthood] (Special edition). *Zeitschrift für Erziehungswissenschaft, 24,* 233–261.

Wolter, A. (2009). Expanding graduate employment and mobilizing social demand for higher education: Recent developments and policy debates in Germany [Special issue on higher education reforms]. *Journal of Adult and Continuing Education, 15*(2), 187–203.

Wolter, A. (2011, February). Hochschulzugang und soziale Ungleichheit in Deutschland [Access to higher education and social inequality in Germany]. In H. B. Stiftung (Ed.), *Öffnung der Hochschule – Chancengerechtigkeit, Diversität, integration* [Opening up higher education: Equal opportunity, diversity, integration] (pp. 9–15). Berlin: Heinrich-Böll-Stiftung.

Wolter, A. (2014). Eigendynamik und Irreversibilität der Hochschulexpansion: Die Entwicklung der Beteiligung an Hochschulbildung in Deutschland [Dynamic and irreversibility of the expansion of higher education]. In U. Banscherus, M. Bülow-Schramm, K. Himpele, S. Staack, & S. Winter (Eds.), *Übergänge im Spannungsfeld von Expansion und Exklusion* [Transitions in the tension between expansion and exclusion] (pp. 19–38). Bielefeld: wbv.

Wolter, A. (2019a). Massification and diversity: Has the expansion of higher education led to a changing composition of the student body? European and German evidence. In P. Zgaga, U. Teichler, H. G. Schuetze, & A. Wolter (Eds.), *Higher education reform: Looking back – looking forward* (2nd ed., pp. 277–292). Frankfurt: Peter Lang.

Wolter, A. (2019b). Opening up higher education for new target groups in Germany. In P. Zgaga, U. Teichler, H. G. Schuetze, & A. Wolter (Eds.), *Higher education reform: Looking back – looking forward* (2nd ed., pp. 391–414). Frankfurt: Peter Lang.

Wolter, A., & Kerst, C. (2015). The "academization"of the German qualification system: Recent developments in the relationships between vocational training and higher education in Germany. *Research in Comparative and International Education, 10*(4), 510–524.

CHAPTER 11

The Abolition of Tuition Fees in Germany: Student Protests and Their Impact

Dieter Timmermann

Abstract

The issue of student fees became controversial in Germany following the introduction of tuition fees in seven of the 16 federal states beginning in 2006. This resulted in resistance and protest movements among students. The author describes his experience as the President of the University of Bielefeld during this period. Student protests and activism, and their support by the majority of the public, resulted in the abolition of tuition fees in all seven of the states by 2013/2014. The author concludes with a discussion of the arguments for and against tuition fees that were raised before and during the tuition fees controversy in Germany, and the various factors that affected the course of events during this period.

Keywords

tuition fees – German higher education – student activism – equality of access to higher education – neo-liberalism in higher education

A Brief Overview of the German Higher Education System

After the Second World War the German higher education (HE) institutions reopened. They were first under the control of the occupying powers, but after the proclamation of the basic law in 1949 (the German constitution) they came under the control of the 11 states (Länder) in West Germany. In 1950 there were 146 institutions, most of them public. In East Germany the HE system followed a separate path laid down by the Soviet Union. In West Germany, the federal government had no role or influence in HE until 1969. Due to growing pressure on the 11 states coming from a growing demand for higher education, from forecasts of manpower needs, and from critiques of the underrepresentation

© KONINKLIJKE BRILL NV, LEIDEN, 2019 | DOI:10.1163/9789004393073_011

THE ABOLITION OF TUITION FEES IN GERMANY

of girls and of children from worker or non-academic families, the states increasingly asked the federal government for financing support. As the federal government, in turn, made demands for more influence on HE, the federal government and the 11 states finally agreed upon a change of the basic law: in 1969 "joint tasks" were introduced into the basic law which allowed the federal government to co-decide on a number of issues in cooperation with the states and to co-finance certain projects, mainly university construction and infrastructure.

The engagement of the federal level of government as well as the growing economy delivering growing tax revenues for both levels of government allowed the HE system to grow due to public investments. Most institutions were and still are public ones financed by public budgets. The specific competencies of the states and of the federal level in HE were laid down in a special law, the higher education framework law. The law was passed in 1976 and rescinded in 2007, as the federal government as well as the by then 16 states (after reunification) came to the conclusion that the federal government should withdraw from HE as a decision making unit and as a financer. This was done in 2007 by changing the basic law again and deleting the relevant articles. In 2015 Germany had 399 HE institutions; 121 (30%) were universities, 220 (55%) were universities of applied sciences (Fachhochschulen), and 58 (15%) were HE institutions for art and music. Of all these HE institutions, 238 (60%) were public, 30% were private and 40 (10%) were church colleges.

Student Financing in Germany

Student fees have always been an issue of controversy in Germany, at least since the second world war. The fact that there was a period up to 1957 without any grant system in the HE system which would have aimed at supporting young people from non-academic background families to move up the social ladder in spite of tuition fees is not present in the awareness of today's students, academics, or politicians. During that period, scholarships were exclusively aimed at highly talented young people, most of them boys from well-off families, graduating from the gymnasium (academic secondary school) and awarded by a group of six grant foundations which had been revived in the late 1940s and early 1950s. It is also not part of the remembrance of our contemporaries that until the mid-1960s, students had to pay tuition fees as well as handset money ("Hörergeld")[1] for each course or lecture they attended. The author himself, who studied between 1962 and 1968, had to pay tuition fees of 150 DM (German Marks) per semester and handset money of about 50 DM, altogether 200 DM per semester. It was only in 1957 that the federal government and the then 11 states (Länder) introduced a scholarship system. The system was named after the town where it was decided upon: the Honnef system of student support (Honnefer Model). It was aimed at attracting students from nonacademic families and opening opportunities of social promotion for them.

As the early manpower forecasting studies diagnosed an existing and growing shortage of academic labor, and as sociological studies identified girls and children from nonacademic background (workers) as well as from rural areas to be the source of future academics to address the shortage it was perceived that in attempts to attract these new target groups to higher education the tuition fees might be an obstacle. So, in the mid 1960s, the tuition fees as well as the handset money for the courses the professors taught were completely abolished. The income loss for the professors was compensated for by raising their regular salaries. In 1971, the Honnef system of public grants for needy students was replaced by a more generous grant system called BAFÖG (federal education promotion law), financed by payments from the federal government and the 11 states. The ratio of contributions was 65% for the federal level and 35% from the states.

This law has had a capricious history, of which only a few aspects can be illuminated here. After coming into effect in 1971, the supportive payment was awarded as a 100% grant. The generosity of the grant awards is mirrored by the fact that in 1972 nearly 45% of all students received some amount of the grant, depending on the income and wealth of their parents. In 1974 the ongoing expansion of higher education in (West) Germany raised concern with respect to the growing cost on the part of the federal as well as the state governments. They then introduced a fixed loan element without interest, whose level was steadily raised, and the recipients had to use the loan part of the payment first. In 1983, the entire payment was changed into a full loan without interest but with a requirement that it be paid back completely. As a result, which was intended, the percentage of students who took advantage of this kind of payment decreased considerably. In 1998 only 12.6% of the student body received grants from the BAFÖG support system.

In 1990 the BAFÖG system was changed into a two pillar model consisting of 50% grant (subsidy) and 50% interest-free loan. The funding rate as well as the allowances were adapted to the income growth of the families, also taking into account the rate of inflation and changing conditions of the student and his family. However, these adaptations did not happen gradually but rather in jumps several years apart. In the mid-1990s the German Student Service started a discussion about a basic reform of the funding system due to the fact that financial support to needy students was not keeping pace with

THE ABOLITION OF TUITION FEES IN GERMANY   207

income growth and inflation. The ideas for reform were intensively discussed but finally rejected by the politicians at the federal and state levels. In the light of a steadily and quickly growing student body the political leaders feared an overtaxing of the federal and state budgets. It was rather surprising that during these discussions about the increasing burden on the public finances caused by a growing student body and a growing sum of grants and loans being provided, a group of economists, as well as university rectors, started a discussion in the mid-1990s on (re)introducing tuition fees at public institutions of higher education as a kind of solution to the financing pressures. This discussion was embedded into a broader and more fundamental debate about the societal role and relevance of state planning and steering (not only in education), the role of the state in a market society, the relevance of markets, and competition and individual responsibility including in (higher) education. This debate was later continued under the heading of the beginning of the expansion of neo-liberalism and the economization of our society, including (higher) education, health and culture. While the red-green federal government[2] set an example of standing against the neoliberal wave by limiting the loan debt of BAFöG recipients to the sum of 10,000 €, it was, nevertheless the first time that in Germany a discussion about tuition fees had happened. Many arguments in favor of and against the introduction of student fees were exchanged. All these arguments popped up again after the federal constitutional court, in 2005, had ruled that the banning of fees for public higher education institutions which had been written into the higher education framework law in 2002 by the red-green federal government was unconstitutional.

This discussion on the good and the negative effects of tuition fees will be taken up in the third section of this chapter, below. The second section will be devoted to the period of the introduction and abolition of tuition fees in seven federal states starting in the year 2006. Section four is left to speculations about the answers to the "why" question. Why were the fees introduced, and why were they given up again after a short period of existence?

In and out: The Introduction and Abolition of Tuition Fees in Seven German Federal States between 2006 and 2015

The Introduction of Tuition Fees

The fee decision by the Constitutional Court in 2005 opened to all (after reunification in 1991) 16 federal states the opportunity to charge tuition fees or to allow all their (public) higher education institutions (universities, institutions of applied sciences, technical universities, HE institutions of music and arts as well as pedagogy) to decide on their own whether to introduce fees or not, and, in the case of introduction of fees, to decide the amount, which could be set between zero and € 500 per semester. Nine federal states did not give the right to charge tuition fees to their HE institutions, while seven of the 16 federal states – all of which were located in former West Germany – passed state bills which allowed their institutions to charge tuition fees.

The tuition fee solutions the respective federal states opted for were as follows. Lower Saxony and North Rhine-Westphalia (NRW) started as the pioneers in 2006. Both federal states asked first-year students to pay tuition fees beginning with the winter semester 2006/2007, and all other students from the summer semester 2007. Lower Saxony imposed state-wide tuition fees of € 500 per semester, i.e., € 1,000 per year. NRW left it to HE institutions themselves to decide whether or not they would introduce fees. In the summer semester of 2007, general tuition fees were introduced in Baden-Württemberg, Bavaria and Hamburg. Students in Hesse and Saarland were required to pay fees starting from the winter semester 2007/2008. Although the details of the regulations enabling tuition fees introduced by the federal states differed (e.g., with respect to different degrees of the institutions' decision-making autonomy), they all followed the same approach: the level of fees was not permitted to exceed € 500 per semester and the income generated had to be used exclusively to improve teaching and student support.

All seven federal states set up their own loan solutions for pre-financing student fees to ensure that those unable to afford study fees, amounting to a maximum of € 500 per semester, could still start and continue studying. The states capped the amount that had to be repaid: this maximum amount included both BAföG debt and tuition fees loan repayment, in order to calm students' fears of accumulating huge debts. The upper limit of repayment was welcomed by the majority of rectors and academic as well as non-academic staff, but most students did not become aware that the upper repayment limit was a very generous gift by the states. They listened to the voices and read the lampoons of those (leftist) student groups who tried to convince them that they would accumulate a considerable debt burden and, therefore, fought against the fees. Most of the Länder offered repayment caps of between € 15,000 and 17,000.

The Bielefeld Case

In spite of all these measures which aimed at relieving students' debt burden, the resistance and protest movement among students against tuition fees was strong and at some places furious (Cologne, Bonn, Münster, Bielefeld). Occupations of hallways and rooms, blocking of access to parts of university buildings where the rector's office and the academic senate met, and personalized aggressions as well

THE ABOLITION OF TUITION FEES IN GERMANY 209

as threats against members of the rector's office and senates, including aggressive actions in private spheres or residence areas were common in those days.

Bielefeld experienced a particularly strong and intense student protest. The protest started unexpectedly early on the first of February, 2006. The rectorate had asked the chair of the academic senate to put the issue of student fees on the agenda of the senate meeting on that date. The aim had not been to decide about the introduction of fees but rather to start a discussion about the pros and cons of student fees. The student members had applied for a shift of the meeting into the largest auditorium. This was accepted by all senate members including the rectorate, which is a member without vote. The aim of the topic was to ask the administration at the end of the discussion to document the discussion on the topic and to draw conclusions as to options of introducing fees (if at all, what kind of exemptions, the size of fees, the composition of the committees which should decide about the use of the fees and the representation of the students within) in order to come to a clear view on the implications of fees for the university. To the surprise of most senate and rectorate members the auditorium was filled with more than 2000 students who were already in an aggressive mood. As a result, the meeting lasted more than two hours, it was pervaded by aggressive interventions, first only verbally, at the end also physically: students approached senate members who had not immediately rejected the idea of fees and threatened them with violence.

When the author reached the rooms in the rectorates' hallway he was surprised to encounter about 200 students in those rooms, including his own office. The attempt to convince the students to leave his office was not successful. The next four weeks were filled with offers to the occupants for discussion, as well as exchange of statements; however, the students were not willing to start oral face to face communication at all. The rectorate asked the police for advice. Interestingly, the police were not ready to expel the occupants; their advice was to stay cool and relaxed, to offer talks and to wait. On our following that advice, the occupation lasted the whole month of February, 2006. At the end of the month, all the occupants had disappeared from our offices. The next meetings of the senate saw intense discussions about fees; commissions (which all have student members) also discussed the issue and developed alternative models. In July, 2006, the senate met for the session in which a decision was to be made. Expecting protest, access to the senate room (on the third floor of the main university building) was restricted; only a small number of students were allowed to be present. The majority of protesters had to stay outside. However, a group was clever; they discovered an opportunity to approach the 3rd storey from outside, using tools, and they managed to climb into an office (through the window) near the senate room. Although the storey was protected by a private security company, protesters were then in the center of the forbidden area. However, the door from that office into the rest of the floor was locked, so the group had no chance to enter the floor. Unfortunately, the head of the security team heard a noise from that office, and in order to see what was going on behind the door he unlocked the door and was overrun by the group. One group member even stole the master key which he had used, so that the group was in the possession of the master key which gave access to every room in the main building.

Noticing that they had the key and also learning that the senate had already decided in favor of fees, the group quickly draw back and did not continue to protest, which seemed strange to us, as we had expected strong confrontations with the group. Of course, at that moment we had not yet learned about the loss of the master key.

The next weeks were full of actions by protesting students. They went into the offices of senate members, but also to some of their private homes and left many traces of vandalism, including ink traces on walls and on office desks as well as feces at the walls of private homes. The highlight was setting fire to the private car of the author in front of his home. The senate had to discuss the fee issue two more times; both discussions were accompanied by police protection of the meetings. In 2008 the protest was gone, the fees were imposed without protest, and they were spent to the benefit of the students, improving the conditions of teaching and learning.

The Use and Distribution of the Revenue from Tuition Fees

Depending on the fee levels and on the exemption or reduction criteria which were awarded to students, the total tuition fee revenues in NRW of about € 283 million accounted for about 10 % of the total universities' public budgets of € 2.73 billion in 2007 (i.e., without third party or private funding of teaching and research). At the end of the fee taking period, in 2011, the fee revenue in NRW came to only € 249 million, which then was only 5.0% of the public higher education budget of € 4,962 billion, a 50% reduction of the ratio.

The regulations in all fee taking states considered exceptions from the obligation to contribute. Generally, the requirement to pay the fees was suspended in cases of a temporary leave approved by the university, a semester spent on an internship or on a study abroad period. Likewise, PhD students and foreign students being supported by official exchange programs such as Erasmus[3] were exempt from paying fees. These general exemptions were complemented by local measures or decisions. Due to student protest and pressure, quite a number of institutions introduced exemptions for students who had to take care of underage children (mostly, one parent was freed from paying) or of family members who had to be looked after due to old age or disease.

THE ABOLITION OF TUITION FEES IN GERMANY   211

Bielefeld University introduced two interesting additional cases of exemption or reduction of the fee burden. The first case referred to students who had taken advantage of the loan from the NRW bank but who did not finish the study program within the expected number of semesters (6 for bachelor's programs and 4 for master's programs). Under the precondition that the loan support had ended, that those students had studied at Bielefeld University at least the last four semesters and that they were very likely to finish their studies within the next two semesters, they would be relieved from paying the fees. The rationale for this solution was the assumption that not only the student should be blamed for the prolongation of the study duration but that part of the reason might lie on the side of the conditions and the quality of the teaching and study system of the university as well as of the faculty.

The second special case of exemptions or fee reductions referred to those foreign students (e.g., from African countries) who were obliged to pay fees but who were not eligible for loans from the NRW bank. So the university waived the fee payment for them as a kind of grant, but expressed the expectation of those students that they would be willing to pay back part or all of this "grant" in the case that they successfully completed their studies and were able to pay it back. That is why the university called this kind of financial support a "false grant" which encompassed a loan possibility.

How were the fee revenues distributed? In the beginning, 23% had to go to the default fund; later it was 14%. About 3% was taken up by the administrative costs of managing the fee processes. In most institutions the remaining amount was distributed as follows: about 50% went directly to the faculties or departments according to certain parameters, mostly student numbers and study program characteristics; about 20% was devoted to project applications from the faculties/departments which had to aim at decentralized measures in a competitive context; and about 30% was devoted to central innovative measures of subject surpassing (interdisciplinary) character initiated by central internal institutions and by the top management of the higher education institutions. All these measures had, directly or indirectly, to be aimed at expanding the human and physical resources available for teaching and learning as well as at improvement of teaching and learning and its conditions.

The Abolition of the Tuition Fees

Before medium-term effects of tuition fees could be seen or felt, the fees were abolished in Hesse after only two semesters (winter semester 2008/2009). Saarland stopped charging general tuition fees in the summer semester of 2010. North Rhine-Westphalian institutions charged tuition fees for the last time in the summer semester of 2011. Two federal states decided to transform their tuition fee systems. In winter semester 2008/2009, Hamburg replaced its fee system (€ 500 per semester) by downstream tuition fees: Gainfully employed graduates rather than students were required to pay for using the resources for their study purposes provided by the state. The graduates were charged € 375 for each semester they had spent at one of the state's institutions if their pre-tax earnings exceeded € 30,000 per year. Students who were willing and able to pay their fees already during their study phase were allowed to do so. If graduates were unable to pay the fees or had to defer the payment, the state (and city) of Hamburg compensated the HE institutions for these expenses.

Changes of government in some federal states (both parties, the Social Democrats and the Greens reject tuition fees on the basis of principle) and political pressure on government caused the abolition of student fees. Newly elected governments in Hamburg and Baden-Württemberg removed the tuition fees (summer semester 2012 in Baden-Württemberg and winter semester 2012/2013 in Hamburg). When a petition for a referendum against tuition fees was launched by political activists in Bavaria, the Bavarian parliament decided to abolish the fees. These were charged for the last time in summer semester 2013. Thus, Bavaria was the only federal state to decide against tuition fees without a change of government. After the 2013 election in Lower Saxony, the abolition of student fees was accomplished in winter semester 2014/2015.

The compilation in Table 11.1 gives a summary of these events.

TABLE 11.1   Dates of introduction/abolition of student fees, by state

Federal state	Effective date of implementation of student fees	Effective date of abolition of student fees
Lower Saxony	From winter semester 2006/2007: student fees for first-year students From summer semester 2007: fees for all students	Winter semester 2014/2015
North Rhine-Westphalia	From winter semester 2006/2007: student fees for first-year students From summer semester 2007: fees for all students	Winter semester 2011/12
Baden-Württemberg	Summer semester 2007	Summer semester 2012
Bavaria	Summer semester 2007	Winter semester 2013/14
Hamburg	Summer semester 2007	Winter semester 2012/13
Hesse	Winter semester 2007/08	Winter semester 2008/2009
Saarland	Winter semester 2007/08	Summer semester 2010

SOURCE: MÜLLER AND RISCHKE (2014, P. 38)

In 2011, the president of the German Science Council (Wissenschaftsrat, an advisory body to the German federal government and the state governments), W. Marquardt, bemoaned that the chance to gain important and interesting insights and empirical evidence from that field test was wasted due to the (too) early closure.

The Reintroduction of Long-Term Study Fees in Some States

Before general tuition fees were introduced, some federal states charged long-term study fees. Following the abolition of general tuition fees, some federal states decided to reintroduce long-term study fees. The basic idea behind these fees is that a state concedes to students a certain number of years or semesters of studying at public institutions of higher education free of charge. Those students who exceed this standard period have to pay fees for each additional semester. The states which have (re)introduced these study account systems are Bremen, Lower Saxony, Saarland, Saxony, Saxony-Anhalt and Thuringia.

The Arguments in Favor of and against Tuition Fees

When it became clear that the decision of the Constitutional Court to repeal the ban on student fees would cause intensive discussions in all institutions of higher education in Germany and that it would be the academic senate that would have to decide upon the "yes or no" to the introduction of fees, the rector and the senate of Bielefeld University tried to structure the discussion by delivering a paper which put together the main pro and contra arguments. Four main arguments based in economic theory were brought forward and discussed: (a) the governance argument, (b) the fiscal argument, (c) the efficiency argument, and (d) the equality of chances argument. The main aspects of these arguments will be presented in the following section, including points subsequently raised by the parties to the discussion, namely a group of economists from the Economics Department, the trustees, the Equality Officer and her Commission, the rectorate, and various groups of students.

The Governance Argument

Advocates of a strict neoliberal market economic order justify study fees by arguing that higher education is a private good. This view implies that the stream of benefits and utility flows only to the students. Therefore, only the students, as the sole beneficiaries, must bear all the cost of their study. This view rejects every argument that raises doubts as to the pure private good character of higher education.

Critics say that this argument is not at all convincing. They argue that free higher education leads to a high level of general education in the population, which in turn fosters higher economic growth and strengthens the wisdom and responsibility of citizens. In other words, it functions as a public good.

From the discussion at Bielefeld around this issue we can draw the conclusion that higher education is neither a (pure) private nor a (pure) public good but a mixed good which has characteristics of both. This means that the students, their families and their peers, but also the society as a whole benefit from higher education. Unfortunately, the benefit to the society is difficult to identify and quantify; therefore, there is much room for speculation. But according to the principle of equivalency of cost and benefit, it can be concluded that both the students and the society, represented by the tax payers, should pay for higher education. Of course, political preferences and political processes may come to divergent conclusions.

The Fiscal Argument

The German Rectors Conference took a decision in 2005 which asked for the introduction of study fees and which heavily relied on the fiscal argument. This argument started with presenting the observation that the institutions of higher education in Germany suffered from a widening gap between growing numbers of students and a level of public funding that was increasing at a much slower rate, or even stagnating. Taking into account the ascending prices of the resources which are used in the production process of higher education, the real value of the expenditures per student was shrinking continuously, and so was expenditure per capita of the population of Germany.

Arguments that fit into this general category include the observation that a "no fees" policy does not fit with the "Social Market Economy" model which assumes that higher education is a public good and should be financed out of tax revenue. Furthermore, in the long run the cost of providing free HE will overstrain the public purse, and the inevitable stagnation or even reduction in per-student contributions from the state will lead to decreasing quality of institutional performance due to overload.

Assuming that fees were to be instituted, university officials and trustees were concerned that the full amount of the fees should flow to the university, that fees should rise (but not too quickly) in the future, and a compensating grant and loan system would be necessary. Furthermore, university trustees were of the opinion that the level of fees should be decided by the state, rather than being left to individual institutions.

The Efficiency Argument

The efficiency argument promises an effective and persistent steering and guiding function of tuition fees on the behavior of students, teaching staff, faculties and departments, and the entire institution. As a consequence of instituting fees, all actors would deal with time and money much more carefully than they do under conditions of 100% public financing. All these actors (students, teaching staff, deans, administrative staff and the institutional leadership) would, according to this argument, develop more cost consciousness. Students would take into account the additional cost of every semester they might study beyond the standard study length, and also look more closely at the benefit of their subject of study with respect to its educational and labor market value.

The teaching staff whose teaching units would have to partially finance their activities through study fees would be expected to invest more time and attention into teaching and its quality in order to offer attractive courses and to attract active, paying participants. It is assumed that study fees increase competition not only between the institutions and faculties/departments but also between the teaching staff, who are spurred towards better teaching and caring about student performance. Such competition would lead to innovations in teaching, as well as improvements in library and IT services.

The introduction of fees would also tend to reduce the number of students who switch fields of study or institution, abandon their studies before graduation, or exceed the normal time to graduation.

Critics of study fees object that rational (economic) behavior of students would mean that students would base their decisions as to study field on the opportunities to utilize their acquired competences in the labor market and their marketability, to a much greater extent than is the case without tuition fees. But they allege that students do not, or should not, become "customers" of a narrow-gauge strictly employment oriented study experience but instead would be imparted "Bildung," i.e. a broadly-based education, including knowledge and techniques that are employment relevant.

This leads to the question of how fields of study that offer non-marketable competencies would fare, particularly those subjects taught in the humanities and social sciences. The question, then, is how the future of these subjects can be ensured in a system of tuition fees. Of course, during the short period of fees at German higher education institutions these possible effects could not be observed. But looking nowadays to the USA, the danger of at least thinning out the humanities' and social sciences' landscape cannot be denied.

The Equality of Chances Argument

The argument for equal chances of access to higher education is the strongest and most important argument put forward by the critics of study fees. They fear that the introduction of study fees would scare off children from families with no history of higher education or from low income life worlds from beginning to study, even if they have earned a university entrance qualification. The fee as such, irrespective of the size of the fee, is said to frighten them off. This fear is combined with and strengthened by the foreseen danger that the level of the fees would not be stable but would steadily increase in the course of time.

The Equality Officer, as well as some of the students, stated that fees would disproportionately affect female students (including future female academics), in the light of gender discrimination in the labor market. Also, students who are parents (particularly single parents) would be particularly burdened by fees, as would part-time students.

Fees would only be acceptable if the fees would be totally covered by grants, so that these target groups would not at all be burdened by the fees. In the sphere of higher education politics this solution does not get any support. What is offered are only loans, which may vary with respect to the interest rate (no rate or a subsidized rate) and the repayment conditions. Fees opponents reject the loan solution, arguing that loans and interest obligations create a debt burden which also has an effect of scaring off these target groups. Furthermore, if loans are to be offered then foreign students from outside the EU must get access to the loans offered by the state bank. But, in general, fees hinder the movement of students and are an impediment to the goal of internationalization of higher education.

However, critics of this position point out that the opponents of fees consistently ignore the fact that the public financing solution is very likely to have unexpected and undesirable income redistribution effects. These effects come from biases between the social and income related structure of the higher education beneficiaries on the one hand and the social and income related structure of those citizens who bear the tax burden. The student population (the private beneficiaries) has a strong bias in favor of children from families which are better off and which have at least one parent with an academic background. In Germany, of 100 children out of this social background stratum, 77 are likely to study, while of 100 children without an academic in the family, only 23 are likely to study; for children who live with a long term unemployed parent, only 2 are likely to study (see Middendorff, Apolinarski, Poskowsky, Kandulla, & Netz, 2013, pp. 11–12). The total tax burden seems also to have a bias in favor of the better off families. Since, in Germany, there is no evidence about the distribution of the total tax burden among all households, we have to trust single studies which have come to the conclusion that higher education graduates bear only 20% of their direct study costs by means of their income tax. In other words, free higher education is in effect a state subsidy to the already well off.

Conclusion

This chapter may have contributed a small amount to a comprehensive view of the controversy around study fees; it may be helpful particularly for those readers from other countries who have been very familiar with student fees for many decades. As the fee period in Germany was not comprehensive and very short, we do not have serious evidence which could help to assess the effects of fees on the students, the staff and the institutions. Looking at the publications of Heine and Quast (2011), Helbig and Baier (2011) and Müller and Rischke (2014), only very moderate conclusions may be drawn at the end. Müller and Rischke (2014) venture to conclude:

1. Tuition fees amounting to € 500 per semester, when coupled with refinancing options, do not have a deterrent or socially selective effect. There is no empirical evidence of deterrent effects that can be clearly attributed to study fees (p. 44).
2. Poorly defined and undifferentiated communication can create uncertainty amongst prospective students via psychological barriers, even in the absence of an objective reason (p. 44).
3. Paying students must be made aware of the improvements brought about by tuition fees. Communication is crucial for acceptance! (p. 52).

Conclusions 2 and 3 will be shared by many actors who have been witnesses of this unintentional field experiment. Conclusion 1 seems to be premature. But what can be said is that at least in NRW and in particular at Bielefeld University the student protests against the introduction of study fees had completely passed away after one year. Students seemed to have accepted the fees and adapted to live with them. Nevertheless, in 2010 the composition of the state government of NRW changed from black-yellow (Christian and Liberal Democrats) to red-green (Social Democrats and the Greens), similar to the other "fee-states" (except Bavaria). In all these states the red and green parties had announced that in case of their victory in the elections, they would immediately abolish the study fees. Besides expecting to get many votes from students the basic reason for abolishing the fees is deeply embedded in the ideological conviction and positioning of a vast majority of the "reds" and "greens." They do not say that access to higher education is a basic right as many students (being members of their parties) do, but they still adhere to the old German tradition which says that education is a public good and has to be financed by the tax payer. Higher education is included in this conviction. The strange thing is that the social inequalities which are still built into the present higher education system as well as in the present tax system, and which work to the advantage of the academics and the well off part of the population, are not on the awareness agenda of the representatives and most members of both parties.

Acknowledgements

I wish to thank Martin Löning, who serves as the archivist of Bielefeld University and who gave intensive support to me by opening records of senate and rectorate meetings to me.

This chapter presents my personal view, as an economist of education, and having served as a professor at Bielefeld University where I was a member of its rectorate for 13 years, including 8.5 years as the rector.

Notes

1 While the tuition fee was a fixed and equal amount to every student who enrolled, independent of the number of courses or lectures or seminars the students attended, the handset money was a kind of fixed price by the course hour that each student had to pay for attending a course, lecture or seminar. At the time in question that price was 5 DM per course hour – i.e., if a student attended a course which was taught two hours a week per semester he or she had to pay 10 DM for listening to the academic teacher during the semester.

2 In Germany, there is an old tradition to name the communist or social democratic party the red party/parties, while the Christian Democrats are called the black party and the liberals are named the yellow party. At the end of the 1980s, parts of the women's movement and of the environmental movement started to progress towards an organizational status which ended in the foundation of a political party which was named "Alliance 90s – the Greens." Later, after the German unification, the party renamed itself the Green party. Since then and currently, a red-green government means a government composed of the two parties: the Social Democrats and the Greens. In our case, the "red-green government" refers to the federal

THE ABOLITION OF TUITION FEES IN GERMANY 219

government of Chancellor Gerhard Schröder (red = Social Democrat) and foreign
minister Joschka Fischer of the Green party.

3 The Erasmus Programme is a European Union (EU) student exchange program
established in 1987. The program is named after the Dutch philosopher Desiderius
Erasmus of Rotterdam, known as an opponent of dogmatism, who lived and worked
in many places in Europe to expand his knowledge and gain new insights.

References

Heine, C., & Quast, H. (2011). *Studienentscheidung im Kontext der Studienfinan-
zierung* [Enrollment decision in the context of study financing]. Retrieved from
http://www.his.de/pdf/pub_fh/fh-201105.pdf

Helbig, M., & Baier, T. (2011, October). *Gebühren mindern Studierneigung nicht* [Tuition
fees don't diminish the propensity to study]. Retrieved from http://www.wzb.eu/
sites/default/files/publikationen/wzbrief/wzbriefbildung1820 11_helbig_baier.pdf

Middendorff, E., Apolinarski, B., Poskowsky, J., Kandulla, M., & Netz, N. (2013). *Die
wirtschaftliche und soziale Lage der Studierenden in Deutschland 2012. 20.* Sozialerhebung des Deutschen Studentenwerks durchgeführt durch das HIS-Institut für
Hochschulforschung, Hannover.

Müller, U., & Rischke, M. (2014). As dead as a dodo? – Student fees in Germany. *Journal
of the European Higher Education Area, 4,* 33–68.

CHAPTER 12

Conditions of Learning at High-Ranked Universities in Four Countries: An International Student's Perspective

Jade Zhao

Abstract

This is an "up close and personal" description of the internationalization of higher education by a student who has attended universities in four different countries and has also taken part in a short term non-university educational experience in a fifth country. She discusses her experience at the four universities under these headings: academic rigour and integrity, participatory pedagogy, academic support, and inducting new international students. She concludes with some recommendations for the reform of the international education process, reform that will result in "authentic internationalization."

Keywords

internationalization of higher education – international students – student experience – participatory pedagogy

Old and New Student Pathways

Increasingly, young people are taking advantage of higher education internationalization by attending universities in countries other than their own. For a young person seeking to broaden cultural horizons, the notion of attending a foreign university has considerable appeal. Hence, in 2016, a quarter of those in Australian universities and more than a million students on U.S. campuses were from overseas. In 2000, some 2 million students were studying abroad; by 2016, this number had risen to 4.5 million. International student enrolment is expected to reach 7 to 8 million by 2025 (Varghese, 2008).

Many students studying abroad are following well-worn pathways but others explore new gateways. Until recently, China sent large numbers of students

© KONINKLIJKE BRILL NV, LEIDEN, 2019 | DOI:10.1163/9789004393073_012

CONDITIONS OF LEARNING AT HIGH-RANKED UNIVERSITIES 221

to study abroad but today also welcomes many foreigners to its universities. Even Japan – an intensely homogeneous society – is offering incentives to lure foreign students to universities. By 2020 Japan plans to have 300,000 foreign students enrolled in Japanese higher education institutions (*The Economist*, 2016). In 2014–2015, there were 975,000 foreigners studying at US universities, many in top-tier institutions with a long-standing tradition of attracting the best and brightest.

Prior to going abroad, the travelling student has plenty to think about. Quite apart from finding accommodation, there are questions about degree require-ments and the expectations of foreign teachers. What do they expect, and am I capable? The fact that a university scores well in global rankings does not guar-antee the competence of administrators, teachers or cooks in university cafe-terias. Will the host university acknowledge my background? Or am I expected to fit into well-established local cultures? Does a high score on *Times Higher Education* "reputation" rankings mean there will be adequate student services, competent teachers and congenial local students?

International students should not expect overseas conditions to resemble those at home. Even if host universities embrace diversity, there are bound to be surprises. However, if the international student finds congenial groupmates, roommates and colleagues, mobility programs can create lifelong friendships and transcend political squabbles (e.g., those between China and Japan).

This is the author's story of life as a foreign student in France, Japan, China and the United Kingdom. Others will have different experiences. However, inside the idiosyncrasies of individual stories are incidents relevant to coop-eration and mobility among 21st century universities.

Foregrounding the Student Experience

My family and I immigrated to Vancouver (from China) when I was 10 years old. On my first day there, I was confused and frightened, but my parents made me feel safe in the new landscape. Despite switching elementary schools five times as we moved from rental home to rental home, I made friends easily and absorbed Eng-lish quickly. My teenage years were spent at Burnaby South High School where I had excellent social studies teachers who triggered my yearning to see and learn in other parts of the world. As a Chinese immigrant to Canada, I was more than ready for an academic journey or long march into a worthwhile career.

Vancouver is a culturally diverse city where routine daily interactions (on the bus, at a restaurant or the local grocery store) involve people from many cultures. My mother has an insatiable curiosity concerning places and cultures. Both my parents were tertiary teachers in China and had high expectations of me – the Chinese "one-child." I was blessed with the financial and social capacity to travel and, because I could not sit still, decided to live in various countries and be open to all forms of learning.

The Vancouver-based University of British Columbia (UBC) was my induction into higher education. As an undergraduate, I was eligible for programs offering exchange, research and study-abroad opportunities with over 200 partner institutions worldwide. After two years at UBC, I took advantage of the Go Global Program in my third year by taking up a one-year exchange to L'Institut d'études politiques de Paris (Sciences Po) in 2010. Classes taken at Sciences Po would be credited to my degree at UBC.

Many Sciences Po classes were taught in French, but with a sufficient number in English to allow for an exchange student to choose a full English year. Although Parisian French does not entirely resemble Canadian French, I had enough French language fluency to appreciate lectures and submit assignments *en francais*.

After returning from Sciences Po and graduating from UBC in 2012, I continued my cross-cultural education by spending a year in a small town in Shikoku, Japan, teaching English on the Japan Exchange and Teaching (JET) program. Although a teacher, I was also there as a learner. From kindergarten (age 3 onwards) onward, children in the school where I taught were in charge of lunch management and classroom cleaning. They dressed in white overcoats and chef hats and carried buckets (sometimes larger than their little bodies!) of rice and cooked vegetables, and cartons filled with milk. They used brooms, mops and brushes to clean classrooms at the end of every weekday. The teachers filled a supervisory role, giving guidance and occasional instructions but giving students space to develop their own understanding of their roles and responsibilities. This is only a small part of what I learned about Japan and its people.

Before my Japanese adventures, I had seriously considered graduate studies. The idea of a "joint" master's degree (involving two universities) was appealing and I looked at various combinations such as Peking University (PKU) with Sciences Po. However, having already spent a year at Sciences Po, it was hard to resist the famous London School of Economics (LSE) brand. Thus, I ultimately settled on the double master of science degree program with the LSE and PKU in International Relations and History. Having immersed myself in Japanese rural life for a year, I now journeyed to my birthplace – China. After one year in PKU, I spent my final academic year at the LSE. At the time of writing, I am living in London and working for one of the LSE's many research institutes. Having landed at LSE, it was hard to leave.

My higher education thus far has involved six years, three degrees (one bachelor and two masters) and four higher educational institutions in four

CONDITIONS OF LEARNING AT HIGH-RANKED UNIVERSITIES

countries: the University of British Columbia in Vancouver, Canada; L'Institut d'études politiques in Paris, France; Peking University in Beijing, China; and the London School of Economics in London, United Kingdom.

I will organize my recollection of life at UBC, Sciences Po, PKU and the LSE around four themes:

- Academic rigour and integrity
- Participatory pedagogy
- Academic support
- Inducting new students

Academic Rigour and Integrity
University of British Columbia

I was happy to see Justin Trudeau become Prime Minister of Canada in November, 2015 and can proudly say I graduated from the same university as he did! UBC has produced many great graduates and is consistently ranked as one of Canada's top three research universities. UBC typically has over 13,000 international students from 155 countries enrolled. International students comprise 23% of the total student body at the Vancouver Campus (University of British Columbia, 2016).

For undergraduates, a system whereby identity card numbers were used instead of student names on assignments ensured the anonymity of work handed in for grading. I took comfort from this because it eliminated bias from the grading system. Final grades were based on participation (usually 20%), coursework (30–50%) that included presentations and papers, and the final exam (30–50%). In some courses, there was the peculiar practice of peer-to-peer evaluation for participation and some coursework (e.g., presentations). I did not like peer-to-peer grading and preferred the expertise of the professor. Most courses were assessed in the traditional manner and feedback was mostly generous and useful.

I cherished my first years at UBC because we students were encouraged to explore numerous subjects. I later found European students were not afforded the same luxury; instead, they had to go into higher education with a clear understanding of what subject was their "major" – the one they wanted to pursue. At UBC, first-year coursework was elementary and foundational, and allowed plenty of time for extracurricular activities and nicely (and, in my view, appropriately) postponed decisions about career trajectories and majors.

L'Institut d'études politiques de Paris

Sciences Po is the alma mater of 13 French presidents, plus numerous French diplomats and politicians, a former UN Secretary General, and former

Canadian Prime Minister Pierre Trudeau. Its library is touted as continental Europe's largest collection in social sciences and humanities. I didn't want to do my study exchange anywhere else. In addition, since over 46% of its student body is from outside of France, I felt I would be a good fit for this place in the leafy streets of Paris.

In addition to its famous alumni, I was also attracted to its working professors – lecturers who worked in the professional world. By that point, the theory-based learning that dominated my first two years of undergraduate studies was becoming cumbersome. I craved practical knowledge and case studies based on current events. These working professors were the perfect antidote to a Chinese-Canadian brain drowned in theory.

Except for some courses conducted in large lecture halls containing over 100 students, most courses were conducted within a seminar format. The *"exposé"* (French word for "presentation") was an integral component of the student experience. Short policy briefs were part of the final grade.

Final exams were restricted to the two main courses, one in each term. There were a total of seven courses per term, one of which was usually a large-lecture-type course. Another was usually a language course and a third reserved for interesting extracurricular activities. I took archery in the first term, a friend took scuba-diving, and another was in a horse-riding course. That was different from other institutions and I deeply appreciated this breath of fresh French creative air.

Peking University

At PKU, professors and students do a delicate dance around "sensitive issues" and must recognize, implicitly or explicitly, Communist Party authority. Criticizing the Party is an offence. Therefore, professors and students have access to only a restricted array of literature. Although many people find ways over or around the "great Chinese firewall," it is dangerous to be caught looking at forbidden websites like Facebook, Google or Twitter.

Universities are controlled by the Communist Party and there is no western-style free speech, academic freedom or university autonomy. This, despite the fact PKU was the cradle of the May 4th, 1919 movement for science and democracy and, in 1989, its students led pro-democracy protests in Tiananmen Square. However, despite harsh politics in Chinese universities (not to mention atrocious air in Beijing), for me, PKU was easy to handle. The regulations were not too strict and classes were conducted in English.

Being fluent in Chinese and English, I had many advantages. By the time I got to PKU, I was able to follow conversation, speak and write in English, French, Chinese, and Japanese, to varying degrees of fluency. However, having

CONDITIONS OF LEARNING AT HIGH-RANKED UNIVERSITIES

immigrated to Vancouver as a child, my Chinese-language abilities were rusty. Because my closest friends at PKU were also foreigners, it took a while to sharpen my Chinese language abilities. However, compared with non-Chinese foreign students, I had many advantages. For example, during lunchtime gossip sessions, local students talked to me because I looked Chinese.

In China, there is a common saying about education: "From primary school to senior high, students are worked to the ground, but once they successfully enter university, life is a breeze." At a superficial level, being a PKU student was relatively easy. A lack of academic rigour meant more time spent outside the school, in the gardens of the New Summer Palace, by the side of No Name Lake or in the Lama Temple. However, there could be profound problems if the student was passionate about censored subjects such as Tibetan autonomy, Falun Gong, or the politics of the South China Sea or Xinjiang.

Foreign students at PKU tended to stick together, and everyone had a story about the lack of academic rigor and integrity. These stories were made doubly alarming by the fact that PKU had received millions of Renminbi from the 985 project, the 211 project, and other Chinese government attempts to improve higher education. As well, PKU is at the leading edge of China's attempts to build world-class universities capable of getting into the top 100 on international rankings (Rhoads, Wang, Shi, & Chang, 2014). Several Chinese leaders (such as the current Premier Li Keqiang) are graduates of PKU, and well-connected faculty members lecture at the Central Party School of the Communist Party of China or advise high government officials.

Like most university professors in China, those at PKU are obliged to produce a continuous flow of articles for publication in journals with a high "impact factor" on the CSSCI – the Chinese Social Science Citation Index. At PKU, students easily got the impression the professor's research output and extracurricular activities (networking for promotion, reputation building or positioning in the Communist Party) were more important than teaching. For example, responding to calls for "student participation," a PKU professor required each student to make a 40-minute presentation. The duration of a class was three hours, and within that, three students had to address the class. That left little time for concrete input from the professor. He sat back, randomly interrupted our presentations and did not provide critical commentary or positive feedback. On another occasion, a PKU professor made derogatory remarks about my "southern" (Cantonese) accent when speaking Mandarin.

At PKU, I opted to write a master's thesis on Chinese-Japanese cooperation to ameliorate air pollution in China. After the year living in Japan, I had developed a considerable admiration for Japanese people and culture. However, because Japanese are routinely vilified in China, this was a risky thesis topic.

Environmental cooperation was the least controversial topic in Sino-Japanese relations. I realized during my research that it was the only area of cooperation transcending political and historical conflicts between the two countries.

As long as I stayed away from politically sensitive topics and didn't stir up conflict with academic staff, PKU was an easy year. Among foreign students, the word was "socialize all you want outside the classroom. Just keep your head down and adhere to the Party line on paper." There was no need to worry about inadvertently mentioning a "sensitive issue" (like Tibet or Falun Gong) during class discussions because they did not exist.

The International Relations Department at PKU did not consider discussion (among graduate students) a priority worth pursuing. Just as citizens should pay attention to the Party Secretary, the role of the student is to listen to professors (Yin, Lu, & Wang, 2014). For me, this active discouragement of student participation was the most appalling feature of Chinese higher education.

The absence of student-teacher interaction at the University is part of a larger problem. Rhoads et al. (2014) used case study methodology to study academic life at four top Chinese universities – PKU, Tsinghua University, Renmin University (known colloquially as Renda) and Minzu University. When asked to identify the dominant "spirit and culture" at their universities, Tsinghua faculty said "applied research," Minzu pointed at "minorities," and Renda said "government relations." PKU (known colloquially as Beida) said "the Beida way" (*Beida jingshen*) but informants were hard-pressed to say what this nebulous (allegedly "mystical") concept involved. Instead, they mostly waffled about the pagoda and lake. In addition, some pointed at Beida's leading role in the May 4th, 1919 and June 4th, 1989 protests at Tiananmen Square.

In 1957, PKU President Ma Yinchu challenged government thinking about population policy and was told "deny your thesis" or "step down from the presidency." Ma chose the latter. Although "the pagoda was seen as a kind of torch or beacon of truth" (Rhoads et al., 2014, p. 71) it did not protect the President or Zhang Weiying, assistant to the PKU President who, in the face of considerable resistance, unsuccessfully tried to scale back government influence and introduce greater competition and transparency at Beida (Zhang, 2004).

In 1989, "the Beida way" also failed to protect PKU student Wang Dan who went to prison because of his leadership at Tiananmen Square. Now, nearly 30 years later, PKU aspires to be "world-class" and was 21st on the 2016 Times Higher Education "reputation" rankings (Ali, 2016). But, despite the ability of marketers to boost "reputation" scores, PKU has a brutal history, a weak identity, missing faculty members and a tendency to inflict slideshow tedium on students.

There are two salient problems at Beida. First, a lack of autonomy stifles academic freedom. Second, professors have "excessive security, decent pay and

CONDITIONS OF LEARNING AT HIGH-RANKED UNIVERSITIES   227

a minimal workload." If Beida wants to be world class, it will involve "rejecting the idea of faculty as cadre in favour of a new model more similar to that of western universities" (Rhoads et al., 2014, p. 77).

London School of Economics

Like Sciences Po, the LSE has a long list of impressive alumni including J.F. Kennedy, Pierre Trudeau and Tsai Ing-Wen, the current President of Taiwan. Furthermore, in a typical year, over 70% of its student body is foreign.

Although the LSE and PKU are partners in the International Relations master's program, they are an odd couple indeed. Compared with PKU, the LSE had stringent academic requirements and there was little time for sightseeing, partying or waffling about pagodas or lakes. Despite its reputation as a hard-drinking place, at the LSE the students spent long hours in the library or the study rooms of student residences.

At the LSE, there was a heavy emphasis on the final exam, which occurred in June. Few marks depended on work completed during the year. Usually, 100% of the grade rested on the outcome of the final exam (although this was beginning to change during my time there). Stress levels in June resembled those for the fabled gaokao (university entrance exam) in China. The inhabitants could smell crunch time in the air. The library remained open 24 hours a day and, at night, turned into a giant dorm room, filled with odours of sweat, coffee, and smelly fast food. Students took to staying overnight, marking their territories with coffee mugs, books and food wrappers. Some brought pillows and coffeemakers and supported each other through the ordeal!

Throughout the term, there were mandatory LSE papers and presentations. But instead of attracting marks, these were regarded as a "practice runs" for the final exam. Foreign and locally-born students took mid-term activities seriously even though they would have no impact on final marks. The months leading up to June were filled with the sound of pen-to-paper, groans and growls and the occasional banging of heads on tables. There was something intensely old school and "British" about the torture of preparing for an all up one-kick-at-the-can final exam.

Participatory Pedagogy

In places with many immigrants – like Vancouver and Hong Kong – there is a continuing preoccupation with so-called "teaching styles" or "learning" styles. According to conventional wisdom, teachers should adapt their processes to the needs and expectations of learners. According to this view, a "one size fits all" type of teaching is bound to privilege some learners while the rest suffer.

Educators influenced by theories of adult education or "andragogy" (see the classic description of andragogy in Knowles, 1970) feel there are universal laws of learning transcending cultural differences. For them, all learners want their experience acknowledged and respected. In addition, they want to be involved in the design and management of their learning experiences. In some ways, these views contradict relativist notions of teaching or learning "styles." Advocates of universal laws of learning are confident that learners (of all ages, cultures and learning styles) will respond positively to participatory and respectful pedagogies. Hence, instead of rigging up a media projector for the next round of slideshow tedium, before the class begins, the instructor will ask "What can I do to involve learners?"

UBC faculty members with commitments to teach at Chinese universities are sometimes (wrongly, in my view) told "Do not try that touchy-feely, group discussion stuff." Why not? "It won't work because Chinese prefer to listen to a lecturer, take notes and regurgitate them on the exam." Fortunately for learners in China, certain foreign (and locally-born) teachers ignore stereotypes like this and, despite the possible disapproval of the Party Secretary who considers "teaching" a top-down, information-giving process, deploy participatory pedagogies involving learners.

Sciences Po expected students to keep up with required readings and know relevant literature. In addition, students were expected to be in a position to discuss the day's news the minute they stepped into the classroom. Most professors held dual appointments. Students were expected to be active self-directed learners and capable of engaging with world leaders in International Relations. If North Korea launched a rocket, class members were expected to be in a position to discuss this with professors within hours of the event. Students were expected to have nuanced and reflective views on international terrorism, peacekeeping and politics at the United Nations. At the LSE, reading lists were impossibly long and students had to quickly find a system to digest essential ones and skim optional material. They also had to conceptually organise and be ready to reflect on large amounts of information.

At the LSE, every course was accompanied by seminars. Typically, a formal lecture by professors was once a week for one hour. There were two discussion seminars per week, usually led by Ph.D. candidates working as teaching assistants. Student-led discussion weighed heavily and some courses even took out 10% of the final mark from the exam to be able to grade student participation. This was reminiscent of UBC where "class participation" could comprise up to 30% of the final grade.

CONDITIONS OF LEARNING AT HIGH-RANKED UNIVERSITIES 229

Academic Support

At each university, there was a different attitude concerning students in need of academic support. At UBC and the LSE, there were a variety of writing, counselling, coaching and other services for students. At Sciences Po, it depended on the professor. I was not aware of the degree to which UBC spoon-fed me until well into my year at Sciences Po. At UBC, student support was dense and repetitive. Bureaucratic necessities were sent in multiple email reminders. There was step-by-step guidance on how to properly complete paperwork and respond to appointments. Coursework requirements were clearly spelled out. Strict guidelines always accompanied any paper, presentation or exam. If the UBC student followed the rules and read prescribed reading materials, a pass would be awarded.

Sciences Po is one of the world's most reputable institutions for the study of Political Science and International Relations. However, the school offered few email instructions to students and when "communications" arrived, they were as threadbare as an old sock. Sciences Po was not in the business of reminding students about deadlines on the road ahead. Students had to grow up fast. In addition, Sciences Po rarely checked on student progress.

At Sciences Po, I enrolled in a course on the history of communism. Being a Chinese, I should have known how to navigate the back alleys of Marxism, Engels and the alleged thoughts of Chairman Mao. But because the course was taught in French, like a Red Army soldier caught in marshlands during the Long March, I was bogged down and making slow progress. I had acquired a workable knowledge of the French language in Vancouver, but in high-speed Sciences Po lectures thick with academic jargon was sometimes floundering. It became difficult when the lecturer said "as was clearly explained last week" and then darted off into other jargon-dense highways or back alleys.

Back in Vancouver I had had an informative conversation with Nobel prize winner Carl Wieman and figured the same approach would work at Sciences Po. Reluctantly approaching the professor, I found he understood my language problem and was supportive and sympathetic. This professor was kind to international students and often stayed behind to talk in an informal and relaxed manner. His specialty was helping students with the dreaded *exposé en français.*

Sciences Po had informal ways of providing services that were part of formal institutional arrangements at UBC and the LSE. At each institution, professors mostly honoured their posted "office hours" (with those at UBC and the LSE sometimes begging students to visit them during office hours as it could be quite lonesome at times). Of the four institutions, it was hardest to track down professors at PKU. Maybe I created this problem by choosing one of the busiest PKU professors as my thesis supervisor. His appointment book was often filled with television interviews, travels and Communist Party activities.

I felt more comfortable with my LSE academic advisor than with my PKU advisor. I also found my LSE advisor more willing to help than the PKU counterpart. However, contacting my PKU advisor provided a good introduction to 21st century technology. The preferred manner of contact was WeChat (the Chinese equivalent of Whatsapp combined with Facebook). I would not dream of chatting with UBC or other western advisers via such an informal channel! WeChat cut through deeply formal professor-student relations in China. It was a startling juxtaposition that reminded me of the ways technology was changing power relations in China.

At PKU, sometimes professors would go missing for several days. Perhaps they were wooing officials for more funding? Or home struggling to finish the latest "high-impact" article? Or developing guanxi (connections) at Communist Party banquets? Whereas a UBC professor would explain their absence, in China, unexplained disappearances were treated like state secrets.

Inducting New Students

UBC, Sciences Po, PKU and the LSE each had unique ways of inducting new students into academic life and culture. UBC had entire programs and activities designed to ease the transition for new students; Sciences Po and the LSE had partial responses to this problem; PKU was very weak in this regard.

University of British Columbia

UBC had a week-long "Fresher's Orientation" filled with rallies, team activities, parties and booths. There were buddy programs such as the "Arts Tri-Mentoring Program" that paired an incoming student with a senior student to share experiences, tips and tricks. Housing was assigned by a lottery system and preference was given to international students and those with no family connections in Vancouver.

L'Institut d'études politiques de Paris

Sciences Po had its one-week orientation to welcome international students and a buddy system where foreign were paired with French students. The French student was expected to provide a broad array of language and other forms of assistance. Most international students were housed at Cité Universitaire for the first month and after that, were expected to find their own shelter.

CONDITIONS OF LEARNING AT HIGH-RANKED UNIVERSITIES   231

I found my own housing via a website called Bedycasa, but this place was not a good fit so I moved to a new abode which I discovered through a French website and after multiple phone calls in French with landlords. This was done without assistance from Sciences Po.

Peking University

At PKU, graduate students in International Relations had one orientation session with Dr. Paul Keenan, our program advisor. The school held a "Welcome Week" to hand out orientation packages and hear speeches by faculty members. There was also a "Club Week" with booths to attract new members. I participated in "Culture Week" where foreign students organized booths to showcase their national cultures and heritages. There were also Chinese and International talent show competitions, but Chinese and international students never competed against each other; it was two separate competitions.

Everyone I knew joined the Western Student Union, mostly for the chance to party and meet other foreign students. As far as I knew, there was almost no formal help on the housing front for us (although it was a different story for scholarship students from the Sciences Po-PKU program). I used *guanxi* (family connections) to get a room at the Global Village where most undergraduate and language program students were housed. The Global Village was just across the road from one of the main gates at PKU so I could walk to class or the library. Most of my program mates used "Beijing Buddies" or an equivalent service to arrange apartments. These were adequate but cost more than 10 times the price demanded from Chinese renters! In China, there is an old tradition of extracting usurious rents from foreigners.

London School of Economics

The LSE hosted a similar array of first-week welcome activities, including student club booths, Student Union-hosted parties, and career events themed on industry, the biggest of which were Consultancy and Banking nights. The housing was simple. Much like the UBC system, it was lottery-based and students were given one of three preferences when they signed up.

One of the most memorable non-academic events was the annual departmental trip to Cumberland Lodge on the grounds of Windsor Castle. Every department held a trip there over one weekend. It was not only a trip to meet and socialise but also an arena for fruitful intellectual discussion. This was one of the most outstanding events of my six years of higher education.

Out of the four PKU graduate programs in International Relations that I know of, mine had the most Chinese nationals in it. Hence, our Chinese program advisor loosely implemented a buddy system where each foreign student was paired with a local so as to receive help. The relationship was reversed at the LSE where we English speakers were expected to assist "foreigners."

A Student Perspective on Reform

Students of higher education who visit university libraries will soon see not much literature on higher education reform is written by students. Instead, it is mostly compiled by professors, government departments and inter-governmental organisations (like OECD or UNESCO). Chinese students are almost never asked to make comments about higher education and even in western countries, individual student stories about university life are too easily dismissed as individual "memoirs" lacking generalizability.

Yet, individual recollections of student life can trigger reform. Here is a small list of famous people and universities they dropped out of – Mark Zuckerberg (Harvard), Brad Pitt (Missouri), Steve Jobs (Reed College), F. Scott Fitzgerald (Princeton), John Lennon (Liverpool College), Paul Allen (Washington), Woody Allen (New York University), Charles Darwin (Edinburgh), Sir Edmund Hillary (Auckland), Bill Gates (Harvard), Larry Ellison (University of Illinois, Urbana and University of Chicago). Do university authorities know why they dropped out? Revealing answers reside in memoirs (e.g., Hillary, 1955, 2003) or biographies (e.g., Becraft, 2014, on Bill Gates; Symonds & Ellison, 2003, on Larry Ellison). Many of these people recalled their higher education as a waste of time punctuated by disorganisation, unprofessional behaviour and lack of student support.

Regarding *international* higher education, in particular, my experiences have convinced me that there are many variations in academic integrity, student services and teaching at the world's leading universities. Even at top universities like PKU, the LSE or Sciences Po, much teaching is mediocre and commitments to internationalization are often superficial. Along with culture shock, the foreign student will find academic programs and teaching not congruent with the high standards implied by "reputation" rankings or promised in recruitment literature.

With my experience at UBC, Sciences Po, PKU and the LSE as the backdrop, I suggest higher education reformers should consider the following:
- the extent to which foreign and local students have opportunities to learn from each other;
- the need for academic freedom and participatory pedagogy for everyone in the university community;
- the need for a diverse and varied curriculum.

CONDITIONS OF LEARNING AT HIGH-RANKED UNIVERSITIES

Learning with (and from) the Locals

During my experiences with international higher education there was a lack of interaction with local students, especially at the two non-anglophone institutions, Sciences Po and PKU. In both places, foreign students noted the difficulties of learning about local norms and culture. My friendships at these two places were telltale signs of this. All close friends were international students like myself. I could have invested more time and effort into the process. However, by the time foreign students arrived at Sciences Po, their French peers were in their second year. Their friendship circles had solidified over a year. Much like in high school, once cliques are formed, it is hard for newcomers to insert themselves. At PKU, it was a similar situation. However, what made it more inconvenient was the fact English-based courses were only available to students in the three graduate international programs of the PKU-based Masters of International Relations (MIR), Sciences Po-PKU and LSE-PKU.

Unless Chinese national students were part of these programs (such as the seven in our group), we did not see another Chinese soul aside from our professors. If newcomers were brave enough to take a Chinese-based course, they would have to pass a Chinese exam to prove their language proficiency. None of us did that so we were stuck with each other.

Academic Freedom and Participatory Pedagogy

Chinese authorities yearn for PKU (and Tsinghua) to enter the Shanghai Jiaotong "top-100" universities list. But I doubt that this will happen while Chinese students are lectured at, forced to avoid sensitive issues, and turn in assignments (including master's theses and doctoral dissertations) echoing the Party line. Moreover, there is more to "internationalization" than, for example, listing the number of foreign trips made by professors (see Rhoads et al., 2014).

At each of the four universities, the pedagogy was aligned with the dominant political culture. Hence, at UBC, the LSE and Sciences Po, student views were secured by having them actively involved in the teaching and learning process. In China, students were expected to listen to lectures or watch slideshows. There were vastly unequal power relations in Chinese universities where the student task was to listen and regurgitate on the exam what was said by "experts." Even at one of the top Chinese universities, pedagogy depended on an "empty-vessel" or "stuffed-duck" model.

In 2015, Beijing renounced the notion of China as the "workshop of the world" and committed itself to fostering "innovation" for the 21st century. From what I experienced at PKU, it was hard to imagine much innovation coming out of university classrooms. There were limits on academic freedom (and thus innovation) (Rhoads et al., 2014) and too many lectures that silenced students and rendered their experience (or views) irrelevant. With this as the backdrop, what is the point of waffling about pagodas and lakes?

At UBC, Sciences Po and the LSE, I participated in processes designed to bring everyone into conversations. The best environments were those in which classmates were comfortable with one another. Provided the student body was already diverse, the optimal class size was about 15–20 students, with a knowledgeable, welcoming and understanding professor or teaching assistant who provided encouragement and a wide perimeter for discussion.

The most decisive variable was friendship among colleagues. Being a stranger is not conducive to classroom discussions. However, if each class contains people who are also good friends, it provides a safe learning environment. In order to facilitate such an environment, universities should host events that engage both international students and students who are nationals of the country. In addition to welcoming orientations, social events should be organized throughout the year to forge friendships. Group outings, dances and cultural excursions foster bonds that lead to fruitful conversations.

The Road Ahead

Compared with only 30 years ago, mobility programs have given 21st century university students unprecedented opportunities for personal and cultural growth and career development. Knowing this, there are internationalization offices in many universities and numerous meetings and conferences designed to smooth out the kinks in mobility systems.

Based on my experience at the four universities, it is clear that there are inauthentic and authentic approaches to mobility and internationalization.

Inauthentic Internationalization

In the inauthentic case, the university "vision statement" and "strategic plan" welcomes foreign students and uses "internationalization" as a noun, but this is mostly a marketing ploy and internationalization is a fake. Despite its being in the vision statement, there is only a superficial (or surface) commitment to internationalization.

Where inauthentic internationalization is just a noun, a static concept in the university vision, the student will encounter course outlines entirely concerned with local (rather than global) issues and literature; mono-cultural student services not adapted to the needs of visitors; teaching staff who consider

CONDITIONS OF LEARNING AT HIGH-RANKED UNIVERSITIES

international students a time-consuming nuisance; teachers who expect international students to adapt to the local (hegemonic) system and suppress the need to celebrate (or teach others about) their own culture. They will also experience racism and hear derogatory comments about politics, religion, dress codes and language styles.

Authentic Internationalization

In the authentic case, the university vision statement and strategic plan welcomes foreign students and uses "internationalize" as a verb – a continuous process rather than a static concept. Hence, as part of the process of welcoming foreigners to the university, there is a deep and genuine internationalization of curriculum, pedagogy and student services. As Ms. and Mr. Foreign Student explore the campus and make friends, they will see plentiful and clear evidence of deep commitments to internationalization. The students will encounter course outlines containing international and global content; student services attuned to their needs, struggles and modus operandi; teaching staff who derive genuine joy and pleasure from interacting with foreigners; diverse opinions; courses where international students are provided with ample opportunities to celebrate (and teach) their own heritage and cultures; cultural inclusion; and encouragement to do research on topics relevant to their homeland.

References

Ali, A. (2016, May 4). Japan, China and Hong Kong's universities rise in world reputation rankings. *The Independent*, p. 1.

Brains without borders. (2016, January 30). *The Economist*, pp. 51–52.

Hillary, E. P. (1955). *High adventure*. London: Hodder & Stoughton.

Hillary, E. P. (2003). *View from the summit: The remarkable memoir by the first person to conquer Everest*. New York, NY: Random House.

Knowles, M. S. (1970). *The modern practice of adult education*. New York, NY: Association Press.

Rhoads, R., Wang, X. Y., Shi, X. G., & Chang, Y. C. (2014). *China's rising research universities: A new era of global ambition*. Baltimore, MD: Johns Hopkins University Press.

Symonds, M., & Ellison, L. (2003). *Software: An intimate portrait of Larry Ellison and Oracle*. New York, NY: Simon & Schuster.

University of British Columbia. (2016). *Fact sheet update 4*. Retrieved from http://news.ubc.ca/wp-content/uploads/2016/03/2016_867_Factsheet_update4.pdf

Varghese, N. V. (2008). *Globalization of higher education and cross-border student mobility*. Paris: International Institute for Educational Planning, UNESCO.

Yin, H. B., Lu, G. S., & Wang, W. Y. (2014). Unmasking teaching quality of higher education: Students' course experience and approaches to learning in China. *Assessment and Evaluation in Higher Education, 39*(8), 949–970.

Zhang, W. Y. (2014). *Daxue de luoji* [The logic of the university]. Beijing: Peking University Press.

PART 3

Students and Their Influence on Higher Education Policies

∴

CHAPTER 13

Student Policies and Protests: The Student Movements of the 1960s and the 2012 Canadian "Maple Spring"

Hans G. Schuetze

Abstract

Student unrest and protests are as old as universities and were mostly in reaction to unsatisfactory conditions or policies affecting students. The student movements of the 1960s in the Americas and Western Europe were different as they were in support of, or in opposition to larger social and political issues most of which had little to do with actual student issues or policies. Examples were the opposition to the Vietnam war and the support of social and civic causes such as Women's Liberation and Antiracism. Because of the broad and general nature of these causes students had no immediate or direct impact in spite of the wide publicity of their protests, yet they were quite influential in the longer run. In contrast, the 2012 "Maple Spring" in Quebec and the less widely reported protests in Germany against university tuition concerned a typical student issue and were successful in the short run. This chapter recalls briefly the causes and events and analyzes the differences between the broad movements of the 1960s and the more focused protests some 50 years later.

Keywords

Quebec Maple Spring – 1968 student movement – student protests – Vietnam war – Free Speech movement – Paris 1968 – university tuition

Introduction: The 2012 Maple Spring Student Protests in Quebec

The Maple Spring[1] took place in 2012 in Quebec, Canada's second most populous province which has, like all Canadian provinces, the responsibility for education. It was the name of a wave of long-lasting student protests against the provincial government's plans for increasing university tuition in Quebec.

© KONINKLIJKE BRILL NV, LEIDEN, 2019 | DOI:10.1163/9789004393073_013

The protests were directed against the plan of the government to increase user fees for public services. University tuition fees were to grow by roughly 75 percent over five years. Students claimed the increases would keep individuals from low income families from participating in higher education (HE). They argued also that the planned hikes "constituted a significant ideological shift away from the promises made during Quebec's 'Quiet Revolution' of the 1960s to freeze tuition at a low rate and eventually abolish user fees for education as a means of reversing systemic inequities and building a more equitable society" (Spiegel, 2015, p. 771).

The government justified the increases by arguing that the entire public sector would need to undergo significant funding cuts or increases of user fees in order to make up for huge budget deficits the province was facing. It also emphasized that universities in Quebec had the lowest tuition fees in Canada and the planned tuition increase would bring tuition in Quebec just up to the level of the other Canadian provinces. The government promised, however, to increase financial aid for students from low income families to compensate for the rise in tuition.

In spite of these arguments and the promise of additional aid for needy students, student organizations and social action groups opposed to the fee increases stepped up protests, claiming that education was a public function and an individual right and should, therefore, be funded from the public budget, and not by the students.

While opinion polls showed that many Quebecers sympathized with the students, initially the majority did not support the protests, especially not in Montreal where most of the demonstrations took place and where main streets, public places and subway stations were often blocked and traffic paralyzed or slowed down by the protests.

The students organized strikes, boycotting lectures and seminars and putting up picket lines to prevent students opposed to the protests from entering buildings and attending classes. Whereas many faculty members and sessional lecturers sympathized with the demands of the students, most universities did not formally endorse nor join the strike.

In order to quell the protests and disruptions of public life the government introduced an emergency law prohibiting protests on or near university campuses. The law required prior approval by the police of all gatherings of more than 50 persons and imposed draconian penalties for defying this requirement – an attempt by the government to regain control of the situation by abridging the right to peaceful assembly.

In defiance of this law students stepped up protests and demonstrations, now supported by larger parts of the population. Using mobile phones and

STUDENT POLICIES AND PROTESTS

social media, they organized protests in a flexible and mobile way, often surprising and frustrating the police who were trying to control the situation.

Moreover, students and their organizations were successful in forming a larger coalition with groups who, like the students, saw the tuition hikes as a neo-liberal violation of the social contract. In Montreal, students brought together between 150,000 and 200,000 protesters; around a thousand of whom were arrested and fined for unlawful assembly. People manifested their support also by banging pots, pans and lids in the streets, public places and subway stations.

Convinced that the majority of voters were opposed to the disruptions and defiance of the public order, the Liberal government called an election. It was won by the main opposition party, however, which had sided with the students' cause and promised to cancel the plans for the hikes. When the *Parti Québécois* formed the new government, it called off the tuition hikes.

In an effort to discover the reasons why the Maple Spring was successful while other student protests were not, I look back at some major student movements in the 1960s in North America and Europe which are often seen as models for successful student activism.

Student Activism and Movements in the 1960s

Long before the Maple Spring, there had also been massive protests in many other countries which were student led or where students were prominently involved. However, important as some of them were locally or nationally, news about them did not spread to other countries except much later when new communication technologies such as TV and satellite communication allowed media attention and coverage to spread news of these events world-wide in real time. Thus student unrest and demonstrations in the 1960s and thereafter gained high visibility and became models for similar action in other countries. Not all of these were led by students nor concerned with typical student issues or particular student policies such as access to higher education, unaffordable tuition fees, or rights of students.

Latin America saw massive student protests in the late 1950s and 1960s, for example in Mexico, Brazil, Argentina and Chile protesting the rule of autocratic, military regimes, poverty of most of the population and the lack of basic rights and freedoms. For example, in Mexico where the economy had grown considerably between 1940 and the end of the 1960s, this had not reduced but rather exacerbated social and economic inequality. Access to higher education and in particular to the small prestigious, highly selective university sector was open mainly to the children of the rich land owners and ruling class (Pensado, 2013).

Protests by the "New Left" culminated when Mexico organized the Olympic Games in October, 1968. The protesters argued that hosting the Games, which for the autocratic government was an important high prestige event, would cost the country money that was urgently needed to fight poverty and under-development. When days before the opening of the Olympics some ten thousand protesters gathered peacefully in the Square of the Three Cultures in Mexico City, the police and army crushed the demonstration using assault rifles and tanks and killing some 40 protesters on the spot while many others were arrested, tortured or killed in custody.

Most student demonstrations in the USA between 1964 and the early 1970s were part of larger protest movements, especially against the Vietnam war and the military draft but also in support of social and civic movements, for example Women's Liberation, Anti-Racism ('Black Power'), and the rights of the Mexican immigrant farm-workers ('Chicanos').

The first major student protests to make world-wide headlines were the demonstrations in 1964 by students of the University of California (UC) Berkeley protesting the ban imposed by the university administration against students' plan to hold an anti-Vietnam war rally on campus (the demonstrations became known as 'Free Speech' movement). When students then occupied the central administration building some 800 students and supporters were arrested.

Many other student protests sprang up all over the US following the widely-reported Berkeley events, many of them in protest against the US involvement in Vietnam. For example, in the spring of 1968 protests erupted at Columbia University in New York City after students discovered the cooperation of Columbia with the Pentagon on some war-related activity. Students occupied some university buildings for several weeks until the New York police stormed the buildings using riot gear and tear gas and arresting students.

Protests against the war and the draft continued on many campuses. Prominent became the protests at Kent State University in May 1970 when students burned down a ROTC building[2] and the National Guard shot and killed four of the student protesters. In reaction to the killings more than 450 university, college and high school campuses across the country were shut down by students.

In Western Europe, major student protests occurred basically in all countries at the end of the 1960s. Many were in protest against the Vietnam war but most had also other, partly local causes.

In France, the May 1968 movement started as a small protest action at a suburban university campus outside of Paris when angry students complained about crammed facilities and restrictive housing rules. When the

STUDENT POLICIES AND PROTESTS

administration did not respond students occupied the central administrative offices. The rector called the police who arrested the intruders and closed down the campus.

The students took their protests to the streets of the Latin quarter in Paris where they got lots of attention from the public and support from other students. Some students erected barricades in the streets and police started chasing and clubbing the protesters. using tear gas and arresting hundreds of students. When more students joined the protesters the following day and more barricades went up to prevent the police from making more arrests the government sent in para-military riot troops causing the escalation of protests and street fighting. Television pictures of the barricades, riot troops and unarmed students, burning cars, and ambulances quickly reached the rest of France igniting more protests and strikes in other large cities.

Reacting to the massive demonstrations of a million people and the general strike that had been called by the trade unions, the government retracted ordering the re-opening of the university campuses and the release of arrested protesters. By this time, however, the students were calling for more far-reaching policy changes and changes to the traditional hierarchical education system. Many workers who had followed the call by their unions for a general strike refused to go back to work, even after employers had agreed to significant wage increases. Many spontaneous strikes took place which the unions could no longer control with the strikers and protesters now demanding the abdication of the government and new elections. The government finally gave in and called new elections. Frightened by the war-like scenes in the streets of Paris and other big cities and afraid of anarchy, voters re-elected president de Gaulle's conservative party with a large majority. With that, the strikes and demonstrations came to an end; workers returned to their workplaces and students to the classrooms and libraries.

When the government in West Germany[3] pushed legislation through parliament in May 1968 that were to give the government the power to suspend parliamentary rule as well as some civil rights guarantees in times of emergency, major protests erupted at many universities. These protests co-incided with major demonstrations against both the US war in Vietnam and the nuclear re-armament of NATO countries.

A year earlier there had been violent clashes in West Berlin between students and the police after the police had killed a student who, together with thousands of others, had peacefully demonstrated against the state visit of the Shah of Iran, an autocrat who persecuted and tortured dissenters in his own country. Iran was an important oil producer and cold war ally of the American and the German governments.

Students were also demonstrating because of the lack of reforms of higher education. Although student enrolment as well as the numbers of academic teachers and researchers had doubled in the previous ten years, the strongly hierarchical university structures and the non-inclusive governance system had essentially remained the same as before the war. Students called for reforms that would give students and young researchers both voice and vote in university governance.

The conflict culminated in April 1968 when a well-known student leader was shot in the street at Berlin by a right wing gunman which caused widespread and sometimes violent protests at all universities.

While West German students were protesting against the war in Vietnam, the plans for changing the constitution in times of emergeny, and the lack of higher education reform, their peers in East Germany were living under the authoritarian, repressive and anti-democratic rule of the Communist Party. For them to challenge the iron fist of the party would have required an uprising that would have led to mass arrests, harsh penalties and increased oppression. Rather than to the student protests in West Germany students in East Germany were anxiously looking at events in neighboring Czechoslovakia where the head of the Communist party, Alexander Dubček, had promised reforms that would create "socialism with a human face," challenging both the communist doctrine of the dictatorship of the proletariat and the Soviets' grip on his country. When the peaceful revolt of the "Prague Spring" was crushed in August 1969 by an invasion of Russian and other Warsaw Pact troops, the hopes of East Germans for democratic reforms came to a sudden end.

Causes, Contexts, Patterns and Outcomes of Student Protest Movements

Discussing the contexts, causes, patterns and outcomes of the Maple Spring and the student movements of the 1960s, one must be aware of the differences in the cultural and political contexts in which they occurred and the causes that brought the protesters into the streets. The student protests in the US and Western Europe some fifty years earlier were different in several aspects from those recent ones in Quebec – even if, on the surface, pictures and patterns looked similar: unarmed students and fellow-protesters voicing their demands mostly peacefully while the police were armed and in riot gear, using clubs, tear gas and sometimes guns as they broke up crowds and arresting protesters.

In the following section I discuss the political, social, economic and cultural context of the protess, the main causes of student discontent, the support

STUDENT POLICIES AND PROTESTS

students had for example from political parties, trade unions, the media, and the general public.

Context and Causes

In the US, the massification of higher education and economical and social factors played a role in the genesis of a youth protest culture. A CIA report on "Restless Youth" from September 1968 (cited by Klimke, 2011, p. 1) summarized this development:

> Youthful dissidence, involving students and nonstudents alike, is a world-wide phenomenon. ... Because of the revolution in communications, the ease of travel, and the evolution of society everywhere, student behavior never again will resemble what it was when education was reserved for the elite. ... Thanks to the riots in West Berlin, Paris, and New York and sit-ins in more than twenty other countries in recent months, student activism has caught the attention of the world.

Besides these general factors, the student movement in the US was part of a widespread opposition against the war in Vietnam. The 1964 Free Speech movement at the Berkeley campus of the University of California actually started with a rally on the campus against the war and the military draft. At the same time, other political and social causes ignited and fueled student protests: the fight for gender equality (Women's Liberation) and against racism (Black Power) were other important causes.

Some analysts saw the student movement primarily as a rebellion against the parent generation and their values and life style (Feuer, 1969; Bell & Kristol, 1969), others as a political coming-of-age of the post-war generation (deGroot, 1998; Horn, 2007; Lipset, 1970). The protests in the US and in Europe were also part of a major cultural revolution. Bob Dylan's song "The Times They Are A-Changing" expressed and mirrored the feelings of a new generation and new age. Writers like Jack Kerouac (*On the Road*), Hermann Hesse (*Steppenwolf*), and Albert Camus (*The Rebel*) gave this new generation an identity and a voice. In the US, the hippie movement propagated a new lifestyle, breaking with the bourgeois values and conventions of their parents' generation. Drugs, independence, and opposition to power and authority (as expressed in the musical "Hair") were part of this new lifestyle. The "sexual revolution" ("Free Love") which was made possible by the availability of birth control pills giving women unprecedented personal freedom.

Although the anti-Vietnam-war movement was also fueling student unrest, students in Western Europe protested primarily society's old power structures that had not changed much, in spite of new constitutions having come into force after the war. The government in Germany young people lost confidence in the new democratic governments when it was discovered that many personalities in public life, for example judges, high level administrators and government ministers, had been active members of the Nazi party and collaborators with the Nazi government and its institutions during the "Third Reich." Students were especially enraged upon discovering that some of their professors had been propagating Nazi ideology such as racist theories and fascist models of law and government.

In France, authority was challenged because of the wide-ranging powers that the constitution gave to the president and the weak role the opposition played in the system. But there were other political issues at play, such as the war of independence of France's former colonies in North Africa, the role of the military and the resistance by many of the French settlers and eventually their return (*"pieds noirs"*) to the homeland. At the same time, the media revealed that many former Nazi collaborators who had worked during WW-2 for the Vichy government, which ran the occupied parts of France working closely together with the Germans, were still holding influential positions in French public life after the war.

Although students in France and West Germany were also challenging bourgeois values and life styles, they were more political than most of their counterparts in the US. An active and visible minority among them was advocating alternative political concepts, especially communist (Marxist or Trotzkyist) rule. They denied or played down the fact that Marxism, at least in the form of the 'dictatorship of the proletariat,' did not work without bloody oppression, as the uprisings of workers and students in Eastern Europe had shown.[4] It was for this reason that most students did not follow their ideological direction even if supporting many of the protest actions they were organizing.

Causes and Objectives

Although the higher education systems in the US and Western Europe had massively grown after WW-2 in terms of institutions, students and academic staff, this expansion had happened without much re-thinking and discussing of the changing functions and purposes of universities in a modern, democratic society. Students in France and West Germany insisted that universities could not be reformed top-down by state bureaucrats or senior academics and administrators making all important decisions without consultation. New structures and participatory processes were needed that would give students and the non-professoriate academic staff (i.e., long-term assistants and junior, non-tenured professors) voice and vote in the reform process.

STUDENT POLICIES AND PROTESTS

In the U.S. three major causes of student discontent and activism can be distinguished, which partly overlapped and fed into each other. The first was a general discontent and politicalization of students. Coming mostly from middle class families and participating in higher education in much greater numbers than the generation of their parents, students were more critical of formal authority and unafraid to challenge it when it was unresponsive to their demands. This critique was first formulated in a comprehensive fashion in the Port Huron Manifesto of 1962 by the Students for a Democratic Society (SDS) and served as ideological platform and point of reference for much of the 1960s. The Manifesto criticized American society and its capitalist foundations and called for an active, egalitarian and participatory democracy. Universities, being "the only mainstream institution that is open to participation by individuals of nearly any viewpoint" were seen as central to achieving this vision. However, for universities to assume such a role would require major reforms:

> An alliance of students and faculty ... must make fraternal and functional contact with allies in labor, civil rights, and other liberal forces outside the campus. They must import major public issues into the curriculum – research and teaching on problems of war and peace is an outstanding example. They must make debate and controversy, not dull pedantic cant, the common style for educational life. They must consciously build a base for their assault upon the loci of power. (SDS, 1962, p. 18)

Another major cause cause of student activism was support of the Civil Rights Movement. The fight of black and other racial minority students against racism and for equal access and treatment activated many students to protest in their support. "Women's Liberation" was another major cause that involved student activism. Although the battlefield of the fight for equal rights for women and racial minorities was much larger than university campuses and classrooms, these larger political conflicts were fertile grounds for student activism (Rhoads, 2016).

The third and probably most important cause of student protest was the opposition to the war in Vietnam. Students protested with marches, sit-ins, strikes and the occupation of campus buildings against "US imperialism" and demanded that the government withdraw US forces from Vietnam. America's war in South East Asia became one of the main political controversies and cause for student activism in the entire Western world, generating a vigorous and polarizing debate and militant action.

Organization and Mobilization

Although there was a high degree of spontaneity and ad hoc action systematic organization was of central importance. As a look at the major protest movements of the 1960s and the Quebec 2012 Maple Spring shows, how students organized themselves and how they organized their activities had a significant impact on their effect.

Most universities in the West have a multitude of social or cultural circles or associations, sports clubs, and political groupings of different kinds in which students engage. Besides these voluntary organizations, students automatically become members of student associations or unions when they enroll in university. These latter associations have the mandate of administering various student affairs (for example housing, child care, employment services) and represent the students' views vis-à-vis the university leadership. These organizations also often speak on behalf of their membership to the (public) media on student issues; however they have no general 'political' mandate and must stay therefore within the mandate of student relevant questions.[5]

A main problem for organizers of student action was to broadly engage and forge – often ad-hoc and temporary – coalitions of different social and civil rights groups, not just of students. To gain the attention and support of the media and of influential personalities and eventually the public is of utmost importance. For example support by public intellectuals and writers are important: Some of France's leading intellectuals, among them the philosopher Jean Paul Sartre, supported the students' cause and marched with them in the streets. Likewise, many intellectuals supported the students' cause in Germany, thus the philosophers Theodor Adorno and Herbert Marcuse[6] and the writers (and later literature Nobel laureates) Heinrich Böll and Günther Grass.

When Quebec students in 2012 started strike actions against the plans for substantial tuition hikes, several student organizations that had in the past successfully mobilized their members[7] agreed to closely collaborate. Unlike student organizations in other Canadian provinces, Quebec student organizations are known for their militancy and have a long history of organizing strikes, some of which have been successful (Bégin-Caouette & Jones, 2014).

The 2012 strike action was the longest and by far the best organized. Protest actions included frequent nightly demonstrations, traffic blockages and other activities over six months. Students found original ways of getting the attention of the media and keeping their cause alive by various creative means, for example students of theater presenting silent choreographies in Montreal subway stations. Moreover, the organizers, aware of the importance of publicity, spread news of the strike and its cause to forums outside Quebec, for example

STUDENT POLICIES AND PROTESTS   249

the Cannes Film Festival and the Saturday Night Live show in New York City (Bégin-Caouette & Jones, 2014). All these actions demonstrated that this strike against tution fees was not just a one-time protest but an ongoing fight for fair access, part of the specific Quebec student culture.

Impact and Outcomes

Most student protests did not yield immediate or direct results as far as the broad political causes and issues were concerned that had brought students to the streets. In many ways, however, the protests created or contributed to an increasing awareness of the causes and issues the students were protesting or supporting. This was clearly the case of the political and military dominance of the US in the Third World. The end of the war in Vietnam was the result of many forces and actions, of which the student protest and engagement were a visible part.

There were also some more direct results with respect to the demands from the protesting students. In Berkeley, the university administration did allow "free speech" on campus, i.e., debates, demonstrations, teach-ins, and sit-ins against the Vietnam war and in favor of the various social causes that students supported. In New York, Columbia University canceled collaboration with the institute that had close connections with the Pentagon and the Vietnam war.

Student protests in West Germany put into the spotlight the Nazi past of some of the leading members of the political and cultural elite, as well as the continuing racist tendencies and undemocratic structures of society. As a consequence of student protests many former Nazi officials and academics in the public realm resigned or lost their job.

Although there was no direct and immediate impact, in the medium and longer term the 1968 student movement caused a fundamental liberalization of German society in many ways – political, social and cultural. A few higher education reforms were the result when some provinces (Länder) changed their university laws, giving students and young researchers representation and vote in formal governance decisions.

Some former student leaders and activists chose "the long march through the institutions" by going into politics. Tom Hayden, the author of the Port Huron Manifesto and civil rights activist, served 18 years in the California State Assembly and State Senate. In Germany several activists helped to form an ecological basic-democratic movement which eventually became a political party (the "Greens") and, especially for young people, an alternative to the established parties. Best known were Daniel Cohn-Bendit ("Dany le Rouge"), one of the leaders of the May 68 French student movement who later became a member of the European parliament, and Joschka Fischer, a well-known student activist who became the leader of the Green Party and in the early 2000s became Germany's Foreign Minister and Deputy Federal Chancellor.

In France, after the May protests the newly elected government of president de Gaulle appointed Edgar Faure as minister of education; many of the student demands were met by major reforms of higher education which, among other things, gave universities more autonomy and students more participatory rights.[8]

The protesting students in Quebec had two main goals, closely interconnected: the abolition of all tuition fees for post-secondary education and the rescinding of the increases of tuition fees mandated by the government. Both were genuine student issues, as they concerned questions of affordability of and access to higher education. The call for a total abolition of fees was directed against a more general, larger development, namely the erosion, as students and other opponents of the government saw it, of the social contract of the "Quiet Revolution," the major social and political transformation that had taken place in Quebec in the 1960s (Bégin-Caouette & Jones, 2014; Bissonnette, 2015). This larger goal was not attained, as tuition fees remained in place. The students were partly successful, however, when the new government did not go ahead with the tuition increases.

"Outcomes" are not always permanent. After the Free Speech Movement of 1964 had been successful in that the university leadership allowed political debate and demonstrations on campus, the conservative California governor (and later US president), Ronald Reagan who had been critical of the students' demands and protests, appointed a new Board of Regents which fired the liberal university leader and ordered a reversal of some of the university's student policies. However, the opening of university campus facilities to political debate and demonstrations survived (Freeman, 2004).[9]

In Quebec, the newly elected government that had promised a reversal of the tuition increases mandated by the previous Liberal government did not last long, and after new elections a Liberal government came back into power. It has not gone ahead with raising tuition, but since the structural deficit of the provincial budget is still the same, it is probably just a matter of the government waiting for the opportune moment to do so.

Conclusions

Students have been prominent actors in many revolutions and revolutionary movements. They have influenced society as agents of change, either demanding change, or protesting change. They have sometimes acted on issues that were directly affecting their own conditions of living and learning, but more frequently they protested, together with other groups and forces, larger societal issues.

Partly as a result of the demands by the 1960s movements, many of the policies and conditions of higher education have changed over the last 50 years. At least four factors have profoundly changed since the 1960s: the massification of higher education and the differentiation of higher education institutions, which have opened access for many young people who before and right after WW2 were not eligible; the recognition of student rights and participation in university governance; in Western Europe the increase of university autonomy; and the financing of HE whereby students are required to shoulder a much higher share of the costs of their education. This latter issue, while not of much importance in the 1960s, is now a major topic for political discussion and in many countries the main cause of student discontent and protest actions. The Maple Spring was not the first and will not be the last example of protests against the rising financial burden students are expected to bear.

Importantly, there is a significant difference between student protests in the 1960s and now with regard of the organization of student actions: the role that new information and telecommunication technologies and the social media play. Although in the 1960s new media like television and satellites contributed to the wide diffusion of the images of the protests, the Internet and social media that have been developed in the 1990s and subsequently have not only further magnified the news and made it available at any time and any place, they have also become a major instrument of mobilization and the flexible and efficient organization of protests (Epstein, 2012). Different from the media of the 1960s, these new media also allow protests and support of demands in other forms besides in-person gatherings and actions of various kinds in the streets and on campuses. In particular, on-line petitions and discussion forums, advocacy and networks of emotional support allow protests and protesters to be local and, at the same time, global (Castels, 2012).

Have students themselves changed and their propensity to engage in political and social causes declined? Some analysts suggest that in Western societies "students are becoming more individualistic and perhaps more interested in subjective well-being, self-expression, and quality of life" (Altbach & Klemancic, 2014, p. 3) and therefore less willing to engage in protest actions in support of democratic rule and human rights.

Although the Quebec Maple Spring and other, more recent student protests, for example in Chile from 2006 to 2013, and the "Fees-must-fall" protests in South Africa (2015) suggest that fees and other "student issues" are still important causes, other more political motivated protests (such as the Tahrir Square protests, the Gezi Park protests in Turkey and Hong Kong's "Umbrella Movement") suggest that students continue to engage, often in alliance with other groups, for political causes and remain a potent force of protest, even if the modes of involvement are changing.

Notes

1 A play on words as "maple" in French is "érable," which sounds like "Arab"; the term "Arab Spring" alluded to the widespread protests in 2011 against authoritarian governments in Tunisia, Egypt and other Arab countries. The maple leaf is a symbol of Canadian unity and shown on the Canadian national flag.

2 The Reserve Officers' Training Corps (ROTC) are a group of college and university-based officer training programs for training students to become officers for the US Armed Forces.

3 After WW2 Germany was divided into the Federal Republic of Germany and the German Democratic Republic. The former was a member of the NATO, a military alliance of Western countries while Communist East Germany belonged to the Warsaw Pact, a military alliance under the command of the Soviet Union.

4 In Eastern Europe, student protests were part of a larger political opposition to the oppressive communist regimes that had been installed by the Soviets after WW-2 and were tightly controlled by Moscow. Uprisings in Eastern European countries, such as in East Germany (1953), Poland (1956) and Hungary (1956) were part of the opposition against the Soviet regime and their puppet governments in Berlin, Warsaw and Budapest. Although the protests in Czechoslovakia in 1968 were different in that they were led by a communist leader trying to reform, not abolish communism, they were all crushed by Sowjet tanks because of their perceived threat to the Soviet rule of the communist bloc. Although students were visible as part of these protests, and some of them were killed and and many arrested. students were not the leaders of these uprisings.

Likewise, when much later, in 1989, peaceful demonstrations against the communist regime in East Germany made the Berlin wall come down and, with it, the iron curtain in the rest of Europe, students did not play a prominent role. Partly this had to do with the way young people in communist Germany (and other communist countries) were carefully screened before being admitted to higher education. Youth whose parents were members of the communist party or one of its sub-structures, or who came from an industry or farm worker family background, had privileged access while others from bourgeois or business or from practicing Christian families had very little chance to be admitted to university studies.

STUDENT POLICIES AND PROTESTS   253

5 This line between student issues proper and statements of a political nature is sometimes difficult to draw. For example, in Germany mandatory student organizations successfully lobbied for a national student-aid program but were kept, ultimately by court order, from speaking out against organizing activities protesting the Vietnam war. The introduction of student fees was clearly a 'student matter' and student associations had the mandate for organizing strikes, sit-ins, and other forms of student action. The protests against state visits of foreign dictators (the Shaw of Iran) or the US involvement in Vietnam, triggers of the large-scale student demonstrations in Germany in the late nineteen sixties, were clearly of a "political" nature and outside the student mandate.

6 Marcuse was teaching at the time at the University of California, and his writings, especially his treatise on "the one-dimensional man," were also influential among Berkeley and other US student activists.

7 The *Féderation étudiante universitaire du Quebec* (FEUQ), and the *Association nationale des étudiants et étudiantes du Quebec* (ANEEQ), as well as the *Association pour une solidarité syndicale étudiante* (ASSÉ). Together with other non-student groups that were against fee increases and in support of a strike they formed a larger coalition with the acronym CLASSE (the additional "CL" standing for "*coalition large*"; the acronym suggesting a matter of class struggle).

8 Faure later became chairman of a UNESCO commission on the development of education and the main author of the 1972 UNESCO report *Learning to be: The world of education today and tomorrow* which became an influential reference point for education reforms in many countries.

9 More than fifty years later the principle of "free speech" at universities is being challenged anew in Berkeley and other US universities, this time, however, not by the government or university presidents but by radical groups insisting universities should limit free speech in order to guarantee "safe spaces" and "political correctness."

References

Altbach, P. G., & Klemancic, M. (2014). Student activism remains a potent force worldwide. *International Higher Education, 76*, 2–3. Retrieved from https://doi.org/10.6017/ihe.2014.76.5518

Bégin-Caouette, O., & Jones, G. A. (2014). Student organizations in Canada and Quebec's "Maple Spring." *Studies in Higher Education, 39*(3), 412–425.

Bell, D., & Kristol, I. (1969). *Confrontation: The student rebellion and the universities.* New York, NY: Basic Books.

Bissonnette, J. F. (2015). Resisting the discipline of debt: The unfulfilled radicalism of the 2012 Quebec student strike. *Theory and Event, 18*(3).

Castels, M. (2012). *Networks of outrage and hope: Social movements in the internet age.* Cambridge: Polity Press.

DeGroot, G. J. (Ed.). (1998). *Student protest: The sixties and after.* London and New York, NY: Longman.

Epstein, I. (Ed.). (2012). *The whole world is texting: Youth protest in the information age.* Rotterdam, The Netherlands: Sense Publishers.

Faure, E., & International Commission on the Development of Education. (1972). *Learning to be: The world of education today and tomorrow.* Paris: UNESCO.

Feuer, L. S. (1969). *The conflict of generations: The character and significance of student movements.* New York, NY: Basic Books.

Freeman, J. (2004). The Berkeley Free Speech movement. In I. Ness (Ed.), *Encyclopedia of American social movements* (pp. 1178–1182). Armonk, NY: M.E. Sharpe.

Giroux, H. A. (2013). The Quebec student protest movement in the age of neoliberal terror. *Social Identities, 19*(5), 515–535.

Horn, G. R. (2007). *The spirit of '68: Rebellion in Western Europe and North America, 1956–1976.* Oxford: Oxford University Press.

Klimke, M. (2011). *The other alliance: Student protest in West Germany and the United States in the global sixties.* Princeton, NJ: Princeton University Press.

Lipset, S. M. (1970). *Students in revolt.* Baltimore, MD: Discover Books.

Pensado, J. M. (2013). *Rebel Mexico: Student unrest and authoritarian political culture during the long sixties.* Stanford: Stanford University Press.

Rhoads, R. A. (2016). Student activism, diversity, and the struggle for a just society. *Journal for Diversity in Higher Education, 9*(3), 189–202.

Spiegel, J. B. (2015). Rève général illimité? The role of creative protest in transforming the dynamics of space and time during the 2012 Quebec student strike. *Antipode, 47*(3), 770–791.

Students for a Democratic Society (SDS). (1962). *Port Huron statement.* Retrieved from http://www2.iath.virginia.edu/sixties/HTML_docs/Resources/Primary/Manifestos/SDS_Port_Huron.html

CHAPTER 14

Collective Student Action and Student Associations in Quebec

Alexandre Beaupré-Lavallée and Olivier Bégin-Caouette

Abstract

Student associations have been a part of Canada's higher education systems for over a century, especially in the province of Quebec. Their formal roles and responsibilities as well as their impact and their inner workings are ill understood, even though they are ever-present in public space. Quebec student associations have used a remarkable arsenal of legal and political means to achieve their goals. Societal change, however, might be swinging legislation and civic rights momentum in Quebec in a direction that could force the student movement to alter its approach to advocacy and social contestation. This chapter describes the organization of student associations in the province. It further describes the rights provided to associations in the legal and legislative context of the province, as well as the recent challenges to these rights. Finally, we test the *orientation-focus* framework (Altbach, 1968) on the events of the Maple Spring of 2012.

Keywords

Maple Spring – student associations – Quebec higher education – orientation-focus framework – student activism

Introduction

Student associations are an inherent part of the higher education landscape in the largely French-speaking province of Quebec (Canada). They have undergone well-documented changes since the late 1960s, gaining legal protection, pushing affordability and social change agendas, and being credited with government turnovers (Bégin-Caouette & Jones, 2014). In 2012, social media and global attention came together to push the Quebec student protests to the fore

© KONINKLIJKE BRILL NV, LEIDEN, 2019 | DOI:10.1163/9789004393073_014

of public awareness. The spring social phenomenon which lasted well into the summer was quickly dubbed the *printemps érable* ("Maple Spring"), a play of words on the previous year's *printemps arabe* (Arab Spring).

Yet, despite its media presence, the student organization has been surprisingly little studied. Of the general literature on student associations, Altbach (2007) said that "[s]tudent movements and organizations at the postsecondary level have an immense and *often ignored* impact not only on students and student cultures but also on academic institutions and sometimes on society" (p. 329, emphasis added). Likewise, Robinson (2010) observed that "[i]n spite of their active presence in Canadian higher education, the role and influence of these [...] student associations has been all but ignored in the literature and certainly merits further attention" (p. 92). In Europe, "it is rather surprising how little scholarly research exists on student representative organisations" (Klemenčič, 2012).

This chapter's aim is twofold. It first complements the existing literature by presenting an overview of the student movement in Quebec that highlights its key legal and organizational characteristics. Second, it argues that Altbach's orientation-focus theory (1968) provides a robust analytical tool to analyze the social institution of student associations, and illustrates this through a brief analysis using the lens of the Maple Spring.

Student Associations in Quebec: Historical, Organizational and Legal Considerations

Student associations, clubs and media have been part of Quebec higher education since its inception. Gagnon (2008) places their first activist purpose in the 1950s. When Quebec Premier Maurice Duplessis refused to allow federal funds to be transferred to universities, the Catholic French-Canadian Youth Association denounced the decision with a call for a strike (Bégin-Caouette & Jones, 2014; Gagnon, 2008).

In 1963, the student organizations from three Quebec universities founded the *Union générale des étudiants du Québec* (UGÉQ). Through its six years of existence, it set the path for a first cycle of radicalization, with rhetoric requesting, among other demands, that hierarchical barriers between students and professors be brought down and that universities be co-managed (Gagnon, 2008). UGÉQ folded in 1969 and was replaced with the equally assertive *Association nationale des étudiants et étudiantes du Québec* (ANEEQ) in 1975. In 1981, tensions between reformist and activist tendencies came to a head when the ANEEQ's *university affairs caucus* split from the organization to form its own federation of associations dedicated to university affairs and espousing a more reformist philosophy: the *Regroupement des associations étudiantes universitaires* (RAEU). That same year, a federation of college student associations was created, the *Fédération des associations étudiantes collégiales du Québec* (FAECQ) (Bélanger, 1984). These two associations would evolve into the *Fédération étudiante universitaire du Québec* (FEUQ) and the *Fédération étudiante collégiale du Québec* (FECQ), respectively. The ANEEQ dissolved a few years later, in 1994, amidst internal strife. The more radical wing of the student movement, which represented students from both colleges and universities, founded the *Association pour une solidarité syndicale étudiante* (ASSÉ) in 2001. Two opposite ideals of the student movement—a more utilitarian, pragmatist wing and a more idealistic, radical wing – were thus already in place in the late 1970s.

Today, student associations in Quebec are part of a uniquely structured higher education system. The *Report of the Royal Commission of Inquiry on Education* (Royal Commission of Inquiry on Education in the Province of Quebec, 1967) called for the creation of a post-secondary system divided into two discrete, sequential types of institutions: colleges and universities. Generally speaking, students are required to complete a two-year program at a college before applying at universities, usually for three-year bachelor degrees.

Colleges and universities tend to differ in their organization. Universities usually align with the classic model of discipline-based academic units (such as departments), which are grouped in larger structures (faculties or schools). Colleges, on the other hand, tend to have much flatter organizational structures, without schools or faculties.

As in many other jurisdictions,[1] Quebec students have their associative structures imbedded in the legal framework of higher education. The *Act respecting the accreditation and financing of students' associations* (the *Act*) grants student associations official recognition[2] and determines the nature of the membership, the financial relationship between the association and its members, the legal status of the association and its status within the institution (Klemenčič, 2014). As it turns out, the *Act* gives accredited associations access to considerable material and symbolic resources (Bégin-Caouette & Jones, 2014; Klemenčič, 2014; Lajoie & Gamache, 1990).

The *Act* makes membership automatic and grants the associations the right to collect dues from their members, the payment of which is enforced by the obligation to pay the dues in order to register (Article 54). Associations must be incorporated under the *Business Corporations Act*. Finally, the Act grants accredited associations a monopoly on student representation in the unit covered by the accreditation, excluding all other groups (Article 28).

The *Act* seems to go out of its way to ensure that associations will not depend on the institutions' authorities to function. Colleges and universities are removed from the decision-making process regarding the fees levied by the association. The obligation of incorporation precludes administrative intervention in the association's affairs, a level of autonomy that should technically allow the association to "hold authorities accountable to student interests" (Klemenčič, 2014, p. 401).

At the same time, we present the hypothesis that the *Act* facilitates the daily operations of associations in two ways. First, the *Act* mandates the institution to collect said dues together with the tuition fees (Article 53). Second, it mandates the institution to provide the accredited association with the names and addresses of the dues-paying members. These obligations relieve associations of having to devote time to gathering basic resources or information. In addition, the monopoly of representation conferred upon accredited associations further alleviates the political necessity of having to periodically defend their legal legitimacy when participating in institutional governance. The implications of such advantages are considerable, at least from an organisational standpoint, as the associations can use the resources that would have been devoted to fundraising for other purposes, such as community organization, lobbying, research and professional staff budgets. Research has yet to compare the impact of this shift of internal resources allocation on the efficiency of student associations.

Defining Student Associations

We use the term "student association" to describe the organization legislated by the aforementioned *Act*: an incorporated entity whose membership is made up exclusively of students from a definite unit of accreditation and which enjoys a monopoly over the representation of students' interests within said unit of accreditation. While this definition matches the *Act*'s intent, it does not present a definition of what "students' interests" means.

The aforementioned *Act* spells out the areas covered by the term *students' interests*, as the legally imposed mission of student associations is to represent students and their interests, "particularly respecting teaching, educational methods, student services and the administration of the educational institution" (Article 3). This definition is very similar to that provided by Klemenčič (2014) for *student governments,* which "represent and defend the interests of the collective student body" (p. 396).

Maroy, Doray, and Kabore (2014), through the analysis of the public discourse at the provincial level, confirm the contemporary cohabitation of the two duelling ideologies identified through history. One[3] considers the student as being primarily *a student* and assumes that organizations' focus should be to defend and enhance students' education and living conditions (Altbach, 1968; Maroy et al., 2014). This philosophy is best illustrated by the lobbying history of the *Federations*, which have focused on a freeze of tuition fees in order to foster access (Bégin-Caouette & Jones, 2014; Maroy et al., 2014), increased scrutiny of institutional administrations in order to insure efficient internal resource allocation (FEUQ, 2007; Maroy et al., 2014) and increased sharing of power within institutions (FEUQ, 2007). Compromise is often perceived as necessary because achieving the end becomes a justification for giving something away, an uneasy relationship explored in more detail by Klemenčič (2012).

The second ideology has been upheld by the *Association pour une solidarité syndicale étudiante* (ASSÉ) and is much more paradigm-shifting (Maroy et al., 2014) as it places the student at the centre of a broader social struggle against neoliberalism (ASSÉ, 2015; Maroy et al., 2014). It will usually reject compromise as a means of action (Bégin-Caouette & Jones, 2014) and adopt a more militant approach to mobilization. It also tends to embrace adjacent social causes such as gender equality, environmentalism and LGBT advocacy.

This dichotomy between a reformist, transactional student-centred philosophy on the one hand, and a more militant, activist and confrontational philosophy on the other, is also found in research regarding national student organizations in Europe (Klemenčič, 2012). Student associations are seen as either *interest groups* or *social movements*. The former establish a trading relationship with the State, one based on reciprocal benefit, a preference for lobbying over conflict and an emphasis on "issues directly affecting students" (Klemenčič, 2012). The latter tend to amalgamate student interests with resistance in a global fight against values (such as neoliberalism or capitalism) rather than specific events or policy items.

Much like Maroy et al. (2014) and Klemenčič (2012), Altbach (1968) uses dichotomies to characterize organizations and movements. However, he provides *two* spectra of analysis: one for the orientation taken by movements, and the other for the focus of their action.

The *orientation* spectrum ranges from a "normative" end to a "value" end. *Normative* orientation is the propensity of a movement to limit its actions to one specific issue, such as a tuition-fee hike or reduced financial aid. *Value* orientation, on the other end, is the action aimed at larger, ideological issues, such as feminism or class warfare.

The *focus* spectrum ranges from an "etudialist" to a "societal" focus. Altbach describes etudialism as student- or campus-centered activism, regardless of its cause or origin. The issues at hand tend to be more concrete for the average student and limited in scope to the student status. The societal focus, on the other hand, aims at a broader perspective and views student issues within a larger context reaching beyond the university. Thus, the variety of societal issues tends to be wider than that of purely student issues, as they can be of political (elections), macro-economical (capitalism) or social (poverty) in nature.

Having set the conceptual context of the study, we will first analyze the legal framework in which student associations operate, and contrast its key principles with the aforementioned concepts of common core, voluntary participation, and limited responsibility. We will then proceed with a preliminary analysis of the Maple Spring events and fallout using Altbach's orientation-focus theory.

The Maple Spring: A Summary

In 2010–2011, at the urging of the university presidents' association, the Liberal government announced tuition fees would be increased by $1,625 over the five following years, starting from a base of $2,200 (Maroy et al., 2014). While the Fall semester of 2011 was spent educating students and creating coalitions (Bégin-Caouette & Jones, 2014; Rashi, 2011), ASSÉ took a page from its 2005 campaign and widened its tactical membership to any association, even those members of the Federations, which shared the goal of abolishing tuition fees altogether and recognized striking as a legitimate mean to achieve that end (Bégin-Caouette & Jones, 2014; Nadeau-Dubois, 2013).

The notion of "strike" itself is blurry, as students in Quebec do not have the right to "strike" in the same way salaried workers have the right to collectively cease work as a means of exerting pressure on employers before or during collective bargaining negotiation (Labour code). As the relation between the HEIs and students is not the same as the relation between an employer and an employee, many argue that there is no "right to strike." De facto strike action is, therefore, often referred to as "boycotting" (Weinstock, 2012b).

In reality, students' associations use boycotting in much the same way as labour unions use strikes; boycotting is widely used and often successful in achieving its aims (Bédard, 2006; Bégin-Caouette & Jones, 2014; Lacoursière, 2007). Student associations use general assemblies or referenda to conduct strike votes that they then enforce by physically blocking access to classrooms and other facilities – with the aim of creating enough pressure so that administration will give in to their demands.

Universities have reacted very differently over time and from one institution to the other. In some situations, the institution will recognize the decision as legitimate and "suspend classes" for the duration of the strike/boycott ("Étudiants en grève au cégep de Sherbrooke," 2015). Others, as was the case during the 2012 Maple Spring and the 2015 spring action, use legal means to enforce the accessibility of their buildings (*Université du Québec à Montréal* c. *Association facultaire des étudiants en arts de l'Université du Québec à Montréal*).

There was very little challenge to the student associations' practice of striking or boycotting until the events of 2012 (Makela, 2014). In March of that year, the *Law Students' Association* of the Université de Montréal filed a provincial injunction to ensure that students would have access to institutions. While the application was denied (Lemay & Laperrière, 2012), it set the tone for a series of legal challenges, which came in two flavours: institutional (initiated by colleges or universities) and individual. While individual challenges aimed at providing individual students access to their classroom or their education (Makela & Audette-Chapdelaine, 2013), the institutional challenges tried more often than not to provide a safe working environment or general access to the buildings and classrooms.

In response, the government enacted Bill 78 in May 2012, *An Act to enable students to receive instruction from the postsecondary institutions they attend*, which was designed to reduce the impact of the protest by forcing professors to teach their courses and by forbidding associations from blocking the entrance to universities and colleges, thus almost nullifying associations' means to enforce strike votes. Associations that did not comply with the legislation could lose their official recognition accreditation and be subject to fines. Importantly, the legislation also included provisions that were designed to limit protests, including requiring that the itinerary of every protest march of more than 50 people had to be provided to the police at least eight hours in advance (Bill 78, 2012; Weinstock, 2012a). This *Act* actually fanned the flames of public outcry, as more social groups joined in the protests. Altercations between police and protesters were daily news footage. It became obvious that the student protests provided a catalyst for those portions of Quebec society that felt that the Liberal government had lost its legitimacy to govern the province.

In August of 2012, Premier Jean Charest dissolved the Provincial Assembly and called a general election for the following month, which his Liberal Party lost to the Parti Québécois (PQ), thanks in part to the PQ's promise to convene a summit on higher education. The summit was called only a few months after the election.

The Federations and the ASSÉ displayed widely divergent attitudes towards the Summit. The Federations' demands included a freeze on tuition fees, the creation of a *Conseil National des Universités* (a state agency monitoring quality, accessibility and management) and a modernization of the financial aid infrastructure (Corriveau, 2013). Meanwhile, the ASSÉ demanded that the Summit consider the abolition of tuition fees altogether, a core demand of the association. When the government refused to allow this possibility to be discussed at the Summit, the ASSÉ threatened to boycott the Summit (Shields, 2013).

In the end, the Federations came out partly victorious, securing a promise regarding the *Conseil national des universités* and investments in financial aid. On the core issue of the Printemps Érable, however, they had to admit defeat as the government announced a new formula to determine the increase of fees (Maroy et al., 2014). The government announced it would reduce the tuition fee increases to the value of a newly created indicator, the per-capita increase in disposable household income, based on an estimate by the federal statistics bureau, Statistics Canada (*Comité consultatif sur l'accessibilité financière aux études* [CCAFE], 2013).

Most promises from the summit were sidelined, including the much-vaunted Provincial Council of Universities, when the PQ was replaced by the Liberal Party after another election in May of 2014. The new formula for tuition increase, however, remained in place.

Chronologically, it was the beginning of the end for the FEUQ. The Summit was followed by a string of disaffiliations and, in 2015, the two largest member associations left the Federation (Blais, 2015). Faced with dwindling revenues and internal strife, the Federation announced a cessation of its representation activities in April of 2015 (Gerbet, 2015). A clear causality between the results of the Summit and the demise of the FEUQ remains to be established.

Analysis and Further Research Perspectives

The context and the narration of the events provide crucial data for an analysis based on Altbach's orientation-focus theory (1968). The discourse analysis of Maroy et al. (2014), notably, can be used as a first phase of analysis aimed at extracting broad themes (and clear illustrations) from the associations' public discourse.

As we have seen, the Federations' main objective did not waver: The fees increase had to be cancelled. With this came a limited number of well-defined policy demands. The same focus on a limited number of demands would be repeated during the Summit, as financial aid reform, oversight of institutions and tuition fees freeze comprised the pragmatic, almost functionalist approach to negotiations.

However, once the government and the courts started issuing legislation and decisions that reduced or deterred the use of historically potent and effective strategies (boycotting/striking and protesting), the Federations were forced to alter their discourse and include the protection of these rights in their overall campaign. The announcement of the provisions of Bill 78 forced the Federations to publicly withdraw from their traditional negotiation-focused stance, prompting the president of the FEUQ to declare that "the government just declared war on the student movement. It's worse than the increase in tuition fees!" (Chouinard & Journet, 2012).

The ASSÉ's stated objectives went beyond the simple cancellation of the tuition hike and instead proposed a societal project for the higher education system. Opposing "market influences" (ASSÉ, 2009) in education (such as quality assurance and the professionalization of curricula), the ASSÉ suggested the complete abolition of tuition fees along the lines of the UN's "International Covenant on Economic, Social and Cultural Rights," Article 13c of which states that "[h]igher education shall be made equally accessible to all, on the basis of capacity, by every appropriate means, and in particular by the progressive introduction of free education" (United Nations, 1966, as cited in ASSÉ, 2012).

The rejection of market mechanisms colored the other considerations brought forth by the ASSÉ. For example, during the Summit debate on institutional governance, the Association rejected the inclusion of "external" members on Boards in favour of a more traditional interpretation of the concepts of autonomy and collegiality, an interpretation akin to the definition of self-management (ASSÉ, 2009).

While Maroy et al. (2014) argue that the summit delivered an overall victory for the FEUQ, others argue that the association actually suffered a tactical defeat (Asselin, 2015). By imposing a moderate, incremental tuition hike, the PQ essentially took away the FEUQ's primary argument for its existence – tuition fees freeze – and left it to redefine its identity, without providing the Federation with a major victory to show to its members. For many students, the only outcome of the summit was that the bottom line of their bill would keep rising, albeit more slowly.

The difference between the two groups is glaring and illustrates rather well the two ends of the *orientation* spectrum. While the Federations adopted a normative stance, limiting their actions to demanding a small but well-defined number of demands, the scope of the ASSÉ's discourse went much larger than the matters at hand and tried to address the issue of marketization of higher education. The ASSÉ's actions are definitely over at the *values* end of the spectrum.

The same analysis is not so easily done for the focus spectrum. All associations claimed to place the student at the centre of their discourse. Yet, neither shied away from widening the debate to the subject of the overall performance of the Liberal government. The Federations' demands and program has a larger proportion of student-centred issues compared with the paradigm-changing demands and objectives of the ASSÉ, but even the Federations strayed away from a purely *etudialist* focus by spending quite a lot of resources lobbying, for example, for the *Conseil National des Universités*, although its direct impact on students *as students* was never made clear. On the other hand, the ASSÉ did make a conscious effort to make explicit the effects of their demands on students (notably through websites and pedagogical video packages).

This is where the lack of scaling becomes a detriment to the analysis. Since the actions of the groups do not fit exactly either of the ends of the spectrum, we are left with little or no indication as to how far from each end the groups really stand.

In addition to the lack of scaling, two more perspectives are neglected by the orientation-focus theory. The first blind spot is the inability to explain how a student organization manages to exit the realm of higher education politics and mobilize non-educational agents, be they economic or social. The second blind spot relates to the analytical void about the preferred mode of action, the organization's *modus operandi*.

These issues can be addressed using existing literature. First, identifying associations as *pressure groups* (Bégin-Caouette & Jones, 2014) could provide further insight into the associations' linking up with other organizations. This cooptation of emerging social organizations provided the basis for a concerted effort to channel social protest. However, such occurrences are rare, mostly *ad hoc* and do not explain the movement as a whole.

What is interesting is that despite the sheer number of external agents who joined in the social upheaval during the summer of 2012, the core of the active movement consisted of student associations, as we have defined them, rather than issue-specific student advocacy groups (with pro-feminism or environmental agendas, for example). While the latter did participate in the debate and the mobilization (Lamoureux, 2012), the organization and the enforcement of strikes in institutions remained the sole responsibility of the institutionalized, academic-unit-based student associations.

In reality, labeling student associations as pressure groups in the sense of Pross (1986) rather speaks of a latent potentiality for action, one which lies in the collective, if inconsistent, pooling of resources. This consideration of *resources* could help link the associations' position on Altbach's scales with the yet unexplored issue of resource acquisition and allocation.

The second potentially useful perspective is the corporatist/militant dichotomy suggested by Makela and Audette-Chapdelaine (2013). Its emphasis on the relation associations have with institutional power distribution is revealing of an underlying conception of the higher education institution and of higher education in general. More importantly, in order to fully interpret the relationship that a specific association shares with the institutional power distribution, symbolic or not, the analyst must first consider the patterns of *institutional action*. The inclusion of action as an analytical concept could expand the scope of inquiry of the orientation-focus theory to a point where it could provide a much more accurate descriptive analysis of student associations.

Conclusion

A first consideration regarding the analysis is obfuscated by the obvious tension between the normative Federations and the values-oriented ASSÉ. What is fails to reveal is how *similar* the two groups are if we disregard ideological considerations. Both provincial associations worked according to the same pattern: Local associations, whether from academic units or campus-wide, would vote to affiliate to one of the two groups. Dues were levied and paid to the provincial level by the affiliate level. Decision-making happened in various forms of group meetings, and one needs to stretch the analysis to the perception of the legitimacy of decisions to find a divergence. For example, the ASSÉ viewed their Council as a conduit between individual members in local, general meetings and the provincial executive. Their perception was that the Federations left too much power to a rising class of locally and provincially elected officers to dictate the provincial strategy, thus depriving individual members of a say in the conduct of the campaign (ASSÉ, 2015). There has not yet been an in-depth, comparative analysis of the decision making process of the provincial associations. Moreover, the provincial-level analysis of discourse (Maroy et al., 2014) or action (Bégin-Caouette & Jones, 2014) fails to describe how the basic units of the provincial associations, the member associations, actually used their legal rights and subsequent organizational configuration to their advantage.

And yet, the extent of the legal and organizational autonomy of local and institutional associations is considerable, and "the legitimate power conferred on student governments as a key university constituency or stakeholder through legislation and institutional rules can be significant" (Klemenčič, 2014, p. 399). The *Act* grants accredited associations extensive rights in terms of financial leverage and monopoly of representation. It also grants them protection against outside interference or contestation of their legitimacy. Moreover, the legal delimitations of jurisdiction, sometimes interpreted as restrictive, actually drive home the monopoly aspect of their autonomy. Finally, the obligation to conform to certain regulations (such as incorporation, respect of accounting norms or corporate responsibility considerations) has, in larger associations, spawned a whole professional sector of employees who must compensate the annual turnover of elected officials with additional human capital resources and expertise.

The stratified structure of the student movement created by the *Act* has placed various constituents of the movement in either category of two descriptive dichotomies. We used Altbach's (1968) orientation-focus spectra to qualify the whole of the movement but the orientation spectrum seems more revealing. On one end, associations that limit their members' identity to that of *students* tend to meet the needs and tackle the issues that affect that particular aspect of their identity. On the other end, associations that believe that students are members of the society as a whole tend to use the student movement as a leverage point for demands that go beyond the higher education level and enter the realm of societal protest. The coexistence of these two philosophies creates pressure and friction that ultimately produce internal conflict, external dissociation of discourse and operational shifts, depending on who is elected in which association.

Yet, the omnipresence of striking and boycotting as a means of leveraging pressure for major issues, with a surprisingly high success rate (Bégin-Caouette & Jones, 2014) and by associations at both ends of either spectrum of analysis, suggests that Altbach's dichotomies cannot capture the nuances of the cultures of student associations. Reformist organizations do use tactics that go beyond the "logic of influence" (Klemenčič, 2012).

The mass of yet-to-be-discovered data about student organizations and movements in Quebec (as in Canada) is staggering. Jones's 1995 survey of the financing of these massive lobby-like corporations which, in Quebec, have a legal monopoly over student representation, is about the most recent microeconomical data set we have. While the 2005 and the 2012 protests have sparked a string of books and testimonies, their value remains at that exact level: testimonial, perceptual and anecdotal evidence. Finally, while the organizations have a tendency to publish memoirs, research and memos about basically every aspect of higher education, they stop short of studying themselves.

The unknowns are considerable. For example: What is the socioeconomic profile of elected student leaders? How is student democracy articulated? Are the concepts of efficiency and efficacy shared uniformly across the movement?

What services do student organizations offer and how do they complement, supplement or compete with the services offered by their college or university? Are there patterns to be found in negotiating tactics?

Further research should, therefore, focus on two main areas. First, a serious, historiographical effort must be made to study the institutional, political and cultural evolution of the movement. The 2012 Maple Spring was not an accident. At least two other large-scale student mobilizations have occurred in the last 20 years: the protests against tuition fee hikes in 1996[4] and the protests against cutbacks in financial aid in 2005.[5] These three events are memorable because of their sheer scale, but a careful examination of existing literature reveals another event that should be considered as a turning point: the 2000 *Sommet du Québec et de la jeunesse* (Quebec Youth Summit) of 2000.[6] These four events should serve as the four reference points, and the events leading up to them and their fallout promise to be as analytically revealing as the events themselves.

Second, associations themselves should be studied more closely in order to understand their dynamics and potentiality. Particular emphasis should be placed on how they have reacted to exogenous and endogenous pressures and change. Since these organizations rely in part on institutional memory to perpetuate their mission, there is sufficient rough documentary data available to start an exploratory, descriptive, yet exhaustive study.[7]

Acknowledgements

A first version of this chapter was presented at the 11th Workshop on Higher Education Reform in St. John's, NL, Canada, on August 28th, 2014. The authors express their gratitude to the organizers and the participants in the conference for their highly relevant comments and contributions.

Notes

1 Ontario enacted Bill 184, an *Act respecting student associations at post-secondary educational institutions in Ontario*, in 2011.

2 The *Act* only applies to associations covering an academic unit (in universities) or an institution. Provincial groupings of university and college associations were not included in the *Act* and remain unregulated.

3 The authors attribute this first ideology to the *Fédération des étudiants universitaires du Québec* (FEUQ) and the *Fédération des étudiants collégiaux du Québec* (FECQ), respectively representing university and college students.

4 In 1996, the Quebec government announced its intention to raise tuition fees by 30%. Student mobilization forced a reconsideration of the initiative; the government eventually announced a 10-year freeze on tuition fees (Coalition large de l'Association pour une solidarité syndicale étudiante [CLASSÉ], 2013; Lacoursière, 2007)

5 In 2004, the government announced that it would convert $103 million worth of financial aid grants into loans. A year later, the decision was rescinded, although the ASSÉ's coalition denounced the agreement (CLASSÉ, 2013).

6 In 2000, the government conveyed a Summit to discuss a variety of issues affecting Quebec youth (Bureau du Sommet du Québec et de la Jeunesse, 2000). On the first day of the Summit, among many unique events, youth advocacy groups muscled through an amendment to the agenda, forcing the consideration of issues regarding social equity, poverty and education (Tenue du Sommet du Québec et de la Jeunesse, n.d.). The event is interesting for two reasons. First, the *Mouvement pour le droit à l'éducation*, one of the three provincial associations at the time, tried and failed at organizing protests to challenge the Summit, and folded a few months later (CLASSÉ, 2013; Lacoursière, 2007). Second, the Summit was one of the many consultations and initiatives that led to the formal introduction of quality as a steering principle in Quebec higher education (Bernatchez, 1999), which would be embodied later that year by new performance-based funding agreements.

7 Two limits should nonetheless be kept in mind. First would be the sub-conceptualization of the main theory, the orientation-focus theory. The lack of gradation on the spectra makes it very difficult to work into the model the nuances of human actions. The second caveat would be the authors' choice to focus on the contextual analysis rather than on improving existing typologies or analysis.

References

Act respecting the accreditation and financing of students' associations. (2015, c. A-3.01). Retrieved from LégisQuébec: http://legisquebec.gouv.qc.ca/en/ShowDoc/cs/A-3.01

Altbach, P. G. (Ed.). (1968). *Turmoil and transition: Higher education and student politics in India*. Bombay: Lalvani.

Altbach, P. G. (2007). Student politics: Activism and culture. In J. J. F. Forest & P. G. Altbach (Eds.), *International handbook of higher education* (pp. 329–345). Dordrecht: Springer.

Asselin, M. (2015, March 29). Le PQ aurait-il tué la FEUQ? [Did the Parti Québécois kill the FEUQ?]. *Journal de Montréal*. Retrieved from http://www.journaldemontreal.com/2015/03/29/le-pq-aurait-il-tue-la-feuq

Association pour une solidarité syndicale étudiante [ASSÉ]. (2009). *Revendications* [Demands]. Retrieved from http://ancien.asse-solidarite.qc.ca/spip.php%3Farticle19&lang=fr.html

Association pour une solidarité syndicale étudiante [ASSÉ]. (2012). *Pourquoi la gratuité scolaire* [Abolishing tuition fees]. Retrieved from http://www.asse-solidarite.qc.ca/wp-content/uploads/2013/02/memoire-gratuite-scolaire-2012.pdf

Association pour une solidarité syndicale étudiante [ASSÉ]. (2015). *L'ASSÉ*. Retrieved from http://www.asse-solidarite.qc.ca/asse/

Bégin-Caouette, O., & Jones, G. A. (2014). Student organizations in Canada and Quebec's "Maple Spring." *Studies in Higher Education, 39*(3), 412–425.

Bélanger, P. (1984). *Le mouvement étudiant québécois* [The Quebec student movement]. Montreal: ANEEQ.

Bernatchez, J. (1999). L'opération « contrats de performance » des universités québécoises [Performance contracts in Quebec universities]. In P. Doray & P.Chenard (Eds.), *L'enjeu de la réussite dans l'enseignement supérieur* [Success in higher education] (pp. 41–60). Montreal: Presses de l'Université du Québec.

Bill 78: An Act to enable students to receive instruction from the postsecondary institutions they attend. (2012). *39th legislature* (2nd Session, Ch. 12). Retrieved from the National Assembly of Quebec: http://www.assnat.qc.ca/en/travaux-parlementaires/projets-loi/projet-loi-78-39-2.html

Blais, A. (2015, March 28). La FEUQ perd le tiers de ses membres [The FEUQ loses a third of its membership]. *La Presse*. Retrieved from http://www.lapresse.ca/actualites/education/201503/28/01-4856247-la-feuq-perd-le-tiers-de-ses-membres.php

Bureau du Sommet du Québec et de la Jeunesse. (2000). *Document d'information* [Information]. Québec: Secrétariat de la Jeunesse. Retrieved from http://jeunes.gouv.qc.ca/documentation/publications/documents/cahierInformation.pdf

Business Corporations Act. (2015, c. S-31.1). Retrieved from LégisQuébec: http://legisquebec.gouv.qc.ca/en/ShowDoc/cs/S-31.1

Coalition large de l'Association pour une solidarité syndicale étudiante [CLASSÉ]. (2013). *Historique des grèves générales* [Chronology of general strikes]. Retrieved from http://www.bloquonslahausse.com/verslagreve/historique-des-greves-generales

Comité consultatif sur l'accessibilité financière aux études. (2013). *Indexation des droits de scolarité et des frais institutionnels obligatoires et augmentation des montants forfaitaires des étudiants canadiens et étrangers* [Indexing of tuition and ancillary fees, and the raising of complementary fees for Canadian and international students]. Retrieved from http://www.ccafe.gouv.qc.ca/fileadmin/ccafe/50-1130.pdf

Chouinard, T., & Journet, P. (2012, May 18) Projet de loi 78: «une déclaration de guerre», selon la FEUQ [FEUQ calls Bill 78 a declaration of war]. *La Presse*. Retrieved from http://www.lapresse.ca/actualites/dossiers/conflit-etudiant/201205/18/01-4526513-projet-de-loi-78-une-declaration-de-guerre-selon-la-feuq.php

Corriveau, E. (2013, February 9). Revendications au sommet – Les étudiants visent le gel des droits de scolarité [Summit on higher education – Students to demand tuition freeze]. *Le Devoir*. Retrieved from http://www.ledevoir.com/societe/education/ 370230/les-etudiants-visent-le-gel-des-droits-de-scolarite

Étudiants en grève au cégep de Sherbrooke [Student strike at Sherbrooke College]. (2015, November 30). *Radio-Canada*. Retrieved from http://ici.radio-canada.ca/ breve/36659/etudiants-en-greve-au-cegep-sherbrooke

Fédération étudiante universitaire du Québec [FEUQ]. (2007). *L'imputabilité des universités – premier volet* [Universities' accountability – part one]. Retrieved from http://studentunion.ca/docs/qc/FEUQ/2007/FEUQ%20-%20Imputabilite%20 des%20universites%20-%20Premier%20volet%20-%20octobre%202007.pdf

Gagnon, L. (2008). Bref historique du mouvement étudiant au Québec 1958–1971 [A brief history of the student movement in Quebec 1958–1971]. *Bulletin d'histoire politique, 16*(2), 13–52. Retrieved from http://www.bulletinhistoirepolitique.org/ le-bulletin/numeros-precedents/volume-16-numero-2/bref-historique-du-mouvement-etudiant-au-quebec-1958-1971/

Gerbet, T. (2015, April 29). Mouvement étudiant : la FEUQ, en plein doute, se met en veille [FEUQ in doubt, suspends activity]. *Radio-Canada*. Retrieved from http://ici.radio-canada.ca/nouvelles/National/2015/04/29/001-feuq-etudiants-veille.shtml

Jones, G. A. (1995). Student pressure: A national survey of Canadian student organizations. *Ontario Journal of Higher Education*, 93–106. Retrieved from https://tspace.library.utoronto.ca/handle/1807/32180

Klemenčič, M. (2012). Student representation in Western Europe: Introduction to the special issue. *European Journal of Higher Education, 2*(1), 2–19. doi:10.1080/2156823 5.2012.695058

Klemenčič, M. (2014). Student power in a global perspective and contemporary trends in student organising. *Studies in Higher Education, 39*(3), 396–411.

Labour code. (2015, c. C-27). Retrieved from LégisQuébec: http://legisquebec.gouv.qc.ca/ en/showDoc/cs/C-27?&digest=

Lacoursière, B. (2007). *Le mouvement étudiant au Québec de 1983 à 2006* [The student movement in Quebec from 1983 to 2006]. Montreal: Sabotart Éd.

Lajoie, A., & Gamache, M. (1990). *Droit de l'enseignement supérieur* [Higher education law]. Montreal: Thémis.

Lamoureux, D. (2012). La grève étudiante, un révélateur social [Student strikes as a social phenomenon]. *Theory & Event, 15*(3). Retrieved from https://muse.jhu.edu/ article/484449

Lemay, V., & Laperrière, M. N. (2012). Student protests and government somersaults: The Quebec spring from a law and society perspective. *Canadian Journal of Law and Society, 27*(3), 339–450.

Makela, F. (2014). La démocratie étudiante, la grève étudiante et leur régulation par le droit [Student democracy, student strikes and their regulation through law].

Revue de droit de l'Université de Sherbrooke, 44, 307–415. Retrieved from https://www.usherbrooke.ca/droit/fileadmin/sites/droit/documents/RDUS/ Volume_44/44-2-3-Makela.pdf

Makela, F., & Audette-Chapdelaine, S. (2013). The legal regulation of university student associations in Canada. *Education and Law Journal, 22*(13), 267–302.

Maroy, C., Doray, P., & Kabore, M. (2014). *La politique de financement des universités au Québec à l'épreuve du « Printemps érable »* [University funding policy meets the Maple Spring]. Retrieved from http://www.cirst.uqam.ca/Portals/0/docs/note_rech/Note2014-02.pdf

Nadeau-Dubois, G. (2013). *Tenir tête* [Standing up]. Montreal: LUX.

Pross, P. (1986). *Group politics and public policy.* Toronto: Oxford University Press.

Rashi, R. (2011). The Quebec student movement: At the forefront of the fight against austerity. *Canadian Dimension, 45*(6), 10–11.

Robinson, N. (2010). Student leadership, involvement, and service learning. In D. H. Cox & C. C. Strange (Eds.), *Achieving student success: Effective student services in Canadian higher education* (pp. 89–99). Montreal: McGill-Queen's Press.

Royal Commission of Inquiry on Education in the Province of Quebec. (1967). *Report of the Royal Commission of Inquiry on Education in the Province of Quebec* (Vols. 1–5). Quebec: Commission of Inquiry on Education in the Province of Quebec.

Shields, A. (2013, February 14). L'ASSE choisit de boycotter le Sommet [ASSÉ to boycott upcoming Summit]. *Le Devoir.* Retrieved from http://www.ledevoir.com/societe/education/370908/titre

Tenue du Sommet du Québec et de la Jeunesse. (n.d.). *Bilan du siècle* [The century in review]. Retrieved from http://bilan.usherbrooke.ca/bilan/pages/evenements/23157.html

Université du Québec à Montréal c. Association facultaire des étudiants en arts de l'Université du Québec à Montréal (AFEA-UQAM), (C.S., 2015-04-01), 2015 QCCS 1236, SOQUIJ AZ- AZ-51163763.)

Weinstock, D. (2012a). The political philosophy of the "Printemps Érable." *Theory & Event, 15*(3). Retrieved from https://muse.jhu.edu/article/484455

Weinstock, D. (2012b). Occupy, indignados, et le printemps étable: Vers un agenda de recherche [Occupy, indignados and the Maple Spring – Towards a research agenda]. *McGill Law Journal, 58*(2), 243–262. Retrieved from https://www.erudit.org/revue/mlj/2012/v58/n2/1017515ar.html

CHAPTER 15

European Higher Education Reforms and the Role of Students

Pavel Zgaga

Abstract

Students were originally excluded from the Bologna Process, but managed to insert themselves and subsequently have made valuable contributions. Students and their organizations are now significant players within the emerging *European Higher Education Area* (EHEA). They influence policy and the application thereof not only at the institutional level but also at the policy level. They insist that the "social dimension" of the Bologna Process cannot be ignored, that higher education is a public rather than a private good. It should therefore not be "commodified." but must be accessible to all qualified individuals.

Keywords

student engagement – Bologna Process – European Higher Education Area – EHEA – social dimension of higher education

Introduction

European higher education systems have experienced deep changes over the last three decades. National systems have become "more comparable and compatible" (Bologna Process, 1999), governance of higher education institutions has been "modernised" (European Commission, 2006) and their mission has been redefined and diversified (EUA, 2006). The policy making process has shifted to the international (European) level, both within the EU member states ('EU 28') and within Europe at large (48 countries of the Bologna Process).[1] Within these changes, national students' unions played an important role, greater than ever before. The focus of this chapter is on the role of students and student organisations within the emerging *European Higher Education Area* (EHEA). My key thesis is that the "Europeanisation" of higher education, i.e. building of the EHEA,

© KONINKLIJKE BRILL NV, LEIDEN, 2019 | DOI:10.1163/9789004393073_015

EUROPEAN HIGHER EDUCATION REFORMS AND THE ROLE OF STUDENTS   273

has resulted in substantially strengthened position of students and their unions not only in the institutional governance but also in the policy making at the national and European level. This change must first be seen in historical context.

Student Participation in University Governance: 1968 and Beyond

Calls by students to participate in institutional governance as well as in broader social and political arenas have a long history. The literature is rich with references to protests and uprisings throughout the history of universities, but this topic is extremely broad and falls beyond the scope of this chapter (but see Schuetze's chapter in this volume). The history of contemporary student activism is generally seen to begin with the year 1968. The student revolt of May, 1968, in France, which quickly spilled over to other European countries and, just a little later, to other countries outside of Europe, surprised academics and politicians; they began to look for means of reconciliation. This took place in very different ways in different countries and had varying impacts in different countries. For example, at the University of Ljubljana a student radio station was established in 1970 as a "gift" to calm down angry students; however, this station has operated as a "critical voice" ever since, and played a particularly important role at the time of the fundamental political changes around the year 1990. In general, the post-1968 period led to the institutionalization of student participation in university governance. This was a new quality in the history of student activism. When viewed in the broader context, we see that this change was, to a significant extent, a result of the *Zeitgeist*.

Against the background of the "material" history of the post-WW2 period, the gradually emerging ideas of "learner-centred teaching," "lifelong learning" and "learning society" indicated a fundamental change in the philosophy of education. As in other historical cases, we can't overlook the connection between ongoing social and political processes and the theoretical production of new concepts: they are one of the necessary conditions that enable and encourage the emergence of new forms of social life and new institutions. In a relatively condensed form, the new spirit of the times around 1968 can be identified in the study for which UNESCO commissioned Edgar Faure (the French Minister for Education after May '68) and a group of international experts. In the chapter on "Elements for contemporary strategies" two far-reaching principles are emphasised and a recommendation is given as follows:

Principle
Teaching, contrary to traditional ideas and practice, should adapt itself to the learner; the learner should not have to bow to pre-established rules for teaching. [...]

Principle

Any system according educational services to a passive population and any reform which fails to arouse active personal participation among the mass of learners can achieve at best only marginal success.

Recommendation

All learners, whether young or adult, should be able to play a responsible part not only in their own education but in the entire educational enterprise.

(Faure, 1972, pp. 220, 222; italics in original)

From this perspective, the post-1968 period is characterized by promoting the principle of democratic governance. In practice, the principle of democratic governance in higher education institutions often met resistance and remained rhetoric; on the other hand, new and previously unimaginable problems arose in the implementation processes. Questions have been raised, as for example: Should the students' right to participate in decision-making be recognized on all issues or only in a few selected ones? Are only students deprived of the right to participate in the higher education institutions? What about the right to participation, for example, by administrative and technical staff? What about external stakeholders? Should democratic governance follow the principle of "one person, one vote," or should the voices of various stakeholders be "weighted"? If they should be weighted, in what way?

These issues do not belong to the past and are not rhetorical questions; they are even more relevant today than a few decades ago. However, it hasn't been possible to articulate them until the principle of democratic governance has started to prevail at higher education institutions.

The more the principle of democratic governance remained pure rhetoric, the more students were expressing dissatisfaction and resistance. Legislative changes do not compensate for lack of change in the (academic) culture. This is one side of the problem, but there is yet another range of problems brought about by the gradual and often conflicting implementation of the democratic governance principle.

Initially, it was understood primarily as the student right to participate at the *institutional level*. Thus, the French government's "Framework Act for Higher Education" ("*loi d'orientation de l'enseignement supérieur*") of November 1968 granted students "a 50 per cent membership in the corporate university bodies, apart from those dealing with the selection of teaching staff, research and exams, on condition that a suitable number of students took part in the election of their representatives." This law serves "as a relatively moderate example of the avalanche of university laws that, during the 1970s, covered the university landscape in Continental Europe" (Rüegg, 2011, p. 106). However, in their "lab work in sociology" which took place on the streets of many European cities in 1968, students learned that their problems only start but not end at their departments. Universities are placed in a broader social and political context. The principle of participation is therefore not exhausted at the institutional level, but applies to the entire national system of higher education. Over the following decades, the problem of student participation was increasingly shifting to the *national* level.

Compared to the power of student organization at an institution, national student unions have a significantly greater ability to influence strategic decisions such as the university system, scholarships, accommodation, etc. Consultations with students on key system decisions with the relevant national authorities have appeared as a minimal form of their participation at the national level. Until the 1990s this practice was strengthened in many countries; still, problems and obstacles were reported. The decisive pushes came in the 1980s from two directions: from the progressing "Europeanization" in Western Europe as well as from the political democratization in Central and Eastern Europe. As a result, "new European associations and interest groups in higher education" – including *Erasmus Student Network* (ESN) and *National Union of Students in Europe* (ESIB) – "have formed to lobby in Brussels" (Hackl, 2001, p. 103). At this time, student activists in Eastern Europe played a great role in the profound political changes that were occurring there. In this way, the issue of student participation was expanded to the *international* level.

European Students' Unions Address European Ministers of Education

The roots of the ESIB go back to 1982, when the *Western European Students Information Bureau* (WESIB) was founded, with only seven national unions at the time. In 1992 the name was changed to the *National Unions of Students in Europe,* but the abbreviation ESIB was preserved. In 2007 the name was changed again to the *European Students' Union* (ESU) which has been in use since then.[2] Since the 1990s the ESIB/ESU has become the largest representative association of student unions in Europe, although it had to strive for recognition at the EU level until the beginning of 2000 (Klemenčič, 2012a, 2012c). Its rise is closely linked to the profound changes that have taken place in European higher education since the late 1980s, and its position and competencies have been particularly increased by the *Bologna Process.*

The first initiative in the direction of what is now called the Bologna Process occurred in Paris in 1998 (Bologna Process, 1998) but the key event took place in June, 1999 in Bologna. The Bologna conference was jointly organized by the University of Bologna, the Italian Ministry of Higher Education and

Science, the two former European university associations (CRE and EUREC/CRUE; later in 1999 merged into a single current European University Association – EUA) and the European Commission (named the Commission of the European Communities at that time). It was attended by ministerial delegations from 15 EU Member and 12 EU Associated States of that time as well as from the EFTA – The European Free Trade Association – countries (Iceland, Liechtenstein, Norway and Switzerland), by representatives of universities, international organizations (UNESCO, Council of Europe) and by experts in higher education.

The conference was divided into two parts: the first day was "academic" – presenting and discussing the study on *Trends in Learning Structures in Higher Education* (Haug et al., 1999), while the second was "ministerial" with adoption of the final declaration text (Bologna Process, 1999) followed by a solemn signing procedure. The conference was held in an optimistic atmosphere that was typical of the time: not only an atmosphere of broadened European cooperation, but also cooperation between the national education authorities and national Rectors' Conferences and with involvement of independent policy experts. It was also attended by a group of about 20 students; however, this was somewhat unexpected. For a normal participant it seemed likely that the students were there primarily as part of the "scenery." However, according to the envisaged scenario they should not have had any active role at the conference. How did they get there?

Manja Klemenčič, ESIB Secretary General at the time, stated in her recently published memoirs that "an official invitation to participate in the high-level conference to discuss 'the European space for Higher Education' signed by the rector of Bologna University was faxed to the ESIB Secretariat just a month before the event." A few months earlier, students had learned that the conference was under preparation, so they lobbied strenuously to be able to attend. The invitation came from the academic and not the ministerial side: It was the rector of Bologna University who faxed an invitation to the ESIB Secretariat. For ESIB it was important "how to respond to the Bologna Declaration (of which was a draft already obtained)" (Klemenčič, 2012c, p. 17).

The ESIB's "intelligence service" succeeded in obtaining a draft ministerial Declaration before the conference; so they decided to write in response their own declaration and distribute it at the conference. As one of the participants remembers: "fairly unexpected and due to a significant lobby at the event itself, the organisers decided ad hoc to change the program of the meeting to include a plenary address by ESIB Chairperson [sic]" (Klemenčič, 2012c, p. 18). Thus, the ESIB unexpectedly found itself at the European ministerial podium.

EUROPEAN HIGHER EDUCATION REFORMS AND THE ROLE OF STUDENTS   277

It was for the first time in history: It was unexpected both by the ministers and by the students.

This was certainly a great success for students. Viewed from today's point of view, we can say that this was the first step towards student participation in the European higher education policy making process. Things have started to move faster even in their home countries, because developments at the European level began increasingly to influence the national policies. Of course, a number of further steps were necessary, which took quite a long time, but the breakthrough had been achieved. Let's look at this breakthrough in somewhat more detail.

European students gained the right to formal participation in governance structures at the level of higher education institutions through processes and reforms that followed the student revolts of 1968; in some countries, the participation of students was at the time already regulated at the national level (Bergan, 2004). At least formally, students in some countries had the ability to influence higher education reforms without occupying the streets with banners. Two decades later, around 1990, two important processes occurred in parallel: (1) the formation of ESIB resulted in the first influential pan-European student forum, which greatly enhanced students' potential power within the on-going Europeanization process; (2) among its many results, the Europeanization process created a pan-European ministerial higher education policy forum – the Bologna Process. If the ministers of 29 countries gather at a conference on the future of European higher education, then students must participate, even if they were not invited.

What they wanted to say at the conference is summarized in the *Bologna Students Joint Declaration* (ESIB, 1999). This document proves that students were familiar with the ideational background of the Bologna Declaration, including some of the background dilemmas and controversies about its content. The students commented on the following four points in the official declaration:

1. First of all, *we do not think that European institutions of higher education lack 'competitiveness' at the international level.* [...] Still, the best way to improve attractiveness and the quality of European higher education would be to increase public funding.
2. We are firmly committed to a *model of quality education open to the largest number of students.* [...] Therefore, *the declarations must not be a means to install any kind of limitation of the access to higher education.* [...]

3. We think that the *diversity* of the higher education system can also be an advantage at the international level. The attractiveness of a model does not only depend on its uniformity. [...]
4. In order to build the 'European space of Higher Education,' *mobility should become a right for all students.* (ESIB, 1999, pp. 1–2; italics in original)

The document points to three issues which were then at the forefront of discussions. First, there is a somewhat controversial comment on the alleged lack of competitiveness (the word is placed in quotation marks) of European higher education systems and the need to increase their attractiveness (not in quotation marks). This issue was related to the discussion about diversity of higher education systems which was much discussed at the time. The Sorbonne Declaration (Bologna Process, 1998) contained the term "harmonisation" which was very controversial: "no uniformisation," but building on "richness of our diversities." The second point concerned the problem of access to higher education, which wasn't compromised by the beginnings of the Bologna Process in any way; however, as this had been one of its core principles, ESIB had to point it out.

Thirdly, the students' declaration radicalized the issue of pan-European *mobility*. Part of the text (not quoted above) highlights the need for wider use of European Credit Transfer and Accumulation System (ECTS)[3] and the Diploma Supplement (DS),[4] draws attention to insufficient learning of foreign languages, notes problems with the systems of equivalences between European degrees, etc.. When it comes to non-European students, the problem of a lack of scholarships and a too strict visa policy was raised. These are all issues that were discussed in the preparations for the Bologna Declaration or were articulated in the first years of the Bologna Process. With their first "Bologna" document European students demonstrated a good understanding of the issues that led ministers to get together and sign the Declaration.

The document concludes with a political remark that the national students' unions "deeply regret that the students were not involved with the drafting of the Sorbonne and Bologna declarations and to the definition of their objectives even though we are one of the most important populations concerned by potential reforms" (ESIB, 1999, p. 2). Students took the popular rhetoric of "higher education partnership" seriously – and achieved an unexpected political breakthrough.

The second conference of the Bologna Process was held in 2001 in Prague; ESIB was formally invited and actively involved in it, especially proposing the *social dimension* as a new "action line" on the official Bologna list of objectives. In the Prague Communiqué (Bologna Process, 2001) Ministers openly recognized "students are full members of the higher education community" and supported an idea which was eagerly championed by ESIB: "the idea that higher education should be considered a public good" and which "is and will remain a public responsibility." In the further development of the Process these views proved to be of far-reaching importance.

The ESIB's impact during the preparation activities for the Prague conference was surprisingly great. Manja Klemenčič compared the "direct citations from ESIB's Student Göteborg Declaration (ESIB's pre-conference statement) and Prague ministerial Communiqué" and found "ample examples of direct 'uploading' of ESIB's Positions into the Prague Communiqué," such as:

Student Göteborg Declaration (ESIB, 2001a)

> Although the Bologna Declaration pointed out the basic aspect of European dimension of h[igher] e[ducation], it failed to address the social implications the process has on students.
> Ministers also reaffirmed the need, recalled by students, to take account of the social dimension in the Bologna Process.
> [...] we ask you, the ministers responsible for higher education, explicitly to write a social dimension into the implementation of the Bologna Declaration and to preserve higher education as a public good.

Prague Communiqué (Bologna Process, 2001)

> [...] Ministers encouraged the Follow-up Group to arrange seminars to explore the following areas: [...] the social dimension, with special attention to obstacles to mobility, and [...] student involvement. (Klemenčič, 2012c, pp. 26–27)

Last but not least, the Prague Conference formalized the structure of the Bologna Process; ESIB, in parallel to EUA, EURASHE[5] and the Council of Europe, got a "consultative" status (modified to an "observer" status at the Berlin Conference in 2003) in the Bologna Follow-up Group (BFUG),[6] which proved to be extremely influential position within the Bologna Process in the following years. An *observer* does not have voting rights (those rights are with the ministers) but can significantly influence discussion within the BFUG and in the drafting of documents adopted within the Process. ESIB has been using this position with a lot of success.

ESIB/ESU and the "Social Dimension of the EHEA"

Student participation is today "considered one of the foundational values in European higher education" (Klemenčič, 2012b) and "one of the EHEA principles" (Zgaga, 2012). This value and this principle are no longer denied, but their implementation has been often disputed. Nevertheless, within a few years, student participation was established as the norm in the wider European area. In a survey from 2002 respondents were asked: *should the student influence in higher education governance increase*? As expected, 90% of respondents from the student group responded positively, but somewhat surprisingly 70% of ministerial and 72% of academic representatives also agreed (Persson, 2004).

ESIB has been recognized as a "Bologna insider" and within certain constraints it has become co-creator of policy for the EHEA. The following constraints have been most often cited: lack of competence, weak institutional and administrative support, the "fluidity" which is due to the nature of student life (rapid turnover of generations) and "the cultural attitudes of key actors in the higher education community" (Klemenčič, 2014, pp. 406–407) which treat students as "too young" for serious decisions about serious issues. All this may occasionally contribute to the impression that European students are "in the periphery of the Bologna Process" (Cemmell, 2007, p. 251). However, on the other hand, this "peripheral" position has allowed them to articulate ideas that would be much more delicate in any other position.

The perspective from which students addressed reforms in the past has fundamentally changed since they have joined the Bologna Club. This was a shift similar to moving from opposition to government: It may bring some uneasiness. For example, in Vienna in March, 2010 the ESIB representatives attended a ceremony on the occasion of "entering into the EHEA," which was held in the imperial *Hofburg* palace and which continued as a real Viennese dance party, while spontaneously formed radical student groups demonstrated against growing "Bologna style neoliberalism" in the streets. But such is the price of a requirement for participation in governance. "Understanding ESIB as an actor displaced from its sometimes preferred territory of critical positions based on values and norms sheds some light on the reasons as to why it cannot be easily situated within the Bologna Process regime" (Cemmell, 2007, p. 265).

Each initiation is accompanied by a certain amount of uneasiness, but the yield is that the way is open to get a new perspective and new life experience. It seems that student leaders basically understood this logic even before ESIB entered formally into the Bologna Process. The *Student Göteborg Declaration* concluded: "Student participation in the Bologna process is one of the key steps towards permanent and more formalised student involvement in all decision making bodies and discussion fora dealing with higher education on the European level" (ESIB, 2001a, p. 3). Indeed: ESIB has proved to be one of those organisations that "have collectively evolved into a political community at the European level which have become very active in shaping and influencing European policies" (Beerkens, 2008, p. 420).

The operation of ESIB was determined, on one hand, by its "peripheral" role in relation to "senior" Bologna actors and by the related fundamental differences regarding some key issues. On the other hand, it was also determined by the internal dynamics *between* national student associations that can vary greatly. We must distinguish at least between the associations "as a social movement organization" and "as interest groups" (Klemenčič, 2012a, p. 8). Notwithstanding this dichotomy, the perspective of the *social dimension* has constantly guided ESIB's positions over the past fifteen years.

ESIB has been actively involved in the discussion on all "Bologna action lines": the degree structure and credit system, the promotion of mobility, recognition of degrees, lifelong learning, quality assurance, etc. These are the "ministerial action lines," as we mentioned, whereas *the social dimension* was raised originally by the students. It would be interesting to analyze student views on each of these lines, but we must postpone it for another occasion. Instead, we will look more at the "student action line." When it comes to understanding the internal dynamics of the Bologna Process and the nature of the EHEA, this point seems to be crucial.

"Education Is a Human Right and Human Rights Can Never Be Tradable"

This proved especially true in the first half of the 2000s, during the "interlude" of the heated discussions about the General Agreement on Trade in Services (GATS), which evoked the future of higher education in Europe and other world regions. The GATS is one of the main World Trade Organisation (WTO) agreements; it was created in 1995 and its core aim is to promote trade liberalization in all kind of services, including education. In 2001, a new negotiation round began (Doha Round), but the process was generally carried out fairly opaquely. The very idea of liberalization of "educational services" and the nontransparency of the negotiation process aroused numerous protests. In Europe the case overlapped with the "Bologna discussion" and was strongly argued within and without the Process.

Preparation of substantial reforms can never avoid discussion on the very "philosophy of reform"; the debate on such a broad question, such as the purposes of higher education (Zgaga, 2009), started to take a position in the foreground of the Bologna debates. Positions around this issue varied and it was possible to distinguish, on the one hand, views that reduced the purposes of higher education to its economic function (e.g., the European Commission) and, on the other hand, those that advocated "the full range of purposes" (e.g. the Council of Europe). In this regard ESIB took a clear and radical position very early. Soon after the Prague Communiqué students stated:

> Students should be regarded as a core part of higher education, not as consumers that purchase a product. To view higher education as a commodity is to undermine the social role that all levels of education confer to both the students and society. We are strongly concerned with the process of commodification of higher education as evidenced by the negotiations on the General Agreement of Trade in Services. Education is a human right and human rights can never be tradable. (ESIB, 2001b, p. 1)

ESIB also insisted on this position later. It continued to develop it e.g., through its Working Group on Commodification as well as by "coalition-building with central actors, namely the European University Association and the Council of Europe" (Cemmell, 2007, p. 263). The GATS was not associated only with the liberalization of services as understood by WTO and the ministers of economy (some of the ministers of education might have a different opinion on this, but did not participate in the negotiations and were initially even not informed); it also clashed with the very "philosophy" of European higher education reforms.

The problem came to a head in the winter of 2002–2003 when the first drafts of the Berlin Communiqué were appearing. In February 2003 one of a series of BFUG seminars was organized in Athens under the heading "Exploring the Social Dimensions of the EHEA," and just before it a regular meeting of the BFUG took place. The seminar focused on three issues: (1) the social dimension of the EHEA, (2) higher education as a public good and (3) higher education in the GATS negotiations (Bologna Process, 2003b).

The seminar topics also entered the agenda of the regular BFUG meeting. As one can read in the minutes, the European Commission representative tried to calm the discussion: "It was explained that the positions taken cannot be completely open since negotiations are currently taking place. [...] It was stressed though, that there is no intention or reason to go any further with offers." However, "ESIB noted that the Bologna Process seems to become more and more associated with the Lisbon targets[7] and expressed its worry that the Bologna Process may be reduced to a mere instrument to reach these targets, which are mainly an economic agenda" (Bologna Process, 2003a).

The seminar started on a similar note; at its opening a special charm was given by unexpected demonstrations of radical Greek students. With their position, ESIB representatives were not lonely partners in the discussion; principled objections and criticism of the GATS was also raised by other participants. For example, Per Nyborg[8] recapitulated the debate expressing the following dilemma: "Can the Bologna Process based on co-operation and GATS based on competition co-exist in the sector of higher education?" And he answered: "GATS may tempt any government to take its national responsibility for higher education lighter, as higher education more easily may be considered to be a *private good*. That is not a European approach and it should not become one" (Nyborg, 2003, p. 4).

In general, the seminar participants reaffirmed that the main objective driving the creation of the EHEA should be based on *academic values and cooperation* between different countries and regions of the world and not on *economic reductionism*. The announcement of the European Commission that it would not include public education in the negotiation proposal for the ongoing GATS negotiations was assessed as a positive development. In conclusion, they agreed that "the European ministers of education have to insert a joint statement on GATS in their next communiqué" (Bologna Process, 2003b).

However, in the Berlin Communiqué no direct observations on the GATS can be found, but in the preamble the ministers reaffirmed "the importance of the social dimension of the Bologna Process." They continued as follows:

> The need to increase competitiveness must be balanced with the objective of improving the social characteristics of the European Higher Education Area, aiming at strengthening social cohesion and reducing social and gender inequalities both at national and at European level. In that context, Ministers reaffirm their position that higher education is a public good and a public responsibility. They emphasise that in international academic co-operation and exchanges, academic values should prevail. (Bologna Process, 2003c, Preamble)

Finally, ministers welcomed "the commitment of Higher Education Institutions and students to the Bologna Process and recognise[d] that it is ultimately the active participation of all partners in the Process that will ensure its long-term success" as well as recognizing that "students are full partners in higher education governance" (Bologna Process, 2003c).

The polemics surrounding the GATS were episodic in nature and have weakened since 2005, but the debate on the social dimension has remained high on the agenda and can be repeatedly found in the texts of subsequent ministerial communiqués, e.g., "The social dimension of the Bologna Process is a constituent part of the EHEA and a necessary condition for the attractiveness and competitiveness of the EHEA" (Bologna Process, 2005); "the student body entering, participating in and completing higher education at all levels should reflect the diversity of our populations" (Bologna Process, 2007); and participating countries "will set measurable targets for widening overall participation and increasing participation of underrepresented groups in higher education" (Bologna Process, 2009).

Conclusion

Claiming that this particular element of the debate on the future of European higher education resulted from active student opposition to "neo-liberal ministers" would be quite an exaggeration. The question of the social dimension of higher education within the Bologna Process has become an issue of importance that all the players are aware of; however, reactions to it were naturally different. Certainly this issue was brought into the debate by students and without them it would not have received so featured a position in shaping the general European as well as particular national policies.

In the first years after its creation, the Bologna Process was considered a "success story." As always happens with such stories, they sooner or later meet with criticisms and opposition. Of course, within the Process sometimes better and sometimes worse solutions have been adopted, so that it has been conducted with high points and low points. When it comes to political processes, including reforms of higher education, such oscillations should be treated as a normal phenomenon.

The problem that should get more attention – both in theory and in actual politics – is that fundamental reforms, as engendered by the Bologna Process, typically concern the fundamental dilemmas of the time. On the one hand actors are faced with the dictates of contemporary global economic competitiveness, while on the other hand they are aware of the principle of public good, which in the European tradition can't be easily given up. On the one hand, "in a changing world, there will be a continuing need to adapt our higher education systems, to ensure that the EHEA remains competitive and can respond effectively to the challenges of globalisation" (Bologna Process, 2007); on the other, there is a continuing need to "increase our efforts on the social dimension in order to provide equal opportunities to quality education, paying particular attention to underrepresented groups" (Bologna Process, 2010). This is one of the dichotomies that have always accompanied the Bologna Process.

The question is, therefore, whether *economic competitiveness* and the *public good* are compatible at all: "Is it consistent to proclaim at the same time [...]

EUROPEAN HIGHER EDUCATION REFORMS AND THE ROLE OF STUDENTS   285

the international competitiveness of higher education and its being a 'public responsibility' and a 'public good'? Or does competitiveness entail that higher education eventually becomes a marketable service?" (Hackl, 2001, p. 115). In Europe, the question is harder than it looks at first glance. Among other things, it requires careful consideration of the general principles on which educational reforms should be based. In this regard, European students insist: "No person should be confronted by any barrier to higher education, and it is a societal responsibility to make sure that everyone has actual equal access to higher education" (ESU, 2012, p. 1).

Notes

1   In recent decades, the European organisations and bodies have developed into a complex and – for an ill-informed reader – rather complicated system. For these readers, some brief general information may be useful: The Bologna Process is an intergovernmental action of 48 European countries (i.e. not an initiative or activity of the European Commission or the European Union; even if the former has equal place with individual countries). The Council of Europe should not be confused with the European Council. The European Council is a body of the European Union and has almost nothing to do with the Bologna Process. The Council of Europe is not a body of the European Union but the continent's leading human rights organisation which is – among other issues – very active in the field of educational policies. Although it has only a consultative role in the Bologna Process it plays quite a prominent role.

2   The way European student organisations at the national level are organised is extremely diverse. According to Rok Primožič, a recent ESU chairperson, unions in the northern part of Europe (i.e. UK, Ireland, Norway, Sweden, Denmark and Finland) are the oldest and best financed. In the South (i.e. Spain, Portugal, Italy, France) more diverse systems of student organisation exist. Germany represents an example of a "hybrid" student organisation (between a social movement and an interest group); as higher education policy is done on the state (*Länder*) level the national union is weak. The systems in the post-Soviet and post-Yugoslavian countries are again different; most of the organisations have been established by national legislation, usually following the Bologna Process recommendations; they are often (but not always) strict on not creating internal groups based on political affiliation (Primožič, 2016; see also Bergan, Klemenčič, & Primožič, 2015).

3   ECTS – European Credit Transfer and Accumulation System, designed to make it easier for students to move between different countries; see http://ec.europa.eu/education/ects/ects_en.htm

4 DS – Diploma Supplement, a document stipulated by the Lisbon Recognition Convention (1997) which is issued to all graduates for the reasons of transparency and recognition of acquired qualifications see http://www.enic-naric.net/fileusers/ THE_DIPLOMA_SUPPLEMENT.pdf

5 EURASHE – the European association of (non-university) institutions in higher education.

6 BFUG – the coordinating body between two ministerial conferences.

7 The so-called *EU Lisbon Strategy* is mentioned (see Council of the European Union, 2000).

8 At the time Chairman of the Committee for Higher Education and Research of the Council of Europe; later, from 2003 to 2005, Head of the Bologna Secretariat in Oslo.

References

Beerkens, E. (2008). The emergence and institutionalisation of the European higher education and research area. *European Journal of Education, 43*(4), 407–425.

Bergan, S. (2004). Higher education governance and democratic participation: The university and democratic culture. In S. Bergan (Ed.), *The university as res publica* (pp. 13–30). Strasbourg: Council of Europe Publishing.

Bergan, S., Klemenčič, M., & Primožič, R. (Eds.). (2015). *Student engagement in Europe: Society, higher education and student governance.* Strasbourg: Council of Europe Publishing.

Bologna Process. (1998, May 25). *Sorbonne Joint Declaration. Joint declaration on harmonisation of the architecture of the European higher education system by the four Ministers in charge for France, Germany, Italy and the United Kingdom.* Retrieved March 13, 2016, from http://www.ehea.info/Uploads/Declarations/SORBONNE_ DECLARATION1.pdf

Bologna Process. (1999). *The European Higher Education Area. Joint declaration of the European ministers of education.* Retrieved March 13, 2016, from http://www.ehea.info/ article-details.aspx?ArticleId=43

Bologna Process. (2001). *Towards the European Higher Education Area: Communiqué of the meeting of European ministers in charge of higher education in prague on may 19th 2001.* Retrieved March 13, 2016, from http://www.ehea.info/article-details. aspx?ArticleId=43

Bologna Process. (2003a, February 18). *Minutes of the Bologna follow-up group meeting under the Greek presidency* [From the author's personal archive].

Bologna Process. (2003b). *General report. Bologna follow-up seminar "exploring the social dimensions of the European Higher Education Area"* [From the author's personal archive].

Bologna Process. (2003c, September 19). *Realising the European Higher Education Area.* Communiqué of the Conference of Ministers responsible for Higher Education, Berlin. Retrieved March 13, 2016, from http://www.ehea.info/article-details.aspx?ArticleId=43

Bologna Process. (2005, May 19–20). *The European Higher Education Area – Achieving the goals.* Communiqué of the Conference of European Ministers Responsible for Higher Education, Bergen. Retrieved March 13, 2016, from http://www.ehea.info/article-details.aspx?ArticleId=43

Bologna Process. (2007, May 18). *Towards the European Higher Education Area: Responding to challenges in a globalised world.* Retrieved March 13, 2016, from http://www.ehea.info/article-details.aspx?ArticleId=43

Bologna Process. (2009, April 28–29). *The Bologna Process 2020 – The European Higher Education Area in the new decade.* Communiqué of the Conference of European Ministers Responsible for Higher Education, Leuven and Louvain-la-Neuve. Retrieved from http://www.ehea.info/article-details.aspx?ArticleId=43

Bologna Process. (2010, March 12). *Budapest-Vienna declaration on the European Higher Education Area.* Retrieved March 13, 2016, from http://www.ehea.info/article-details.aspx?ArticleId=43

Cemmell, J. (2007). European students in the periphery of the Bologna Process. In V. Tomusk (Ed.), *Creating the European Area of Higher Education: Voices from the periphery* (pp. 251–268). Dordrecht: Springer.

Council of the European Union. (2000, March 23–34). *Presidency conclusions.* Retrieved March 13, 2016, from http://www.europarl.europa.eu/summits/lis1_en.htm

ESIB. (1999, June 19). *Bologna students joint declaration* [From the author's personal archive; photocopied document, 2 stapled pages; signed by 16 national student unions].

ESIB. (2001a, March 25). *Student Göteborg declaration.* Retrieved March 13, 2016, from http://www.esu-online.org/news/article/6065/142/

ESIB. (2001b, November 18). *Brussels student declaration.* Retrieved March 13, 2016, from http://www.esu-online.org/news/article/6065/141/

ESU. (2012). *ESU policy on the social dimension.* Retrieved March 13, 2016, from http://www.esu-online.org/news/article/6064/2012-Policy-Paper-ESU-Policy-on-Social-Dimension/

EUA. (2006, March 12). *A vision and strategy for Europe's universities and the European University Association (EUA).* Retrieved March 13, 2016, from http://www.eua.be/activities-services/publications/eua-policy-positions.aspx

European Commission. (2006, May 10). *Communication from the commission to the council and the European parliament.* Retrieved March 13, 2016, from http://eur-lex.europa.eu/legal-content/EN/TXT/?uri=URISERV:c11089

Faure, E. et al. (1972). *Learning to be: The world of education today and tomorrow*. Paris: UNESCO.

Hackl, E. (2001). The intrusion and expansion of community policies in higher education. *Higher Education Management, 13*(3), 99–117.

Haug, G., Kirstein, J., Knudsen, I. (1999, June 18–19). *Trends in learning structures in higher education*. Project report for the Bologna Conference, The Danish Rectors Conference, Kobenhaven. Retrieved March 13, 2016, from http://www.eua.be/eua/jsp/en/upload/OFFDOC_BP_trend_I.1068715136182.pdf

Klemenčič, M. (2012a). Student representation in Western Europe: Introduction to the special issue. *European Journal of Higher Education, 2*(1), 2–19.

Klemenčič, M. (2012b). The changing conceptions of student participation in HE governance in the EHEA. In A. Curaj, P. Scott, L. Vlasceanu, & L. Wilson (Eds.), *European higher education at the crossroads: Between the Bologna Process and national reforms* (pp. 631–653). Dordrecht: Springer.

Klemenčič, M. (2012c). How ESIB got into the Bologna Process. In *ESU turns 30! Fighting for student rights since 1982* (pp. 17–28). Brussels: ESU.

Klemenčič, M. (2014). Student power in a global perspective and contemporary trends in student organising. *Studies in Higher Education, 39*(3), 396–411.

Nyborg, P. (2003, February 19–20). *Higher education and GATS. The European approach*. Bologna Follow-up Seminar, Athens. [From the author's personal archive.]

Persson, A. (2004). Student participation in the governance of higher education in Europe: Results of a survey. In S. Bergan (Ed.), *The university as res publica* (pp. 31–82). Strasbourg: Council of Europe.

Primožič, R. (2016). *A brief overview of student organizing in Europe and funding of student unions*. Retrieved March 14, 2016, from http://ceps.pef.uni-lj.si/images/stories/doc/primozic.pdf

Rüegg, W. (Ed.). (2011). *A history of the university in Europe, vol. IV: Universities since 1945*. Cambridge: Cambridge University Press.

Zgaga, P. (2009). Higher education and citizenship: 'The full range of purposes'. *European Educational Research Journal, 8*(2), 175–188.

Zgaga, P. (2012). Reconsidering the EHEA principles: Is there a 'Bologna philosophy'? In A. Curaj, P. Scott, L. Vlasceanu, & L. Wilson (Eds.), *European higher education at the crossroads: Between the Bologna Process and national reforms* (pp. 17–38). Dordrecht: Springer.

Printed in the United States
By Bookmasters